MW01624096

How Could I Not Have Known?

CHANA ROTENBERG

How Could I Not Have Known?

A True Story of Strength, Courage, and Unwavering Faith

Originally published in Hebrew as *Eich Lo Yadati?*
Written by Miriam Aflalo
(*Ginzach Kiddush HaShem,* 2017)

Translation: Yocheved Lavon
Editing: Eva Hollander
Typesetting: E. Chachamtzedek

ISBN 978-1-68025-367-2

Comments are welcome:
chanarotenberg@gmail.com
972-52-763-9940

DISTRIBUTED BY:
Feldheim Publishers
POB 43163 / Jerusalem, Israel
208 Airport Executive Park
Nanuet, NY 10954
www.feldheim.com

DISTRIBUTED IN EUROPE BY:
Lehmanns
+44-0-191-430-0333
info@lehmanns.co.uk
www.lehmanns.co.uk

DISTRIBUTED IN AUSTRALIA BY:
Golds World of Judaica
+613 95278775
info@golds.com.au
www.golds.com.au

Printed in Israel

הספר יצא לאור בסיוע של

מכון "גנזך קידוש השם"

מרכז הארגונים של
ניצולי השואה בישראל

המשרד
לשוויון חברתי

Dedicated with love
to my dear

Mother שתחי'

heroine of this book,
who is my source of
inspiration and strength.

Dedicated to the Eternal Merit of…

My dear father

Rabbi **Shulem Duvid HaLevi Ish Horowitz** *z"l*

who departed to his eternal rest on 28 Cheshvan 5772

My brother

Rabbi **Mordechai Tzvi HaLevi Ish Horowitz** *z"l*

who departed to his eternal rest on 25 Iyar 5736

My father's family:

Rabbi **Mordechai Tzvi HaLevi Ish Horowitz**

of Krakow *Hy"d*

and his wife, **Frumet**, née Baron *Hy"d*

their children

Yisrael Yitzchak *Hy"d,* **Avraham Leib** *Hy"d*,

Miriam Neicha *Hy"d,* **Chana Devora** *Hy"d,*

and HaRav **Chaim Eliezer Horowitz** *Hy"d*

his wife, Rebbetzin **Rivka Baila** *Hy"d*

and their children

Sara Yocheved *Hy"d*

Moshe Leib *Hy"d*, and **Faiga** *Hy"d*

My mother's family:

Rabbi **Yitzchak Aryeh HaLevi Ish Horowitz** *Hy"d*

his wife, Maras **Tzirel Faigel**, née Goldsobel *Hy"d*

and their children

Maras **Pesya Morocco** and her family *Hy"d*

Sorche Weinberg and her family *Hy"d*

Zlata Horowitz and her family *Hy"d*

Bas Sheva Kocanski and her family *Hy"d*

Frieda Weissgol and her family *Hy"d*

Meir *Hy"d*, **Mendel** *Hy"d*, **Hershel** *Hy"d*,

Moshe *Hy"d*, and **Yisrael** *Hy"d*

ת.נ.צ.ב.ה

A Letter of Blessing and Approbation from
Rabbi Yisrael Meir Lau

Mrs. Chana Rotenberg of Jerusalem sent me a copy of her book *Eich Lo Yadati?* [Hebrew edition], which contains the perceptions of a second-generation survivor, who grew up in the shadow of the Holocaust during the period of silence and repression of those experiences. The book combines the story of the miraculous survival of her parents, who both separately endured the horrors of the Shoah in their youth, lost their whole families, and merited after the war to raise a beautiful family of sons and daughters, outstanding Torah scholars and prominent personalities in their own right.

Mrs. Chana Rotenberg is the daughter of the distinguished Rabbi Shulem Duvid Horowitz *zt"l* — a man of noble spirit, learning, and from a prominent family — left alone after losing his parents and siblings early on during the enemy occupation of Poland. As a survivor he emigrated to Belgium, married, and settled in Antwerp, where he was at the forefront of every effort to reestablish Torah Judaism. In his final years he came on *aliyah* and made his home in Bnei Brak, attaching himself to the Rebbes of Gur. The episodes of suffering he endured, and of the suffering endured by his wife, may she live and be well, who also went through the Shoah, are interwoven throughout this book. Their story teaches the reader the power of faith and trust in Hashem by showing how people can lose their entire world and go on to build a new future with incomparable courage and resilience. Their daughter, although a second-generation survivor, has merited to fulfill the mitzvah of "Remember what Amalek did to you… do not forget," the mitzvah not to forget what that cruel nation inflicted on our people. In addition, the book fulfills the last wishes of the martyrs, may their blood be avenged, members of the author's extended family — pious, innocent, and upright people who perished and whose final request was that their memory be preserved and perpetuated.

As the years pass, and the survivors still among us, who will never forget the events of those days, dwindle in number, the importance of books such as this one grows. The author is the wife of a *talmid chochem* and the mother of *talmidei chachomim*. She has merited raising a new generation that upholds our holy Torah and is continuing the path forged by its ancestors, may the memory of the righteous be for blessing and their blood avenged — and that is the best possible victory over the wicked nation that sought to erase the Jewish people from the world's memory. May all of Heaven's blessings accrue to her and to all of her offspring.

Rabbi Yisrael Meir Lau
Chief Rabbi of Tel Aviv-Yafo

Rabbi Dovid Skolski

General Director
Kiddush Hashem Archives

Tishrei 5777

Many books have been written about the Shoah, long tales of blood, fire, and smoke, pages filled with memories that refuse to loosen their grip, endless lines laden with longing for mother and father, brother and sister, friends, neighbors, and all the holy, pure individuals who were murdered in those years of slaughter in the Valley of Death that was Europe.

Rivers of words and oceans of stories have rushed in torrents over the past seven decades since Nazi Germany laid down its weapons after the terrible destruction it wrought. Six million profiles have been sketched over the years, some more and some less, some plainly and some only in allusion. The common denominator among them all is their belonging to the past, to a world that once was and is no more. They were wiped out without a trace.

Very few books on the Holocaust include hope along with atrocity, rebuilding along with destruction, or a future along with the past that was erased. The core of these few books is usually the spirit that rose above the suffering of the body and survived seven levels of Gehinnom with true, steadfast heroism. It was this spirit that overcame helplessness and despair, defeat and devastation. This spirit brought forth glory from the ashes, defied death and chose life, and built a future on the ruins of the past.

The wonderful book you are reading is of that rare breed. With an artist's hand and in rich, flowing language, this book bridges the generation gap, skipping lightly between the suffering of those who survived the Holocaust and a privileged sector of today's youth.

The story told by Mrs. Chana Rotenberg, daughter of Rabbi Shulem Duvid Horowitz of blessed memory, an outstanding Agudath Israel activist, and his wife, may she live long and be well, is a rich tapestry, in which her parents' secret past before and during the war years in Poland is interwoven with vibrant scenes from her childhood in Antwerp, all leading up to her present-day role as a public speaker on Jewish heroism in the face of the Holocaust.

Through the trip to Poland that forms the framework of the book, Mrs. Rotenberg takes a creative educational approach to the mentality of today's young adults, who find the terrible events of the Holocaust hard to grasp. At the various stops on their itinerary, she relates her parents' experiences in the towns and cities, ghettoes and extermination camps of Poland, thus forging a personal link that connects the students to their people's past.

It is a powerful story that takes the reader on a rough journey through pain and sorrow, hope and joy. Yet the central axis of the story is unshakable faith, and this is the source from which the survivors draw the strength and vitality that saves them. This unshifting faith, too, is what enables them to move forward to the future and pave the way for generations to come.

Our organization, the Kiddush Hashem Archives, which works to preserve the memory of the spiritual heroism displayed by mighty Jewish souls during the Holocaust, sees it as a unique privilege to publish this book, which affords a rare glimpse into the soul and spirit of those who rebuilt the foundations of the Jewish world, while sketching the biographical background of the suffering those heroes endured.

The Kiddush Hashem Archives was privileged to have one of this story's heroes, Rabbi Shulem Duvid Horowitz of blessed memory, serve on the senior staff of our organization and give many days of his precious time to advancing its goals.

We hope and pray that this book, written in a style that crosses the cultural boundaries between sectors of modern Jewry, will find its way to the reader's heart and claim its rightful place in the literature of the Holocaust, fulfilling the wish of its distinguished author to hand down the legacy of unswerving faith from that generation of giants to the present generation and those to come.

With great respect,
Rabbi Dovid Skolski

A Letter from
Rebbetzin Esther Farbstein
Holocaust Researcher and Historian

Dear Chana,

Your family's history, and the way in which you have internalized your role as a second-generation survivor, have been a part of my life for years, and it makes my heart swell to see the story in writing at last, and in such an original way.

Every memory is a link to the past, but your story is a manifold link — a link to a family, a link to the Jewish people and its heritage, a link between Jew and Jew, person and person, and most of all, a link between past and future, an amazing bridge between a generation that was and the generation now flourishing in our Land.

Your reader follows you on a fascinating journey from Lodz to Jerusalem, from Bnei Brak to Krakow, from North Tel Aviv to Bayit Vegan, and takes part in the Jewish landscape of today which contains it all, but the thread that holds it all together is spun of faith and eternal Jewish values. You weave that thread through the story with your typically light touch and your ability to connect with any Jew, whatever his background.

Your special gift for speaking — for bringing a memory to life and making the audience feel that they, too, share in this obligation — comes through in the written story, as well.

My warm wishes go out to you on the publication of your book, and my blessings:

May it be G-d's will that your impressive extended family bring you much satisfaction and joy, that your mother continue to be a wonderful inspiration to you and to all of us, in robust health to the age of a hundred and twenty, that you should be blessed with the strength to continue your remarkable work, and that we should go on working together in friendship and with a sense of mission.

May it be G-d's will that what we have drawn from previous generous should pass on to future generations, and in that merit may we soon see complete redemption, as our Sages taught: "Whoever mourns for Jerusalem merits to see its joy" (*Taanis* 30).

Esther Farbstein
Jerusalem

Rabbi Eliyahu Ilani

Chairman, Nefesh Yehudi

How much knowledge, wisdom, and beauty were in that world… the world that went up in the flames of the Holocaust. How much can we draw from them to enrich the wellsprings of our lives. How much is it our duty to learn from them. In our trips to Poland, Nefesh Yehudi strives to fill the tremendous void left by the Shoah, and Chana Rotenberg, who takes part in these trips, has taken a great step toward fulfilling this impossible task. When she stands there, in that valley of death, and tells students about her parents and their world, about the greatness of spirit, the elevation, the humanity that emerged under those subhuman conditions, even the leaves shed tears.

In the book you now have in front of you, she seeks to continue that enormous task. The story of her childhood home, intertwined with vignettes from our trips, provides a unique glimpse into a charmed world that was, and which she tries to recapture for us. Her parents symbolize that rich world, and their story represents its pure essence.

Nefesh Yehudi has a longstanding relationship with the author. Her son, Rabbi Nechemia Rotenberg, has coordinated Nefesh Yehudi's activities in Vienna almost since our organization's inception. The mission she carries out on our trips, the work of art she presents in this book, and the parents she portrays are the best explanation for her son's accomplishments. The story of our trips, as told by her faithful hands, adds another layer to our family connection, and we are very proud and delighted for her.

Eliyahu Ilani

Contents

A Song of Thanksgiving

Song and praise to the Eternal Living G-d
Who has brought us to this point with
His merciful and loving Hand…

I am sincerely grateful to the many people who helped to transform this book from a relentless, but unfocused, urge to a tangible, readable reality:

- First of all, my dear parents, who raised me with self-sacrifice and devotion, surrounding me with kindness and generosity. My father, of blessed memory, who was saved from the inferno to serve as a fiery pillar of faith for everyone around him, with true Chassidic feeling and warmth. My mother, may she live long and be well, whose gentle, radiant personality is like a lighthouse of lovingkindness and unlimited giving for everyone she meets, but for us especially. May I merit to continue on their special path and bring them much *nachas*.
- My father-in-law, Rabbi Eliezer Rotenberg of blessed memory, an outstanding educator and a man of perfect integrity, and my mother-in-law, Mrs. Penina Leah Rotenberg of blessed memory. Her nobility of spirit and refined character traits shone on everyone who came into contact with her. She and her husband were our link to the wonderful generations of yesteryear.
- The talented writer and teacher Mrs. Miriam Aflalo, of whom I must say, "My book is her book." It was her pen that described my thoughts and feelings, her artistry that breathed life into the words, her craftsmanship that

untangled and edited the bundles of stories I conveyed to her. Miriam listened with rapt attention to every detail and managed to capture the spirit and atmosphere of my childhood home in Antwerp, as well as the emotionally charged journey through Poland with a group of Israeli graduate students. She fully entered into my experience and knew how to express all that I had to say, what I didn't know how to say, and what I left between the lines. I certainly don't know where to find the words to thank you, Miriam, for making a precious dream of mine come true by writing this book.

- My chief guide and mentor when I set out to do the background research for this book was Rebbetzin Esther Farbstein, a leading Holocaust historian in the chareidi community and a trailblazer in teaching the many episodes from that period which highlight the spiritual courage and heroism of our people. Rebbetzin Farbstein has been like a good angel, standing behind me, gently hitting me on the head, and giving me tools to cope and to bring this material deep into the heart of my audience. Through her books, lectures, and incisive personality, she has guided me past the many obstacles I encountered on the way.
- Nefesh Yehudi, the wonderful organization that brings secular Jewish students into contact with their spiritual heritage. It was an honor for me to meet their chairman, Rabbi Eliyahu Ilani, and their educational director, Mrs. Yael Zehavi, who both show astounding dedication to their holy work and who deserve endless admiration. The trip to Poland described in this book is distilled from the various Nefesh Yehudi trips I was privileged to accompany.
- Reb Aharon Wolfson, the guiding spirit and major supporter of *kiruv* today, whose concern for Nefesh Yehudi never wavers.

- The rabbis who led the Nefesh Yehudi trips were also indispensable to this book: Rabbi Yaakov Estreicher, Rabbi Dov Rosenblum, and Rabbi Natan Rosen. All displayed a remarkable ability to transform an experience from harrowing to empowering. This is no easy task, but when it is approached with all one's heart, with wisdom, and with insight, it has impressive and far-reaching results.
- The Ginzach Kiddush Hashem Archives and their head, Rabbi Dovid Skolski, for all the support and direction over the years. Our connection began with my father *z"l*, who ceased his public activities after coming on *aliyah* to Eretz Yisrael, but agreed to serve as a member of this organization and contribute to preserving the memory of the Holocaust and its spiritual heroism in any way he could.
- Mrs. Tova Yoskowitz, a senior staff member at the Archives, has always been there to provide me with didactic aids, and she has always urged me to go out and speak publicly about the spiritual heroism of our people during the war years. Her confidence in me is not to be taken for granted, and I am very grateful to her.
- My students at various seminaries, graduate programs, and lecture circuits, from a variety of cultures. Each has offered me their own sort of appreciation, and I've been enriched in a new way with every encounter.
- The friends, acquaintances, and colleagues who listened to segments of my story with patience and empathy, offering compliments and constructive criticism. And most of all I thank them for encouraging me to carry on and bring this work to completion.
- And last but not least, always foremost in my thoughts, I thank my dear family — my sons and daughters-in-law, my daughters and sons-in-law, who were with me all the way from the moment I began this project in earnest. Their

enthusiastic responses spurred me on, and their enlightening comments added a special touch to the final version.

- Especially, I thank the one who has been at my side all along, encouraging me ceaselessly, my esteemed husband, Rabbi Yeshayahu Pinchas Rotenberg *shlita,* who reviewed the text meticulously and put his mind and heart to the task of ensuring that a true and accurate story would emerge.

May it be the Creator's will that just as I have been privileged
to learn and to teach, to understand and leave this legacy,
so may we all merit to preserve and fulfill the mission
to which it obligates us. For there is much more
here than the written word can say....

Preface

Mexico City, July 1991

It's the middle of a summer day, and the whole family is gathered around the massive table in the dining room, near the picture window that looks out over the spacious, well-tended garden. In a few moments, we will witness an extraordinary event — a total eclipse of the sun. Scientists from all over the world have come to Mexico to document the phenomenon.

The children were sent home from school early, and my husband is home from the *kollel* where he teaches. People were asked not to be out in the streets, because looking at the sun, even during an eclipse, can damage the eyes.

At about one p.m., it begins. As if a curtain were slowly drawn, the sky grows gradually dimmer, and for a few brief moments, it is nearly as dark as night. An awed silence comes over us… stars appear… we hear the sounds of nocturnal animals aroused from their sleep… we hold our breaths…

I wonder if the others can hear my heart pounding. The darkness is thick and heavy, and it casts a feeling of foreboding over the world. Suddenly I don't know what I'm doing here in this dark place, thousands of miles from my home in Jerusalem and from my parents in Belgium. "Oh, please, bring the light back!" I find myself silently praying. For six endless minutes the darkness persists, and none of us utters a sound. The children look at me anxiously. And then, as if the curtain were slowly pulled back again, the sky starts to brighten. The stars fade away into the blue of midday, and the sun blazes once again in all its glory. We all step out into the garden, sighing with relief, grateful for the sun as if we've never seen its light before, enjoying its rays of warmth. That was a powerful experience that has stayed with me ever since.

When I decided, at last, to fulfill my life's dream that was buried deep inside me and allowed me no peace of mind — to tell the story of my parent's experiences during the Holocaust — the memory of the eclipse came back to me vividly.

Before the war, my parents were children growing up in warm, happy families, under comfortable circumstances, in thriving Jewish communities where their family members were prominent Torah scholars. Suddenly, the shadow of death and destruction fell over their world. It seemed as if the sun would never return. But incredibly, they survived and found the strength to rouse themselves from the ashes, push the darkness far away, and rekindle the light in their lives. Under these amazing circumstances I was born, and it is my privilege to bring you the story told in this book — the story of two edelweiss flowers that remained upright and blooming after the fiercest of storms passed over them and the sun came out to shine on them again in all its glory...

Chana Rotenberg
Jerusalem, 5778 (2018)

Introduction

HAR SINAI STREET LOOKS like any other street I've seen in Bnei Brak, with a shul at the beginning of the street, a falafel shop in the middle, an endless stream of pedestrians, cars maneuvering around each other, and a frenetic feeling in the air.

I find the building and press the intercom button. I'm rung in, and finding myself in a private stairway, I feel as if I've stepped into the past. All along the staircase, the wall is hung with framed pictures and hand-painted porcelain plates, wooden decorations and artificial flowers. Even the banister is old-fashioned, and a homely fragrance envelops me.

This is where Mrs. Horowitz lives — the lady I wrote about, Chana's mother. So many times I've thought about her, imagined her feelings, and felt that I admired her or just wanted to hug her, yet we've never met before. A few more steps, and I'm about to meet her.

It all began a year and a half ago, when I got a phone call from a woman named Chana Rotenberg, inquiring, was I the one who wrote the column on the weekly Torah portion in a certain magazine?

"Yes, that's me," I replied.

Well then, she would like to meet me. She had a project in mind that might interest me, and she felt it needed to be discussed face to face. Would that suit me?

She spoke with a subtle European accent that I couldn't place. I felt something interesting at my fingertips. I agreed to meet.

There was a window in my teaching schedule between two history lessons, and I jumped through it, straight into the lobby of the Jerusalem Gate Hotel.

From five meters away, I felt the energy of the woman sitting near the end of one of the coffee tables. This was she… there wasn't a doubt in my mind. She was just as I thought she'd be: animated and smiling, overflowing with pleasantness.

The waitress brought us two bottles of mineral water and two glasses and left us alone. Chana began to tell me about her dream. She had a story that was precious and sacred, and she simply had to publish it as a book. She would like me to write that book for her.

"Your biography?" I asked trying to get some sense of where this was going.

"No, no," she said. "It's the story of many people and many things, and a lot of different times and places. It's many stories that come together, and I want to write them all and tell them all and find a place for all of them in a book and in the hearts of all the people who will read it… but I really have no idea how to do it! And that's why I asked you to come…"

I began to understand that I didn't understand a thing….

"You see, the story doesn't begin in Poland before the war and end in the Diamond Bourse in Belgium. It continues way after that, and in fact it isn't really over yet, and if I knew how to write it, I would do it myself."

I looked at her, and I could see she meant it… but I didn't know how, either.

"Shall we begin?" I asked.

"Yes, let's begin," she agreed.

And so we met once a week, maneuvering between my teaching schedule and her lecture schedule, finding a quiet hour over two bottles of mineral water, a tiny mp3 player that I never managed to get to work properly, and a pen that I related to better.

On the street outside, Jerusalem's Central Bus Station bustled, drivers honked their horns and filled the air with soot; in the mall below us people looked for sales and sat at tables munching pizza.

But I wasn't there. I was pulled completely into Chana's stories, oblivious to the world around me, tearful, astonished, and wondering a thousand times by what merit I'd been chosen to be part of this amazing venture.

The meetings went on for a year. Chana told me the stories, I took notes, and the waitress knew what to bring us without even asking what we were having... those two funny ladies who came every week and drank water.

Chana captivated me. Her stories swallowed me whole; I would get lost in them, and then I'd have to ask her to stop for a moment, because I'd forgotten to take notes.

There were stories about her father and stories about her mother, about the Holocaust and the period of rebuilding, and about those who were there before the Holocaust. There were stories about the wonderful university students she'd come to know, and stories about her own life growing up in Antwerp's Jewish quarter. And all of it as true and real as if it happened yesterday.

We decided from the beginning that this wouldn't be a book where the writer fills in the gaps with her own narrative, as she imagined it. It would be very accurate, down to the color of the shoes, the bow in the hair, and the little story of the trick that was played at the summer camp in Luxembourg.

All the stories of the students, all the dialogue, and all the tearful songs, were taken down carefully, reflecting Chana's memories as faithfully as possible in the pages of this book.

Chana told me the stories, and I wrote them up. Chana made corrections, and I incorporated them.

After working with Chana for a year and a half, I felt that I simply must go to Har Sinai Street in Bnei Brak and meet her mother, a woman whom I could only imagine, and who, according to my reckoning, must have reached a very advanced age...

The woman who greeted me at the door was everything I hadn't imagined.

She stood straight, a lovely princess with a blond wig, blue eyes, a string of pearls on a perfectly ironed dress, and a smile that held all the kindness and humility in the world. She greeted me with warm words and two matching kisses.

Then she quickly disappeared into the kitchen and returned with a big silver tray, laden with freshly cut fruit, little pastries, two cups, and a sugar bowl. With the agility of a young girl, she put down the tray and asked if I'd prefer coffee or cola.

Somehow, I couldn't think of anyone else I knew who was so quick and energetic... except for Chana.

There was a thrill in that moment, finding myself in that European-style sitting room with the low, polished sideboard, the old, velvety sofas, and the big chandelier, dripping with crystals.

And the pictures... every wall was full of them! In black and white and in color, dozens of frames with sweet faces looking out of them. The entrance, the hall, the kitchen and the living room were covered with pictures like wallpaper, with hardly a space between them — pictures of grandchildren and great-grandchildren, family pictures at weddings, and studio pictures of toddlers.

I took a deep breath. Was this how people felt when they met the figures they'd secretly admired?

But Mrs. Horowitz couldn't understand why I was standing there like that, hardly breathing. Why wasn't I sitting on the sofa? I was her guest, wasn't I?

I sat down, sinking into the soft plush and sensing how everything around me was speaking.

"You ask, and I'll translate," said Chana, and then exchanged a few words with her mother in French.

"I understand French," I was happy to inform her.

So we spoke in French, with my Israeli and their Belgian accents, and as I felt the warm embrace of that house, I knew that the lady I'd just met was worthy of much, much more than I'd written about her.

Miriam Aflalo

CHAPTER 1

A New Story Begins

THIS ISN'T A STORY that began "one day." The story was there all the time, a chapter here and a chapter there, scattered around me, pages flying in the wind. But I never thought I had a story.

A long time passed before something changed. Something within me pushed its way up to the surface, arranged itself, and gathered all the scattered pages into one neat pile.

Maybe it was my guests who came from Vienna. Perhaps they inspired me to gather up the pages.

It was an ordinary, planned visit, with the guest beds ready, the cakes in the freezer, and someone going to pick up my son Nechemia, his wife Chaya, and their children from the airport for another happy reunion.

Their visits are a semi-regular arrangement. We wait until enough time has passed to start missing them intensely, and then we find any handy excuse — a bar mitzvah or a school vacation — to ask them to come and see us for a few delightful days.

For them, it's a chance to get reacquainted with all their Israeli cousins, to thaw the Austrian German off of their tongues and go back to chatting in fluent Hebrew; to get tanned by the Israeli sun and walk once again on the path of pale Jerusalem stone that leads up to our building in Bayit Vegan.

The visit began like all the others, with kisses, unloading the suitcases, and my saying all the usual "Bubby things" like, "How you've grown!" and, "Who is this little one that we hardly know?" And then we all went up to the apartment, filling the stairwell with our high spirits.

We sat down for a festive meal, home style. Yesterday the big pots had come out of their dark corner, and since then I'd been busy filling them with everything that I remembered they liked. There's nothing like a mother's home-cooked food when children of any age come back to visit.

So there we were, with steaming plates and clicking forks, enjoying the meal and most of all, talking. My husband wanted to know what was happening in Vienna, which was so very different from Jerusalem, yet was coming out of its eighty-year coma and beginning to sprout new buds in its Jewish community. Nechemia and Chaya lead a large organization of Jewish students in Vienna, the local branch of the worldwide Nefesh Yehudi, which seeks to foster a deeper and stronger Jewish identity among students in Israel and around the world. It keeps Nechemia and Chaya busy with work day and night, organizing lectures and learning groups, meeting students for personal conversations, and constantly hosting guests.

Jewish identity in Vienna has been growing steadily and gaining momentum, like a locomotive that keeps adding on more cars even as it speeds up: schools, shuls, kosher restaurants, and many new members of the community. The sidewalks of Vienna have known Jews for at least a thousand years, but the Jews there now don't necessarily know the heritage they possess. Recently, they've started wanting to know.

"This year we took the students on a trip to Poland," Nechemia was saying.

"You have no idea what that place does to every Jew who sets foot there. It almost forces you to feel connected; it gets into your bones so you can't get away from it. You realize more than ever how Jewish you really are, and how close Judaism is to you."

"A trip to Poland... a trip to Poland... a trip to Poland..." the words were like fireworks exploding inside me.

"Everything you've always wanted to say to the students about *emunah*, about strength, about the Divine plan, and the purpose of the Jewish People, you can say it best there, in Poland."

Nechemia talked, and the words set off sparks within me. "Poland... a trip to Poland... students... you can say it there..."

Could it be... that this was exactly what I needed?

I got up to serve the fancy dessert I'd made. Absentmindedly, I sliced it and handed out the portions. I felt like a robot running on the wrong program. Finally the words came out, almost weakly: "I want to go to Poland, too... No, I don't want to — I have to! I must!"

Nechemia looked at me in surprise. At that moment, looking a bit lost, I wasn't the mother he knew.

"Well, then, you should also go!" he said gallantly, and got up to get a little more chocolate cake for his wife.

"What do mean by 'also?'" I asked him. "I have no intention on joining some trip for retired people organized by some workers' union, with a guide giving touristy explanations. I need to go with people who can really share the experience with me — people I can cry with, people I can talk to, straight to the heart. If only I could go with young students who use their brains for thinking... but who would give me that opportunity?"

My husband tried to calm me. "What's the problem, Chana?" he said. "We have Nefesh Yehudi* here in Israel, too, and there

---

*Nefesh Yehudi (literally, "Jewish Soul") is an organization that provides secular university students in Israel (and in several places abroad) with an open window to the world of Judaism. Its goal is to afford the students opportunities to encounter and experience Judaism directly through study of Jewish texts, lectures, invitations to experience Shabbos with observant families, and educational trips such as the trip to Poland mentioned here.

are flights to Poland all the time. All we have to do is talk to the right people and find out how to arrange all the logistics. I'm sure you could get a place as a guest lecturer on a trip for students, and they'll be happy to hear what you have to say. But... are you sure you want to?"

I knew why he was asking that. And he knew that I knew. Was I really sure I wanted to do this?

"Yes, I'm sure!"

In the evening, after our guests had settled down for the night, we sat in the living room to talk about it. A comforting Yerushalmi breeze stole into the house. Now was the time for me to look for the right string and start pulling it — and the sooner, the better.

It didn't take long to get in touch with Nefesh Yehudi's coordinator in Israel, Yael Zehavi, and with the organization's chairman, Rabbi Eli Ilani. Yes, a trip to Poland was planned. But they were both rather skeptical. This was a trip for female students with an academic mindset, not for a bunch of enthusiastic high-school girls.

Did I understand that Nefesh Yehudi is not the right forum for nostalgic family stories, however touching they might be? A trip like this was not meant to be a purely emotional experience. These young ladies would need intellectually satisfying answers.

"Are you sure?"

Suddenly I found myself without words, as if I'd lost my script. "Are you sure?" they asked me. It was an echo of my husband's question. Was I sure?

No, I wasn't. But I needed to do it. And I had something to say. Of that I was sure.

And with that answer, I began to realize that I did have a story.

CHAPTER 2

A Forbidden Library Book

Antwerp, 1967

The silence in the library was thick. In the reading nooks, the people sat as if sculpted in one piece with their chairs, and not even a rustle was heard when they turned a page.

I was alone this time. My sister was busy, and none of my friends could come with me. I'd planned just to pop in quickly and go home, but instead, I found myself pacing back and forth on the wooden floor, gazing intently at the books on the juvenile literature shelves, and hearing the echo of my breath. It was no use, the book I wanted wasn't there.

From moment to moment, I was losing my patience. The library was overheated, and I felt the heat climbing from my feet to the tip of my hat. Mama always insisted that we dress warmly when we went out, but the radiators won out over her warnings. I opened the gold buttons on my gray wool coat, pulled off the hat Mama had knit for me the summer before, and stuffed it in my pocket.

I was looking for the latest volume of Enid Blyton's Famous Five series. All week, the girls in school had been talking about it, and I didn't want to be out of the loop. I went from one shelf to the next, quickly skimming the French titles, and wondering where the book could be. I was already familiar with most of the books, and I think they knew me almost as well. But the one I wanted just didn't seem to be there.

The librarian was busy with a balding man and a pile of books like a small mountain, and since interrupting was out of the question, I started browsing around in other sections of the library, glancing back at the librarian's desk every few moments to see if she was almost finished with the voracious reader.

Without knowing quite how, I suddenly found myself in front of a shelf holding Holocaust books, which were held back by a rope, on which a sign was hung, stating clearly in French that these books were only for readers aged sixteen and up.

Sixteen… and I was only twelve. What was in those books that I was too young to read? It must be awfully interesting…. Suddenly determined, I tossed my short hair and made up my mind: Somehow, I was going to get a book from here. If I could just think of some way of fooling the librarian, or smuggling a book out…. There was no way I could look sixteen, since I actually looked about ten.

I was feeling brave. I just had to wait for an opportunity. Then I saw Bella, my friend Debbie's older sister, and I knew the moment had come. I chose a title and asked her to take it and check it out for me at the desk in her name. She studied my face for a moment, without even reaching for the book, as if to see if I was really serious about reading it. Quickly, I thrust it into her hand before she could say no. "Please," I wheedled. "Just take it out in your name, that's all I'm asking!"

It was snowing lightly when I left the library. I buttoned up my coat and put my woolen hat back on. Ensconced in my leather bag was a forbidden book. I started brainstorming for ways to keep it concealed from Mama. After all, it wasn't meant for anyone younger than sixteen, and Mama never liked it when we broke rules.

At home, I read it whenever I was safe from watchful eyes. I found myself transported to a terrible, surreal world of atrocity. These were the first Holocaust books, published in the 1950s, compiled from diaries, documents, and personal testimonies, unvarnished and with zero aesthetic distance. They most certainly were not for children, especially not for children born in the postwar years, like me.

We all knew that there had been a Holocaust. We knew our people had been decimated; we even knew about the camps. But we didn't feel personally connected to it. For me, it was like reading about the Inquisition— a dreadful but faraway world of dungeons, instruments of torture, and masked inquisitors.

With wide eyes, behind the closed door of my room, I read this forbidden book, this book meant for grownups.

That first book was followed by another, and then another. Debbie's sister would exchange the books for me every time, never omitting that gaze of perplexed surprise.

Of course, as my furtive reading became a habit, I stopped being so cautious. And one day, it happened. A friend came knocking at the front door, I put the book down on the desk in my room and forgot it there. It was a book by Simon Wiesenthal, and it was lying out in the open for a good few hours.

My mother passed through the room, picked it up, stared at the cover for a long moment, and then looked at me silently.

I lowered my eyes.

Mama didn't yell at me. She never lost her temper. She just took it away, asked me when I planned to go back to the library to return it, and told me she didn't want me reading it anymore.

"Yes, Mama," I said obediently. And I didn't read any more of that book.

But the rope strung across that library shelf, now coupled with Mama's prohibition, kindled my imagination even more. I sneaked more Holocaust books into the house, hiding them more carefully now, and I read them at night by flashlight, under my blanket.

To me, it was a kind of scary thrill, one big horror story that had nothing to do with me, and never would.

CHAPTER 3

How Could I Not Have Known?

I WAS ON A TEL AVIV campus, telling the story of the forbidden book to a group of students. It came after a long interview with Yael Zehavi, the return of my guests to Vienna, and a deep inner struggle between fear and desire.

Yael Zehavi had asked me to give an introductory lecture at the university, and after that, to bring my parents to meet with the students, so they could meet the protagonists before hearing the stories.

A small group of young women sat before me in student chairs of orange plastic. Loose-leaf binders were open in front of them, pens were ready, and they weren't writing anything. Strips of light from the fixtures in the ceiling shone up at me from the polished floor, and I drew a bit of encouragement from their glow for this first-time lecture of mine.

When I arrived, concealing my chattering teeth, they looked at me as if they knew what I was about to say. Most of them were already working toward their master's degrees, and there wasn't much about life that was news to them.

I could almost hear their thoughts. "Another one from the second-generation… Now she's going to start telling us about finding loaves of stale bread hidden in the closets… And every time she left half a cracker uneaten, her mother would tell her about waiting in line in the ghetto for a bowl of soup... And then she'll describe the screams in the night from her parents' room, their terrible dreams, the numbers on their arms and the atrocities. Of course it's interesting, but we've heard all these things before."

But they soon realized my story was different, and now they were looking at me with a fresh supply of curiosity, all their previous thoughts erased.

"When I was around your age," I said to the quiet group in the orange chairs, "I knew approximately nothing about all this. I didn't think of myself as 'second generation.' The idea never even occurred to me.

"In my own mind, I became a 'daughter of Holocaust survivors' much later, when my own children were already grown. That was when it hit me like a bombshell. All of a sudden, I realized that my parents had actually *experienced* the Holocaust."

The orange chairs started shifting a bit. Sparks of surprise and curiosity appeared in my audience's eyes as they waited to hear how it happened, who told me, and how I could possibly not have known all those years.

"We didn't live in a vacuum," I told them. "We knew that Papa was from Poland; he told us a lot about his childhood there, about the *cheder*, about his friends and the foods he loved. Mama was from Poland, too, but she hardly told any stories about it...""For us, Poland was a country behind the Iron Curtain that once, long ago, had been our parents' home. A great place for fathers and mothers to be born in.

Yes, the adults would sometimes talk about the '*lager*,' which was a sort of secret code word from a world where children were barred from entering. We knew that '*lager*' meant a camp. We weren't stupid, but we were very innocent, or perhaps, subconsciously, we chose to be that way...

We never asked ourselves, what do they mean by 'camp?' A concentration camp? An extermination camp? It was just a camp. We didn't think beyond that. Why be negative? Maybe there were nice camps that they went to for the summer, with activities and friends...

Yes, there was something vague in the air, like a curtain drawn tightly to hide something, and we weren't allowed to know what that something was. The 'keep out' sign was invisible, but we sensed it, and we didn't go there. It faded over the years, and the red lights around it stopped flashing, but the curtain remained closed, maintaining a permanent silence about something we weren't meant to know.

Children know when they're supposed to leave something alone, even if no one says so out loud. They sense it very strongly.

It was only after we'd all grown up and left home that the curtain was torn away, and we saw that Gehinnom. There was no one there to shield us from it. It wasn't some distant Gehinnom in the past, involving other people. It was my own parents' private Gehinnom, the parents I'd always loved. The people who symbolized perfection and happiness, the essence of the good life, and most of all, they were figures of strength and confidence who positively radiated well-being. What on earth did that Gehinnom have to do with them?

I went looking for the answer to that question: How were they able to go on with their lives, not just to live but to sing the song of life, to raise happy children, when they emerged from that darkness?

After much searching, I found the answer. I understood where my parents came from, where they drew their strength from, what sustained them, and how they could get up every morning to another day of life, children, work, and friends. How they could smile, be joyful, raise us to be good Jews, be active in the community, and remain truly happy... and then, at the end of a long day, take a little sleeping pill so that the children wouldn't have to hear any screams when the nightmares came.

"And I would like to tell you about the answer I found," I

said to the students seated in front of me. "That is actually why I'm here — to talk about strength and might, and where it came from."

From the middle chair, a hand went up. A young woman with shining brown eyes and freckles introduced herself as Ilanit, and she had a question.

She had grandparents who'd been through the Holocaust. They had married in a displaced persons camp and made *aliyah* to the sands of Tel Aviv, to build a new generation there. She knew nothing about these grandparents; they had both passed away. She'd been a small child when her grandmother was taken to her rest in a small funeral, followed shortly afterward by her grandfather.

"When I was older," Ilanit said quietly, "they started teaching us about the Holocaust in school. There were special programs on Yom HaShoah, a research project on our family roots in ninth grade, and a documentation project in eleventh grade.

"Whenever I would come to my mother with questions, trying to find out the names of cities, or any meaningful stories she could tell me about my grandparents' experience, I would come up against a brick wall. She had nothing to tell me; Saba and Savta had taken their secrets to the grave. 'But Mama, why didn't you ask them?!' I would protest, with the impatience of a teenager. 'How could you not have heard any stories from them? Didn't you have to do projects on the Shoah when you were in school?' I couldn't understand her. How could anyone be born to parents who went through so much and not know anything about it?'

"One day, when I'd been pestering her all afternoon with my questions, she burst out in a rage: 'I didn't know, and I didn't want to know. Do you think I would come and ask them about the Shoah? Who needs to ask about something they live with day and night?' My mother is a strong, self-controlled woman. She manages an employment agency, and she never gets upset about anything. But there she was, with all her defenses broken down, and whatever she had left, she was throwing in my face.

"'Yes, my fine young lady who wants to know,' she said to me, 'I had a bad enough time with what I didn't know. I grew up in the shadow of "there"; it was more than enough of a presence in my life without asking any questions. So much of a presence that I didn't want to know any more. I just didn't want to... okay?!

"'I'll tell you what I did know,' she went on furiously. 'I knew it was terrible to leave a bit of bread in my lunch pack, or two sips of milk in my cup. I knew what I was in for if I didn't finish my soup, and I knew that if my class was going on an all-day trip and wouldn't be home until late at night, I would never be allowed to go. And I knew it was very dangerous to get chilled or sick, because I might die. So I couldn't go out in the winter, I couldn't have ice cream, I couldn't eat in restaurants, and I couldn't sleep at friends' homes.

"'I knew that at night, the nightmares came, and I'd hear them screaming in their sleep, right through the thick bedroom wall. Even if I pulled the feather comforter over my head, those screams would invade my dreams, the dreams of a little girl who wanted to remain a child and wasn't able to... I knew that we had no grandparents, no uncles, aunts, or cousins. We had nothing, nothing! We weren't even allowed to be happy, or to laugh out loud. There was a shadow in our house that wouldn't let us be Tel Aviv Sabras like all my friends at school. I knew that Yom HaShoah was a terrible day, and that every day was a bit of a Yom HaShoah. So tell me,' my mother said to me with tears in her eyes, 'do you think I didn't know enough? Do you really think I wanted to know more?'

"So after that, I didn't ask her any more questions. I never spoke about the Holocaust or brought home any material related to it. I even skipped the twelfth-grade trip to Poland. 'Why cause my mother pain?' I thought to myself, trying to imagine those nights she spent in her bed with the screams from her parents' room in the background. 'Why go there, to the place that to her, meant only...'"

Ilanit left the sentence unfinished and went back to the gist of her question. "And now you say that you didn't know. You didn't know that your parents were in the camps, you didn't know that they lost their whole families… but how could you not know? Even if they didn't tell you, how could it be? Didn't you ever ask yourself, where are my Saba and Savta, my aunts and uncles and all the relatives everyone else has? Didn't you wonder why you never heard stories from your mother about her high-school days, or where your father learned when he was a *bochur*?

"Didn't you ever ask yourself what the adults were talking about? Didn't it seem strange to you that there were secrets in your home, that your mother and her friends would make these vague allusions to 'that' or 'there' or the *lager*, or whatever their code was for it in whatever language they spoke, but it always meant this one unknown thing? Wasn't there a mournful atmosphere in your house, sort of an unspoken rule against laughing and having fun?"

"No!" I answered simply. "There was no mournful atmosphere. In the community I grew up in, there were thirty Jewish girls in one class, and we had nice dresses and stylish shoes, we came to class every day with our school supplies in our bags and smiles on our faces. There was only one girl who had a grandmother — and she was the exceptional one. It was such an oddity that we all got to know her grandmother well. 'Imagine that!' we thought. 'Some people have grandparents.'

"Where I grew up, the same secret was in every home. We were all children of Holocaust survivors. I didn't grow up here in Israel; I grew up in Antwerp, Belgium. Maybe that is half of the answer, but the other half is about my parents, about who they were. That part of the answer is what I learned when that curtain was torn away, and that is what I came to tell you about."

CHAPTER 4

A Gift for Mama

BUT ALL THOSE FINE words didn't make it any easier.

A week before the scheduled trip, doubt was still gnawing at me, like a particularly stubborn worm. The roar of my upstairs neighbor's vacuum cleaner added its own nagging message that Pesach was just a few weeks away, and despite my best efforts, crumbs of *chametz* were still happily occupying my kitchen cupboards and forgotten corners of the house. Amid all this disorder and the thousand guests I was planning to have in my home for the holiday, I was actually contemplating a trip to a place where grass grew over scars of the past that would never heal.

What was I thinking? I'd never been a teacher, I had never given a lesson or a lecture, and I had no idea what was really appropriate to say and what wasn't. Was I truly suited to accompany the girls on this trip?

Yes, I really did want to go, but my fears had me on the verge of despair. How would I find the words? What if I opened my mouth and nothing but sobs came out, the only way to give voice to feelings so long locked inside?

My husband had asked me if I was sure. The rush of weeping was what he meant when he asked me that. The moment when it would all be released, uncontrollable as a river behind a broken dam. Did I really want to cry that badly?

Yes, something within me insisted. I want to cry, I need to cry, I have to cry. But once I allowed myself to cry, how would I ever stop?

All that day, the doubts flailed about in my mind, making me dizzy. The big suitcase that I'd pulled out of storage lay wide open in the side room, hungering to be filled. Not a single item had left my closet yet to go and quiet its whining. I was like a mouse in a cage, a mouse on a circling treadmill: I'm going to do this. No, I can't. I'm going to Poland. No, I'm not. Endlessly around and around.

Until evening. That was when Mama called. Her voice was soft. "Chana," she said to me in Yiddish, and for me it was like a *bas kol,* a Heavenly voice sent to guide me: "I just wanted to wish you a successful trip. I think it's a great thing you're doing — a very, very great thing."

Suddenly, I was calm. Suddenly, it was surprisingly clear. "I'm going!" I said to myself. "Mama wants me to go, and now nothing can convince me not to. If my mother wants it, this will be my gift to her — a trip to Poland."

Holland, 1959

One evening, my big sister gathered all of us younger siblings together secretly. "We're going to make a birthday party for Mama," she announced. She arranged us in a little row and taught us a song and two short skits. "We'll give her a present, too," she whispered with glowing eyes.

"A present?" We gazed at her wonderingly with our innocent eyes. "Where will we get money for a present?"

"We're going to make her a jewelry box," she said conspiratorially. "I've got it — I'll show you." She brought out a wooden cigar box, a common item in many Dutch households. The upstairs neighbors had been happy to give her one of their empty ones. It looked strong, but

plain and crude, nothing like a birthday present. But my sister had it all worked out. "Now bring all your most beautiful seashells," she said. Walking on tiptoe, we went to our collections of precious shells, selected the most the colorful and exotically shaped ones we had, the sort you wouldn't find every day on the shores of the Netherlands. One by one, we handed them to her, and she glued them firmly to the plain wooden box while we looked on wide-eyed. This would be a gift that encapsulated all of our love. Our most precious shells! We could have bartered any one of them for at least three crepe-paper flowers in the unofficial children's marketplace on the beach.

When all the shells were in place, she spread lacquer over the whole creation until it shone almost as brightly as our little faces.

In the morning, we were ready. We'd put on our nice pleated skirts, and we stood before Papa and Mama, excited and nervous. We sang our song, acted out our skits, and presented Mama with our gift. She was overjoyed. Surely in all of Holland she couldn't have found a more beautiful jewelry box, covered with shells of infinite love.

CHAPTER 5

Takeoff

ROW 17, MIDDLE SEAT. Suddenly the plane seemed so small, just a low-ceilinged room with tiny windows, with no place to move around and no way of getting out. The seats were very gray, with a pattern of thin, trembly yellow stripes. But the overhead lights were so bright that the yellow stripes stood out all the more.

I found row 17 and the middle seat. I had my carry-on bag with me, and the flight attendant gave me a smile that matched the satin scarf around her neck. It was all so typical, yet it wasn't. In a way, it made perfect sense, yet in all other ways, it made no sense at all. I couldn't make up my mind how I should feel.

"We'll be taking off in ten minutes," the loudspeaker informed me in several languages. "We wish you a safe and pleasant journey. Thank you."

A pretty young woman with long, curly brown hair asked me to excuse her as she wriggled past me to the window seat.

There is something awkward about those rows of three seats in planes, and most awkward of all is to find yourself in the middle seat, cramped between two strangers, not quite knowing what to do with your hands and your feet.

But the young woman next to me didn't seem bothered at

all. She smiled at me as if we'd long been acquainted, and even extended a slender hand, unadorned with rings.

"I'm Shaked," she introduced herself, "and you're Chana." She explained that she'd heard my introductory lecture on campus and was very impressed. She thought it was amazing to bring someone on this trip who'd experienced the Shoah in such a personal way, and she was sure I would add a lot to their experience. Her eyes were smiling and thoughtful at the same time, and despite her almost childlike voice, one could see that she was a serious thinker.

Then she opened the little window shade and spoke half to me and half to the asphalt outside.

"I can't believe I'm doing this," she said. "I closed up my apartment, let my younger brother take my car, and left my dog with friends, even though he's howling there for me.

"I keep trying to convince myself that this is the right thing to do, even if it meant giving up a vacation. And really, Chana, it wasn't an easy decision."

Shaked paused to stow away her coat and arrange her shoulder bag under her seat, and then she turned to me again to share the niggling doubts that still lingered in her heart.

"We finished the semester two days ago, and I had so many plans in mind, and so many places I'd been wanting to go. And Poland wasn't one of them."

Shaked sighed and fixed her gaze on a nearby plane that was just rising off the end of the runway.

"But here you are, despite it all," I remarked.

"Despite it all." She smiled. "In the end, I decided to come on this trip. I spent a lot of time thinking about it, and a lot of time regretting it. But I decided that this time, I'd give myself a meaningful trip — something that was worth giving up a vacation for, and the trip to Africa I was planning. And I really hope it will be meaningful enough, that I won't regret my choice, and I'll come home with something more in my life."

"I hope so, too," I thought to myself silently, and I meant every word. "I hope it will be meaningful for you, for me, for my parents, and my aunts and uncles, and all the members of my family that I never knew."

After some ten seconds of silence, Shaked spoke again. "I hope my dog won't be too angry at me when I come back. You know, to leave her like that for more than a week..."

"Yes, I know, it can feel like a long time. But if it turns out good, the time will go quickly."

The plane rushed along the runway, faster and faster, and suddenly it lost its grip on the asphalt, and we were moving into the blue sky of Eretz Yisrael. The scenery below us tilted, and then the window next to Shaked was filled with the buildings of Gush Dan, small and crowded. My dear Shaked, I thought, this trip has just got to be meaningful. It simply must.

Shaked was leaving her dog behind, and I was leaving everything I had been until then....

CHAPTER 6

Tell Us Something New

A BUS PICKED US UP at the airport. It was modern and sleek, and like a child who knows his way home, it navigated the streets of Warsaw confidently. We found seats haphazardly, after shoving our suitcases hastily into the baggage compartment and fleeing from the biting cold into the comfort of the heated bus. All the girls looked alike now, enveloped in big woolen scarves, gloves, and puffy coats, with only their eyes left to show their first impressions of Poland. And without words, that first encounter had as much to say as any lecture. Frigid Poland... gray Poland.

With my eyes I count the full seats. Fifty girls, university students from all over Israel. Welcome to our Poland trip! Fifty girls! Yael Zehavi had said it would be nothing for me. Where was she now, to make it nothing?

The flight had been very short; it hadn't left me much time for stomach pains and thinking I'd been a fool to take this on. And now I was already here, on the land that had raised my parents, given them a sweet childhood, and then suddenly turned around and sent them flying, with a mighty kick, nearly to their deaths.

They were saved, and they didn't look back. They had no desire to be pillars of salt, self-doomed in refusal to move on.

"Forward! Forward!" they told themselves ceaselessly. "Keep moving — life is calling us! The children are calling us! And the past lies dead among the fire and brimstone that rained down on this place."

Poland ceased to be, so that we could be. And now I am here, retracing their steps, searching for the path they trod and hoping to gather up all the fragments of words and deeds still hovering here.

In Warsaw, the girls walk about dumbstruck. It's a big city with orderly streets; no one could detect that it was bombed and broken. No one could spot, among the masses of people on the pavements, the boys and girls who clung to the walls at night with pounding hearts, waiting for the searchlight to pass, praying with whatever words they had left that they wouldn't be caught. Not yet… they wanted to live…

This morning, Warsaw is still dozing, as on any ordinary winter morning. It stretches under its blanket of snow and opens one eye, giving us a bored look. "Oh… tourists again," it says to itself.

Rotem comes to walk beside me, bringing Tanya along. Rotem is Israeli to the core, with a brownish complexion and dark eyes, and Tanya is from Moldavia, with Slavic features and blue-gray eyes. They've been good friends since high school. Rotem didn't come up to me to ask questions. Earlier that morning she'd sat next to me in the bus that took us from the airport into the city, drinking her coffee, fiddling with her packed sandwich, and looking as though she were hoping for something.

I invited her to share my box of homemade date cookies. "I've never known any kid to refuse them," I said with a smile.

"I'm twenty-four," she confided, "but it's always fun when there's still something to be a kid for. Especially when you get cookies…"

Rotem was captivated by the cookies. "My mother doesn't bake," she said, laughing at herself, "so I always get carried away when I someone offers me something home-baked. In our house, the oven is mainly used as a mirror by people in a hurry. I don't remember any dough ever being put in it. Someday, when I have kids of my own to spoil, you'll give me your recipe and explain how to make things like this, won't you?"

By cookie number five, I knew that her father was a scientist at the Weizmann Institute, and her mother was a doctor at Ichilov Hospital. They had a huge house in Rechovot, near Weizmann, and a top designer had made them a kitchen like something out of a magazine, with French windows and an oak wood floor. But baking didn't happen there.

"My mother is very warm and loving," said Rotem. "I don't want to give the impression that I grew up as a latchkey girl, coming home every day to a fancy, locked door. No, she always finds time for me, even when she has a million things to do... but she just isn't the cookie-baking type. If we want a snack, we can always find plenty in the cupboard, or we can go down to the corner grocery and get whatever we want. But those cookies, you eat with your teeth. Cookies like yours, you eat with your heart."

And now the two girls were walking alongside me as if we were old friends, and very accustomed to touring Warsaw...

"Will you be speaking today?" Rotem asked, lowering her voice.

"No, I don't think so. We didn't have any family in Warsaw."

"Then who will be speaking?"

I shrugged my shoulders. I had no more information than she did. "But why does it matter to you who's speaking?"

"It doesn't matter. You all speak well. I just hope we're not going to hear all the old mantras from high school, about the uprising, and the heroism of the brave Ghetto Fighters who wouldn't go like sheep to the slaughter."

"You don't want them to talk about that?" I had to make sure I was hearing her right.

"Definitely not. I could write a doctoral thesis on Mordechai Anielewicz, just from all the ceremonies we had in high school, and the songs we sang on Yom HaShoah, and all the bla, bla, bla from our high school trip. I came on this trip to hear something different."

She looked at me with eyes so intelligent and serious, and Tanya, walking beside her, silently expressed her agreement. They wanted a different kind of trip.

The streets of Warsaw were still as cold as before, and the girls were still very quiet, but Rotem's eyes were burning with a new depth. "Don't see us like that," her big, dark eyes seemed to say. "Don't see us as that stereotype of the young, brash Israeli. Inside us, there's a sea of longing for something beyond the boundaries of our lives, something from a world we've never known. Inside us, there's a hunger for something new, something we desperately hope will touch us. Inside us is a blank sheet, waiting for someone to write new words that our hearts have never heard before."

CHAPTER 7

A Different Type of Person

I READ THE MESSAGE IN Rotem's eyes, and then an image came up in my mind's eye: an elderly Jew, a Holocaust survivor, speaking from a video screen at Yad Vashem. I sat there on an empty bench, waiting for the video to start again from the beginning. And he began talking about Auschwitz, and about a hat — a hat that meant life or death. If you showed up for morning roll call with your hat on, you could hope for another day of life. If you had no hat, step this way, you must die. The man on the screen stated these facts simply, as if there really had been such a place on this earth.

One evening, he went back to the wooden shelf that served as his sleeping accommodation and found that his hat was missing. Had it been stolen? Or taken by mistake? There was no time to quibble over how it had disappeared. It made no difference. To be caught without a hat was a death sentence.

That night, he lay awake, waiting until everyone else had fallen asleep. He must try to spot a hat that had slipped out of its owner's grasp. Ah... he saw one... on a bunk, peeping out from under a sleeping barracks-mate. Just a few meters away. But would he be able to get it?

In total silence, he moved across the floor, feeling life restored to him with every inch, and knowing that another life would be taken tomorrow morning. But he gave no thought to that. One thought alone occupied his mind: how to get his hands on that hat without waking up the man lying on it. Slowly, with infinite care, he pulled the hat out from under the sleeping man. And at last, the treasure was in his hands, and he could sleep for the remainder of the night.

In the morning, they all awoke to the sound of the alarm and the barking that summoned them to roll call. The usual scramble ensued, and in the midst of it, a desperate cry rang out: "Where's my hat?! Has anybody seen my hat?! It was with me when I went to sleep!"

He heard his comrade's cries and his hand, stiff with cold, tightened its grip on the hat. He followed the other men out to the square where they lined up each morning and took his place, waiting for his number to be called.

He knew that another man went out hatless to the morning lineup. He heard that man's number called, and he heard the shot. He was alive, and someone else was dead. That was the Holocaust.

I remember sitting on that backless bench at Yad Vashem, stunned, looking for some tears to cry with. "Why?" I asked myself. "Why tell such a terrible story, a tragedy so cruel in so many ways? Why choose that story?"

"Because it's the truth. That's what the Holocaust looked like," the bare concrete walls answered me. "Are you really that naïve? Do you think he was the only one who did such a thing? Do you think his story was exceptional?"

The Holocaust brought out the worst in people. It led them to denounce and betray, to cooperate with the enemy in return for slightly better living conditions, even for status.

When they were removed from their homes and herded into ghettoes, they found themselves packed into a few square feet of space in a room shared with several other families. Did I really think they all waited politely until someone graciously made room for them? The reality was full of ugly quarrels, endless frictions, violence, and an underworld mentality.

The deprivation and hunger, the dying children, the exposure to violence with no means of defense, were desensitizing to the point that people could step over a corpse, stopping only to check if it had anything of value — such as a crust of bread — in its pockets.

The atrocities they witnessed stamped out people's humanity, made them abandon their *tzelem Elokim*. This is a sad and painful fact that could fill many chapters. But still — was this the whole book? Were there no other chapters in this terrible saga?

"All right," I said to myself as I stepped out into the sunlight of the Yad Vashem courtyard. "So that was one facet of the Holocaust. People were dehumanized. But there were other people and other kinds of moments, and I'm going to tell that story. I know those other people. I was raised by two of them, and they made other choices and etched them on my soul. That is my task, to spread the word about that facet of the Holocaust."

And now, my boots were crunching on the thin snow that covered Warsaw. A red light stopped us in the middle of crossing a wide street, and we stood crowded on a too-narrow traffic island, in a cloud of vapor created by our own breath. And again, the eyes all around me seemed to speak aloud: "We don't want to be stuck here on this narrow strip of life. We came here for something more, a new perspective. We want to enter into a new story, and we're waiting for you to tell it."

That evening after supper, relaxed and well fed, we gathered in the hotel's conference hall to get better acquainted. Each of us in turn introduced herself and said a few words about her background and current occupation. Well, each woman who stood up and spoke seemed to have more academic credentials than the one before her... B.A., B. Ed., M.S.W., M.A, M.S... senior police detective, hi-tech office manager. My turn was coming closer and closer, and I felt smaller and smaller. I'd never been to college, and I didn't even have one letter after my name. What was I going to say?

My moment of doom arrived. The young lady next to me finished telling the group about all her sociology courses and her research on Africa, and it was my turn now. I took a deep breath, smiled, and said, "I graduated from university with every degree you could name. I have doctorates in many subjects." I had their attention. They waited expectantly, their eyes bright with curiosity or disbelief, and I went on: "I am the mother of eight children and grandmother to more than thirty. I have a degree in cooking, a degree in medicine, a doctorate in adolescent psychology, and another doctorate in early childhood education. I'm an experienced counselor and mediator for all sorts of emotional issues and disputes. I've conducted an endless amount of research."

The round of applause as I finished speaking told me that I'd gotten through to my audience. Here, too, I had another story to tell.

CHAPTER 8
In the Shtetl

In the morning, we traveled on. Next on our itinerary was Tiktin.

It was like going back in time to a Jewish shtetl from days gone by. You could almost hear voices from the houses speaking Yiddish; you could almost see Jewish boys in peaked caps scampering around in the streets.

Our guide had a plan for pulling us back into the past. She brought out a huge plastic bag from the bus's baggage compartment, and announced that we were going to have a wedding. Without even an audition, she started casting members of the group in starring or supporting roles.

In one hand she held a piece of white tulle, and in the other a crown of shiny, white plastic flowers. "Who wants to be the *kallah*?" she asked.

"Me!" cried Yif'at, making a grab for the costume before anyone could beat her to it. "I'm the *kallah*," she announced to all the others who'd wanted the coveted role, smiling as if she'd won the lottery.

"Who wants to be the *shadchan*?" Now the guide was holding up a brown suit with old-fashioned buttons. There was no rush-and-grab this time, but Shaked was willing to give it a try, although she wasn't quite sure what a *shadchan* was supposed to do. Didn't they gossip all the time about everyone and everything?

Of course not, she was told. Not all the time, and not about everyone... they only said what was necessary to promote a *shidduch*. But you could make some fine matches here in the shtetl. Who knows all the girls here better than you?

"Who wants to be the rabbi?" The rabbi? That sounded like a more complex role. "What does the rabbi do at a wedding?" Tanya asked. "I really don't know a thing about rabbis..."

Yes, Tanya was from that place that doesn't know. A rabbi was a Jewish priest; that was about as far as her knowledge of the subject went.

The guide let Tanya try on the rabbinical cloak and top hat. "Okay. You'll do," she decided.

Mother of the bride? The righteous Bubbe? The fisherman? The barber? The *shvigger*?

One after the other, the costumes were drawn out of the bag like rabbits from a magician's hat. Merriment filled the air as the girls put on their costumes, feeling very proud of themselves and waiting for the show to begin.

Last but not least — who would be the *chosson*? Noa shot a mirthful glance at the *kallah*. "What do you say, Yif'at? Will you be my bride?"

"Hey, wait!" said the guide. "That's not how it works. You don't just decide between yourselves. First the *shadchan* has to talk to the parents, and they decide whether it's a suitable match. If they agree to it, then you meet and see how you like each other."

"Right!" said Shaked. "And don't forget that the prospective groom is a widower with three kids and a hunchback, but he has enough money to buy himself this beautiful young bride."

"Can't you be a little more positive?" someone scolded her. "The bridegroom is a tzaddik who learns in a famous yeshiva, and the bride has a big dowry. Her father is the richest man in the shtetl. As the village matchmaker, you ought to know that."

The jovial atmosphere pushed the cold aside. "We have a *chuppah,* a *shadchan,* a nice dowry. Let's get on with it!" said the tour guide. "Where's the rabbi? The modest young maiden has said 'yes' to the outstanding suitor, and the parents drank a *l'chaim.* It's time to set up the *chuppah* in the ancient courtyard of the shul — on the same spot where they made the *chuppah* for all the couples who were married in Tiktin... maybe there was even a *chuppah* here for your grandfather's great-grandmother..."

Maybe.

The authentic-sounding music, the makeshift *chuppah,* and the old courtyard with the grass sprouting up between the stones stirred something in every heart. Yif'at was a blissful bride as she stood beside Noa, while everyone else clapped their hands to the music. It was as if the shtetl had come back to life and its people had come back to take part in the celebration, quietly mingling with the Israeli girls from the university campuses. "You are our own," the ghostly figures seemed to whisper to the circle of dancers in the heart of the shtetl.

"Your history doesn't begin with the 'tower-and-stockade' settlements of the British Mandate period, or with the First or Second Aliyah," they said. "It doesn't begin with the first Zionist Congress in Basel, or the gymnasium in Warsaw. Someone cut out whole swaths of the scroll. They hid the true story from you, the story of a thousand years of Jewish life in the Polish shtetl — right here, where pure-hearted, G-d-fearing people walked, and over there, in the marketplace and the town square. Their houses were just like those, with wooden fences and a *mezuzah* on the doorpost, and *everybody* went to shul, including your great-great-great-grandfather. Even if his grandson was on the *Exodus* and picked oranges in khaki shorts, part of his past is buried here. No — part of his past lives here!"

Perhaps that was what Rotem meant when she expressed her hope that the speakers wouldn't rehash all the old clichés from high school. Rotem's family roots weren't even in Europe; her parents were Iraqi, but what did that matter? Her eyes showed the same hunger as all the others. What difference did it make to the common history of all the Jews, everywhere on the globe? Didn't the Jews of Iraq also suffer from the hatred of their non-Jewish neighbors and from outbreaks of anti-Jewish violence? And on the other hand, wasn't there a large and flourishing Jewish community in Iraq, too, with *batei midrash* and Torah scholars, children learning in Talmud Torah, and mothers kneading challah dough in honor of Shabbat?

So what difference was there? Her veins, too, had been injected with the same one-sided Zionist narrative that is taught in every secular Israeli high school. And now, in her role as the bagel-seller at the wedding, she was waving a wrinkled red scarf for all she was worth, to bring joy to the fictional *chosson* and *kallah* — and to herself most of all.

The girls inhaled the spirit of the wedding and took it to their hearts. Each one snatched a few bars of the elusive strains of music scattered over the shtetl, and together, they crafted one touching melody.

I observed it all from the side, taking a few pictures, watching in fascination, and thinking my own thoughts about the shtetl I came from, perhaps the only one that was still left in Europe after the destruction. A town with all the signs of modernity, veneer furniture and all the rest, but with the same Yiddish, the same *shadchante* who comes around and all the girls pinch each other, and even the same *goyim*, the gentiles of a Jewish shtetl.

Antwerp, 1967

The Diamond Bourse building was impressive, as always, but the outer doors were locked and barred. Debbie was telling us something very interesting, but I wasn't really listening; I kept looking back and stealing glances at the entrance to the Bourse. I knew my father was in that building, and so were Debbie's father and Mimi's father. Almost all of my classmates' fathers worked in the Bourse.

My father was a maikler, a diamond broker. He carried tiny envelopes, concealed in his special leather belt. He would open an envelope carefully, and use a fine tweezer to take out a few stones and examine them thoroughly under a strong light.

My father was there, inside.

And I was longing to see him. I just couldn't wait until dinnertime, when he would come home and we'd all sit together as a family. I had to see him now. The big doors seemed to wink at me invitingly. Debbie and Mimi looked at me, a bit surprised. "What's with you, Chana? We'll be home in a minute; why are you lingering here?" But I let them go on ahead. I smoothed my hair, pulled up my knee socks, and retied the laces of my brown leather shoes. I could go in now. The non-Jewish guard at the door asked for my father's name; he wouldn't let anyone in just like that. Not even a young girl with her socks pulled up straight as could be. "My father's name is…" I paused for a moment, thinking how to pronounce his name in French so this man would understand who I meant… "Salomon David."

But his eyes squinted perplexedly. "Who?" he asked again. "Salomon David," I said clearly, drawing myself up until I was almost standing on my toes. I couldn't understand it. How could the guard not know my father? "Salomon David…" he repeated to himself several times, as if searching for a clue. No one by that name worked in the Bourse, he was sure.

"But…" I began to plead, and suddenly he tapped his forehead and smiled. "Do you mean Shulem Duvid? Shulem Duvid Horowitz?" Laughter played on his lips. "Why didn't you say so, child?"

That night, I lay awake thinking long, run-on thoughts, like dropped balls of yarn that roll away with no one bothering to catch them and roll them up neatly again. My little night lamp cast a small circle of light on the wallpaper, and my blanket was warm and cozy. But still, my thoughts kept rolling away, and I couldn't reel them in and settle into slumber.

Papa had been so happy that I came to visit him that afternoon. It gave him such genuine joy that Mama even forgot to rebuke me for going without permission. I hadn't told anyone about what happened with the guard at the door... but why had I thought he wouldn't know Yiddish? Maybe it was because he had such a stern, non-Jewish looking face... but he did know Yiddish. Nearly all the gentiles I knew could speak Yiddish. The Shabbos goy spoke it so well that sometimes we forgot he wasn't Jewish....

The gentiles all respected us. We were different, and that was understood and accepted. It was as if there were an invisible boundary between us that didn't cause antagonism, but on the contrary, facilitated our relationships with our non-Jewish neighbors.

But the strangest thing happened with Daniel from Kleinblatt's.

Kleinblatt's was the Jewish bakery, and they made the most delicious baked goods in the world. Daniel was their delivery man. Every morning he would buzz at the intercom and ask which bread we would like that day. We knew Daniel almost as well as we knew the bread he brought, and we knew the bread very well indeed, because Mama and Papa ordered the same thing almost every time. They never ordered cake, for example, because Kleinblatt's cakes were so very expensive.

On Fridays Daniel would bring us a piece of Gan Eden — warm, fluffy challahs, sprinkled liberally with poppy seed. The challahs were set aside until Shabbos, and the fragrance that wafted from the loaves was almost heartbreakingly enticing. It certainly taught us to be eager for Shabbos every week.

Our neighbor, an elderly widow named Raizel, also ordered challah from Kleinblatt's, and every Friday when Daniel came around, she would ask him to do her a small favor. She was old and her hands were arthritic, and he was young and good-hearted, as everyone knew, so surely he wouldn't mind setting the Shabbos timer for her. No, of course he didn't mind. In one moment, it was done, and Raizel would thank him and ask him to help her put the pots on the hot plate. As a token of gratitude, she would serve him a slice of hot kugel, and after that she felt she could ask for one last little favor: could he just open the bottle of wine for her? It became a regular part of Daniel's Friday routine to spend a few moments helping the elderly lady, enjoying a plate of kugel, and receiving her lavish blessing every time. He also made sure to brighten her lonely life by chatting with her in his fluent, cheerful Yiddish, since she didn't know much French…

One Friday he arrived as usual and put the challahs in their regular place, but instead of setting the Shabbos timer he sat down at the table with a sigh and looked apologetically at her as if he had some misdeed to confess.

Raizel brought the kugel and sat down facing him, wondering what on earth this little soap-opera scene was all about. The kugel had come out very tasty this week, and Daniel had eaten up his whole portion despite his distress… so what was bothering him?

After a bit of hemming and hawing, he came out with it in his good Yiddish: "I'm happy to help you with the Shabbos timer and the pots, but… uh, the wine… we'll have to stop with that." Raizel didn't know what had gotten into the yungerman. Opening a bottle was suddenly too hard for him?

"You know, I'm not supposed to, um…" He looked down at the table. "I'm not allowed to open your wine."

"You're not allowed to? But my dear Daniel, what do you mean? You talk as if you were a goy, or something!"

"That's just it," he said, his eyes still downcast. "I am a goy. Didn't you know?"

CHAPTER 9

The Forest of No Escape

FOR ALL ITS LIGHT-HEARTED nature, the mock wedding in Tiktin had awakened something deep and uplifting. But after that height of exhilaration came a harrowing experience.

The wedding costumes were gathered back into the huge plastic bag, and we were gathered back into the bus and brought straight to the Lupochova forest. Yes, we were taken there straight from the wedding, just like the Jews of seventy years ago, who were torn away from their joyful celebrations or their everyday lives and taken there, leaving the pot of soup unserved, the apron tossed casually on the chair just for the moment, the smile of the baby who started walking only yesterday.

They didn't go there in an air-conditioned bus; they were loaded onto a tarpaulin-covered truck. But the forest they encountered was the same one we now encountered.

The forest was tall and forbidding, with frozen ground underfoot, silence so thick you could cut it with a knife... and fear. The forest might have been vibrant, and it might have been relaxing. It might have been enchanting, or it might have been green and refreshing... but it wasn't. Not for me, at least, and it didn't seem to be any of those things for the group of young women crowded together, seeking security, warmth, and protection — everything the forest didn't provide.

The rabbi leading the group handed out printed testimonies from the people of Tiktin and asked each girl to find a quiet spot and read the words to herself, there where they were written. To stand with the person who stood there seventy years ago and see that threatening forest through the eyes of that Jew, to feel the helplessness they felt there, the menace snaking among the trees...

I didn't need any testimony — not there, deep in the forest. When I wandered among the trees, I saw millions of frightened, tortured faces peeping out at me. "This is my family!" I wanted to scream. "These are all the cousins I never knew, the aunts and uncles I never met, and all the children they might have had, but never did. Everything that might have been here with us, but is not." And suddenly I realized that all I knew was the stories of those who survived, but I had no idea of the stories of those who were lost.

The forest closes in all around us and the faces hover around me, threatening to take my sanity from me. And then the violin begins to play, as if it were playing itself, the famous melody to *"Gam ki eilech b'gei tzalmaves, lo ira ra, ki Atah imadi."**

The girls begin to sing along, softly, hesitantly. They know the words and can hum the melody. And in no time they feel confident enough to really sing it, the way people sing when they feel what the song is saying.

How did all these girls from Tel Aviv and Herzliya, girls from secular homes and university campuses, know the tune to these immortal words? They'd heard it for the first time only yesterday, and now they could sing it as if it were a part of them. Perhaps

---

* "Even if I walk in the valley of the shadow of death I shall fear no evil, for You are with me" (*Tehillim* 23:4).

this song had always been a part of them, an unknown part, even an alien part, that only one story, a story different from all the others, could bring out from the dungeon of conventions where it was locked up. Tears suddenly joined with the melody, echoed by the wailing of the violin, and the notes themselves seemed to twist in the air, distorted by the weeping, trembling and sobbing along with it. And each girl read out her personal testimony in the forest, stood on the same ground, sharing the writer's last, terrible moments.

Ilanit cried more than anyone else, and she couldn't bear it anymore... she handed back her papers and asked to go back to the bus. The group was almost finished with the testimonies, but Ilanit couldn't wait; she asked to go back now. Her face was streaked with tears and her body shuddered uncontrollably. She walked back alone to the bus to calm down.

As she went, our eyes followed her. Her form disappeared behind a tree and reappeared, again and again as she made her way to the road where the bus waited. "Look at her!" I said to the girls. The frozen forest seemed to stand still, and only the spot of color that was Ilanit moved across that silent space. We watched her, spellbound. I thought of my father, and a chill gripped me. "That was how the Jews looked when they tried to escape to the forest. It wasn't hard to spot them. There was nowhere to hide."

Tears sprang from my eyes, too, when I thought of him, and they froze on my cheeks in that terrible cold. He'd told me once that a kilo of flour or sugar would prevent a Jew from escaping.

I exhaled and inhaled deeply. Ilanit was still walking between the trees, and the leaves over our heads rustled only slightly. The sky was very gray. Was it about to snow on us?

"A kilo of flour, a kilo of sugar, that's all a Jew was worth, and it was enough to justify handing him over to the Nazis. That was the reward they gave to any Polish peasant who handed over a Jew. And the Jews who tried to escape to these forests," I said, waving my hand at the slender tree trunks around me, "would be exposed one after the other for those bags of flour and sugar. That was all that stood between life and death.

"And that was before my father had a family," I said. "Who could escape if he had a wife and little children? Who could run away if she had elderly parents or little sisters? Who could get up and leave their family behind when no one knew what would happen tomorrow?

"The Jews certainly wouldn't. Not the young men who could have managed here on their own, but didn't dare to leave their wives alone. Not the mothers and fathers who had the necessary strength, but had helpless little children and infants. They preferred to die if they must, as long as they could stay with their loved ones and give them any comfort and protection at all, up until the last moment. I ask you: Is that 'going like sheep to the slaughter,' or is that greatness?

"The forest is big," I went on. "Poland is full of forestland, but it's also full of Poles, and the forests were full of them. Full of Poles on the lookout for any sign of a Jew in hiding, so they could hand him over to the Nazis, who were here" — I looked down at my boots — "right on this ground we're standing on."

We lit memorial candles in a silent, fraught moment. I said a few chapters of *Tehillim* as the flames flickered on the stone, and I could feel Rotem's eyes fixed on me.

"I liked what you said," she told me as we walked side by side on the path back to the bus.

"Me? I said something?" And then I realized that I actually had said something. I hadn't even planned my little speech; it had just come out spontaneously. In my mind, I heard my mother softy saying to me, "You see, Chana? You can do it! You've begun your journey of discovery. There is so much greatness yet to be found, and I'm proud of you." And that alone gave me a chill that spread all the way to my fingertips....

CHAPTER 10

The Treblinka Train Station

AFTER THAT DAY OF dark emotions came the night. Like a blanket that can't remove a chill that goes too deep, the darkness enveloped us. Despite all our layers of winter clothing, we couldn't stop our teeth from chattering and our bones from shaking as we got off the bus. Our guide lit red paraffin torches and handed one, flaming and smoking, to each of us.

We trudged along in the dark, the flickering torches casting strange shadows on the ground. Firelight always has a special enchantment, and we felt it, mingled with a sense of dread. I must say there was more dread than enchantment, but after all, who ever said that Treblinka was a lovely place?

There it was, the Treblinka train station, with an old-fashioned, double-sided clock hanging there from its iron arm as if this were a real station, where people could transfer to another train to continue their journey. But no one changed trains here. This was the last stop, and when you exited the gate from here, you went straight to the next world.

The torchlight colored our faces orange and yellow as we made our way cautiously across the field of sharp stones recalling the atrocities that took place here. A field strewn with stones, each inscribed with the names of the villages, cities, and countries the victims were taken from. "Isn't this dangerous?"

someone on my right asked me; I think it was Maayan, but in that flickering light it was hard to identify faces peeping out of woolen hats and tightly-wrapped scarves.

"Isn't it dangerous, to be out here in the dark, when we can hardly see where we're going, carrying flaming torches — and with all this thick clothing on? Somebody might trip and fall, with a burning torch in her hand. Are you sure this is a responsible thing to be doing?"

"I don't know, my dear."

I tried to keep alongside her, to reassure the frightened little girl within that grown woman. And I hoped that the trip organizers had thought of the possible dangers.

It's not really dangerous today, I wanted to add. Not so long ago it was very dangerous indeed to be here. And there was no one to reassure those endangered souls.

"My uncle was here," I finally said. "With his wife and three children. He was my father's older brother, but I never met him, because he never came back from here. His name was Chaim Eliezer Horowitz, and from here, he went straight to Heaven."

I close my eyes and try to picture him. Young, tall, with a glow of dignity, with a toddler in his arms and another child holding his hand. His daughter Yocheved was with his wife. With his wife and three little children he walked here amid a crowd of others....

Several years before that, my uncle, talented and astute, had been a sixteen-year-old boy pressed in the crowd of men around the Gerrer Rebbe's table, seeking spiritual treasures and new insights in Torah. The Rebbe was expounding on a Torah passage, and a difficult question was raised. Suddenly silence fell in the crowded hall. No one had an answer to suggest. But the young boy at the far end of the table had an answer and the men around him sensed it, although he didn't dare to speak up before his elders. They pushed him forward until he was standing in front of the Rebbe, who was waiting expectantly. Now he had no choice, and with trembling lips he suggested the answer he had in mind. The Rebbe gave him a penetrating look and turned to his brother, who sat at his side. "Here," he said simply. "Why shouldn't this young man be your son-in-law?"

My Uncle Chaim Eliezer became the son-in-law of the Rebbe's brother, Rebbe Mendel of Pabianitz.

A prodigious Torah scholar, he was soon appointed as the Rav of Belchatov, and despite his youth he fulfilled his duties successfully, maintaining a happy family life until he was taken to Treblinka in 1942.

No one said goodbye to him before he went. No one.

But after he went, my father received regards from him, in a manner of speaking.

One day, a friend from Antwerp, on a temporary stay in Communist Poland at personal risk, called my father. "I have here some authentic manuscripts written by someone named Horowitz. Are you interested in them?"

"Authentic manuscripts?"

"You see, I was in the town of Rogatchov, and some old, toothless Polish woman came up to me babbling something about a box full of manuscripts left by a *Rabbiner* from before the war. The greedy old thing demanded five hundred dollars for them."

Five hundred dollars was a small fortune. But Papa's friend paid the money, climbed up to the attic, coughing up dust all the way, rummaged around a bit in the box, and found a bundle of letters with the name Horowitz. Papa knew that Horowitz was a very common name in prewar Poland, but still, the name on the letters was his brother's full name: Chaim Eliezer Horowitz. He was stunned.

When his friend returned home, Papa received the letters and opened them with trembling hands. The pages were covered with original insights on the Torah and brilliant questions, written in a clear, dense hand, addressed by a seventeen-year-old youth to Rav Yosef Rosen, the famed Rogatchover Gaon. The return address on the envelope was that of my father's childhood home in Krakow. The letters were undoubtedly written by his older brother.

It was a comforting smile from the Next World, and a treasure to cherish.

On another occasion, it was Naftali Lavi of blessed memory (the older brother of Rav Yisrael Meir Lau, the Rav of Tel Aviv), who was the messenger.

When I was searching for the location of a family burial plot in Piotrikov, I was advised to contact Naftali Lavi. "He's the world's biggest authority on the subject," I was told. I spoke to him, and when I mentioned my family's name he asked me if I happened to have any family connection to Rav Chaim Eliezer Horowitz of Belchatov.

"Yes!" I said as my heart skipped a beat. "He was my uncle."

"Your uncle?!" He, too, was so stunned that for a moment he was silent. "I was there, at the shul in Belchatov, when he was inaugurated as Rav, and I remember his *drashah* word for word."

We arranged to meet, and my father asked him all his questions, down to the minutest details. We showed him the picture, taken by a non-Jewish photographer, of my uncle emerging from the shul on that Shabbos day after his inauguration. They had a long conversation about those days gone by, and it came out that Papa and Naftali had gone to the same Talmud Torah and spent summer vacations at the same camp in the mountains.

My father had found another memory of his brother, and made a new friend as well. But he always continued to search for the older brother he so admired — and only in Gan Eden would they meet again.*

---

*There is a postscript to this story, and it took place on the threshold of Gan Eden.

My husband was chosen as Rav of the Gr"a shul in Bayit Vegan, Jerusalem. This shul, founded by *yekkes* (German Jews), was meticulous about holding a

Silence reigns, and the flames of our torches die down. Now all the girls have someone they've lost, and there is no more Treblinka, only a field of stones....

At the steps of the bus, we blow out the dying flames. Cups of steaming hot soup materialize out of nowhere, thanks to the amazing staff and their meticulous planning, and they are received gratefully.

Quietly, I think of hot soup sent with love into this frigid darkness, and of that Someone who loves you, even in Treblinka.

---

hachtarah, an inauguration ceremony in accord with all the traditions of Ashkenaz. Important *rabbanim* were invited, including Rav Berel Povarsky, *rosh yeshiva* of Ponevezh in Bnei Brak, Rav Tuvya Weiss of the Eidah Chareidis, and Rav Yehuda Adas, head of Yeshivat Kol Yaakov in Yerushalayim. There were many speeches and many guests in addition to friends and family. My father sat there weeping, overcome with emotion. It was obvious that he was experiencing the event on a much deeper level than the rest of us.

Afterwards, Papa told us that he'd felt he was revisiting the experience of his brother's *hachtarah* as Rav of Belchatov. He had been a young child at the time, and his parents hadn't taken him to the event, which was for grownups. But when they returned home, he could feel, almost tangibly, the excitement, the honor, and the joy his father felt. Now, at the shul in Jerusalem, all those feelings came back to him, but with much greater intensity. It was like joining hands with his father, experiencing the very same *nachas,* as if the family were picking up the thread from that distant point in time and continuing to weave its tapestry.

Two weeks later, my father passed away. He had wanted to come to us for Shabbos, to be there for my husband's first Shabbos as Rav of the shul. But at least he was there for the *hachtarah,* on the threshold of Gan Eden.

CHAPTER 11

Returning a Favor in Lublin

THE NEXT DAY FOUND us in Lublin.

In the middle of the city of Lublin, there's a cemetery. Around the perimeter of this cemetery is a very beautiful fence. It's a work of art that looks as though it was accidentally left in the wrong place.

"This fence is here because of my father," I said, with the smile of someone who knows his listeners won't believe him.

"Because of your father?!" Suddenly the fence was even more beautiful.

"My father was here several times in the 1980s as part of an Agudath Israel delegation, when Poland was still a satellite state of the USSR. It was poor and primitive then, and all the newer buildings were built in that gray, depressing, communist style."

Back then, no one had thought of organizing Jewish heritage trips like the many being offered today, and the few Jews still in Poland were disappearing in the melting pot of assimilation. The Polish government, controlled by the long arm of Moscow, had decided that there were too many Jewish cemeteries, taking up too much space, and that some better and more attractive use could be made of those plots of land... soccer fields, for example.

Word of those intentions reached the ears of the Agudath Israel World Organization, which sent representatives on an urgent mission to Poland to try to dissuade the government from going ahead with any such plan. My father, then an Agudah representative in Belgium, was a member of this delegation. It was incredible to us at that time that he was going back to the place where his blood had been spilled on the ground…

With a great deal of diplomacy, money, and public relations, the delegation was successful in its mission of saving Jewish cemeteries throughout Poland — all but the main cemetery of Lublin.

"In Lublin, the cemetery is right in the middle of the city," the mayor of that city argued. "You can't have people buried in the middle of town. It's unaesthetic, and it takes up too much urban land. If a cemetery were something attractive, I'd be willing to leave it there," he huffed into his moustache, "but…"

"But what?" the Agudah delegates thought, and they came up with a counter-proposal. "We can turn that cemetery into an artistic gem…. True, we can't turn the graves into flowerpots, but we can build an impressive entrance, and surround the cemetery with a fence one doesn't see every day… We can make it worth the city's while to preserve the cemetery."

It was a brilliant idea, but what about the cost? They didn't have funding on that grand scale. They returned home troubled, while the mayor of Lublin waited to see what they would come up with.

Then my father remembered someone he knew, a wealthy diamond dealer in Antwerp. Beneath his self-assured exterior, behind the walls of his big, handsome home with the sleek car parked beside it, was a story of unimaginable pain and suffering — his wife's story.

She had been just a little girl when the Nazis goose-stepped into Lublin. Lublin was a city with a very high proportion of Jewish residents, and the Nazis were determined to deport them all and not let a single one slip through their fingers. That required focused efforts and a highly efficient system of mass murder, and the Nazis had no problem with that. They set up their headquarters in Lublin itself, emptying Jewish streets one after the other and sending every family away in their death trains.

The little girl was several years older when she found herself, together with her sister, in that death trap. They wanted to flee, but there was no way out; the Nazi soldiers were swarming everywhere. They were doomed.

And then their miracle happened. A local priest decided to save them, no matter what the risk. He hid them in the Jewish cemetery in the middle of the city. Right under the Nazis' noses, two frightened young girls were hiding among the silent gravestones.

Who would think of looking for them there? It was an impossible place to hide, with no access to a slice of bread or a bottle of milk, or even wild herbs or berries. They couldn't even walk around there without standing out against the pale gravestones.

But the priest took care of them with astounding self-sacrifice. He brought food to them regularly, despite the danger to his own life, and made sure they were protected against the cold. He would come at night, sneaking among the graves, to see how he could be of further help.

And when they heard the trains rumbling through the night, the girls knew they'd been granted another week of life, another miracle.

Eventually, as the city was systematically emptied, hiding in the cemetery became too risky. The priest, taking advantage of the girls' Aryan appearance, arranged forged papers for them. He had them smuggled out to Germany, of all places, where they were employed as household help until the end of the war. No one suspected that the two blond war refugees were Jewish; there weren't any Jews left in the whole region.

The war finally ended, and that little girl left her painful memories of Lublin, and the noble priest who saved her life, behind. She got married in Belgium, to a man who became a successful diamond dealer. And nobody knew.

But Papa knew. Hearts that have suffered develop a language of their own that other people will never understand, and the wealthy woman's difficult past was known to him. Papa went to his friend and asked him, "Would you like to show your gratitude to the cemetery in Lublin?"

"My gratitude? To the cemetery?" The diamond dealer didn't know what Papa was talking about. The priest who'd saved his wife and sister-in-law had already been honored with a Righteous Among the Nations award, and the cemetery, as far as he knew, was just a piece of land. Consecrated ground, but still an inanimate piece of land.

"Yes," said my father, with a sparkle in his eyes. "If you're willing, you can show your gratitude to the cemetery. It is slated to be destroyed, and you can save it."

Papa explained the Agudah delegation's proposal, his friend agreed to fund the project, and the little girl from Lublin closed a painful chapter in her life.

"And here," I said to the girls, as we stood at the imposing entrance to the cemetery, gazing at the beautifully crafted, symbolic design of the fence, "is the result. "We can never know how G-d is sketching out the events of our lives, but eventually they turn out to be a perfect work of art."

CHAPTER 12

A Yeshiva Bochur from Lublin

WE WERE THERE. Yeshivas Chachmei Lublin.

The students were milling around in the plaza in front of the proud building, or climbing the steps, and the round veranda where Rav Meir Shapira used to stand meant nothing to them. Yes, they knew this had once been a big, famous yeshiva, the flagship yeshiva of the Chassidic world in Poland. They'd heard about the redemption of the building, and they understood that they were looking at a piece of history — but they had no acquaintance with the fabric that piece was cut from. Not even a feeling of antagonism or aversion. No questions they'd always wondered about. Nothing.

Nothing ignited them. Neither a glow nor a flash of anger appeared in their eyes at the sound of the words "Gemara," "Torah," "yeshiva students." The words just rolled over them, and although they remained respectfully attentive as they stood gathered in a semicircle in the lobby, their coats still zipped up to the neck, their ignorance was painfully evident.

A song was playing for them in the background: "Tell me, what is sweeter than a page of Gemara?" said the lyrics in Hebrew, but the words and melody failed to touch them. It was foreign, unfamiliar. They were certainly listening and looking at the printed handouts, but they had no idea what was sweet about a page of Gemara. What was Gemara, anyway?

For them, Torah was Tanach, the Hebrew Bible. It was an ancient text about Avraham and Sarah, Hagar and Yishmael, part of their core curriculum in high school. They'd had to pass a final exam on Tanach, among their other requirements for a diploma. But Gemara? The Oral Torah? What was that all about? They hadn't a clue.

Sometimes you want to engage someone in discussion, even in an argument, in order to achieve clarity. You want him to state his opinion so you can show him the flaw in his thinking and explain what you believe to be the correct view. But when you can't even argue with someone, you realize that they are simply uninformed, abysmally uninformed.

Then the song ended, and the air was filled with information and explanations, as one speaker after the other tried his best to fill that abyss of ignorance. And suddenly the girls were clamoring to ask questions. "Maybe sometimes it works better when people are uninformed," I thought to myself, as my neatly-arranged thoughts of the moment before fell into disarray. "When they don't know a thing, you can give them information on a fresh background, with no preconceived notions getting in the way..."

When the discussion was finished, it was time for me to tell my story. With one hand on a white stone column at the entrance to the building, I began quietly: "I knew the young boy who was going to come here to learn, but never got here...."

Every religious Jewish boy who was raised in Poland had a dream that went out with him to play at recess and painted a bright horizon when he daydreamed during lessons. The dream got up with him in the morning, and sneaked under his feather pillow at night. All the boys had the same dream: to be among the scholars learning in this yeshiva.

And it was this boy's dream, too.

I tried to describe him: "...a fifteen-year-old boy who learned in the *yeshiva ketana* Kesser Torah in Krakow. He had *pe'os* alongside his cheeks and a peaked cap on his head. He had a bold look in his eyes and a strong will, a real ambition, to learn Torah in Lublin, in this yeshiva." I paused for a moment, touching the stone column with the whole palm of my hand.

"He knew that the yeshiva would only accept fifteen boys from the Krakow area. But he would let nothing stand in his way. He sat and toiled over his learning until the words were like flames on his lips.

"The entrance examination took place at the end of the year, and it was nearly impossible to pass it. You had to know a hundred twenty pages of Gemara with Tosafos, an incredible amount of material. But this boy refused to see it as impossible. Months of intensive study culminated in an oral exam conducted by three venerable *roshei yeshiva*, who tested him for an hour and a quarter.

"One rabbi tested him in *iyun*, another tested him in *bekius*, and the third rabbi sat by silently, watching the boy's facial expressions and deportment, assessing his character.

"After this arduous exam, the young boy was informed that he would be welcomed as a *talmid* in the yeshiva. His family in Krakow was ecstatic — Shulem Duvid had been accepted at Yeshivas Chachmei Lublin!

"From all of Poland, only seventy youths had been accepted. And he was one of them. The very ground under his feet danced with him.

"The next *z'man* would begin in a month... and then he would walk through these doors as part of the yeshiva. He would sail on the flagship of the Torah in Chassidic Poland!

"He counted the days, flipping the pages on the calendar and waiting impatiently as summer seemed to drag on endlessly. But when the time came to pack a suitcase and buy a train ticket to Lublin, no one packed a suitcase for him, and no one went to see him off at the train station. His dream had evaporated. He would never sit and learn Torah in Yeshivas Chachmei Lublin. The Germans were closing in on Poland's borders. War was about to begin.

"That boy was right here on the threshold, but never got the chance to go in. He was invited, but couldn't come. He was enrolled as a *talmid* in Yeshivas Chachmei Lublin, but never learned here.

"He was my father.

"I think of those years he spent in the death camps, sleeping on wooden shelves, stuffed into cattle cars, put to grueling slave labor… all the years he was supposed to be here, learning Torah with fervor and love, with a decent room to sleep in, and meals served at a table, on a proper plate.

"When the war was finally over, it was too late. There was no yeshiva anymore, and no *yeshiva bochurim*. They'd all gone up in smoke to the heavens, and this building was used as a Polish medical academy."

I lowered my voice at those last words and stopped to calm myself with a deep breath of cold air. The young women standing around me suddenly saw the building differently. They saw it full of young Torah scholars, with the revered *rosh yeshiva*, Rav Meir Shapira, at their head, as if the picture had been frozen in time, and they were standing in it.*

A few years ago, my father was here, together with a group of

---

*Papa heard a fascinating story from his brother, Rav Chaim Eliezer, who heard it directly from Rav Meir Shapira while accompanying him to the train station. Rav Shapira related that he had seen his mother in a dream, and she was shining like a princess, with a huge crown of diamonds on her head. Rav Meir was astonished by the crown, and his mother told him that for every page of Gemara learned by a Jew anywhere in in the world because of the Daf Yomi (daily page of Gemara) program he had initiated, another diamond was added to her crown. This, Rav Meir told my uncle, is the merit of a mother who raises her sons to love the Torah and increase Torah learning in the world.

men who had finished learning a *masechta* in Israel and traveled here to celebrate the *siyum*. Papa was given the honor of reciting the traditional *Hadran*, and there was a tear in every eye as he stood and read, in a choked voice, the Gemara passage about the Jew who does not abandon the Torah, and it does not abandon him.

"Today," he concluded, looking lovingly at the Gemara as tears rose in his eyes, "I had the privilege, at last, of learning Torah in Yeshivas Chachmei Lublin. Today, after almost seventy years, I became a *talmid* of this yeshiva!"

CHAPTER 13

Majdanek: When I'm Thirty

ON THE BUS RIDE to Majdanek, Shilat came to sit next to me. Rotem and Tanya were in front of me, and Yif'at and Shaked shared the seat across the aisle. It was sweet to see how new friendships formed, and funny that there was a social hierarchy even on a trip to Poland with graduate students, as if nothing had changed since high school.

Every slot in the social structure was filled, and even the few who had no place found themselves in the slots for those who have no place.

Even the slot for the chronic complainer was filled. She complained about the weather and about the cucumber that had no flavor. And of course there's always the "Pollyanna" who tries to make everything all right, to convince everyone that the cucumber tastes fine and so do the sandwiches, and that just because we're not used to a certain flavor, that doesn't mean it's not good, and yes, it's very cold and we're all shivering even under all these layers, but that's what makes it fun.

Shilat was next to me now, telling me she recognized the sights on the way to Majdanek; she even remembered the sprawling fields near the entrance to the abandoned death camp. "I have a picture I took here, and here," she said, pointing at the horizon, "I have a picture of me with my whole high school class, and one of me with my best friend from that time. It's so strange to go back in time, and then turn and find you next to me, instead of that shrewish eleventh-grade teacher with the cropped blond hair.

"I remember Majdanek a little too well," Shilat went on. "I was just a seventeen-year-old kid the last time I was here, and it all hit me like a smack in the face. It was too much for me to contain, and when they showed us the crematorium... I fainted.

"I tried to get over it and act normal. I brought home presents from Poland for the whole family, developed the pictures I took with my old film camera, and told them about my experiences. But all my talk was superficial, and inside, I was still reeling from the blow.

"I promised myself that when I was thirty, I'd come here again to gather up all the words and all the sights that I'd left here thrown on the ground because I couldn't take them with me; there wasn't enough room in me to take them. When I'm thirty, I told myself, I'll come back. I'll be bigger then.

"But soon enough I forgot all about my solemn teenage vow....

"I'm studying now for a master's degree, I live in my own apartment, and I manage a clothing store on the side. I always have a thousand things to do, and I live my life in the fast lane. A promise to come back to visit a concentration camp in Poland was low priority, to put it mildly, and the chances of that promise ever surfacing from under a mountain of things to keep me busy were nil.

"But then I got a message from G-d. Straight to my email — an invitation from Nefesh Yehudi to come on this trip. I was in shock.

"I read the message, and I read it again, and I felt that promise coming back to me like a thunderbolt." Shilat played with the long fringe on her shawl, winding it around her slim finger until it looked like an orange cocoon. With her chestnut hair, the autumn colors of the scarf were very becoming, making her look like an illustration from an old book.

"It was surreal — but as real as could be." Shilat threw off the cocoon with one quick movement and held up two fingers. "In two days," she said softly, "I'll be thirty years old."

She stole a searching look at my face to see if I realized how incredible the timing of the email had been, how clearly Heaven-sent it was, and when she was satisfied with my reaction, she began playing again with the fringes of her scarf.

"I knew that this time, there could be no excuses. I packed up my other plans, and I packed my bags and came here… a thirty-year-old woman walking in the footsteps of a scared little teenage girl.

"Tell me, Rebbetzin — if that wasn't a miracle, then what is?"

But to my mind, everything that was happening here was a miracle.

The fact that these intellectual and very busy young women had come here, to try walking a new and unfamiliar path, was a miracle. Here, Jewish faith didn't come bursting out at them by the back door, nor was it pushed on them, missionary-style. It was clearly visible, offered freely to all participants, without hiding behind lofty, pluralistic terminology. They all knew where they would be taken on this trip, and they had met the trip leaders and knew them to be uncompromisingly "ultra-Orthodox." They were aware that on this guided tour, the sights would be shown to them from a perspective of Jewish faith and tradition. Yet they came, not despite all that, but for all that.

They knew the historical facts, and they weren't particularly interested in the dry statistics, or even in the plentiful information the trip leaders could provide. What they wanted was to sing from the heart, to feel from the soul, and to hear all those words they'd never heard before. "Tell us more of that," they said to us with hungry eyes. "Tell us more about ourselves. What does it mean to be a Jew? To be connected to what flourished here, and what was destroyed here…."

The world around them offered endless experiences, obtainable with a few keystrokes and a credit-card number. As Shaked had said to me on the plane, there were so many places to travel to, and a trip to the remains of Jewish Poland wasn't in the same league with any of them. Yet they were here, courageously rising to their soul's challenge, here to grapple with the big questions, to try to get new answers. All their lives, the secular, pioneering Israeli had been idealized as the replacement for the stigmatized Diaspora Jew who had meekly gone to the slaughter, but something honest within them demanded something beyond that shallow narrative — something real. And they'd come here to find it.

And if that isn't a miracle, then what is?

Nearly all these women had been to Majdanek before, on their high-school trips. And the sights to be seen in Majdanek are not easily forgotten, for there are no words with which to process them. Maybe that is why they were all so quiet here, walking sad and silent among the buildings, the barracks, the bare bunks, the shower rooms, the disinfecting rooms, the gas chambers, and the crematorium.

Shining tears hung from their lashes and dropped to their cheeks, only to make way for the others that followed. In Majdanek, there are no words. Only tears, and throats choked up with tears lodged so deep, they can't find their way out.

Crying suits you, Majdanek. Keep it up, because all the tears in the world won't wash away the blood that was spilled here. All the tears in the world....

CHAPTER 14

My Uncle Was Here

ON SHABBOS, WE WOULD go visit Tante Rivka and Oncle Leibel.

Mama would dress me in my best white dress with the round lace collar. I would wear black patent-leather shoes, and all the way I would watch them to see they weren't getting dirty.

My sister wore a dress like mine, and shiny black shoes adorned her feet, too. But she talked with Mama all the way and didn't pay attention to her shoes.

My brother talked with Papa, and I stayed out of the conversations. I was happy just walking the well-known route I loved, on the day I loved so much, knowing my cousins were waiting to play with me and show me something they'd built. The grownups would sit around the table and eat cake from fancy china plates with little silver forks. But I didn't care about the cake, and not even about the chocolate that Tante Rivka would sometimes hand out. We were going to see the close relatives I loved so much, and that was all that mattered.

Oncle Leibel was much taller than Papa. He always stood straight and looked polished, as if his clothes had been freshly laundered and pressed just a minute ago. Even his handkerchiefs were ironed meticulously, and Mama once said to Papa that you could tell that Oncle Leibel was an aristocratic Gerrer chossid from Warsaw.

Oncle Leibel never got angry or upset. He was always level-headed and calm.

He had a spodik, too. Aside from Oncle Leibel, only one other man in Antwerp, a chossid from Eretz Yisrael, had a spodik, and he carried it to shul in a box. Oncle Leibel was also our chazzan. He led the prayers in a strong, beautiful voice that always thrilled me. Something inside me seemed to blend with my uncle's voice when he prayed.

On Rosh Hashanah, there was a capella in the shtiebel, and since we lived so close by, Oncle Leibel would bring the whole choir to our house for Kiddush during the break before the shofar blowing. We would dash around, preparing hot tea with honey for all of them, and meanwhile they would do some final rehearsals of the newest Gerrer melodies from Eretz Yisrael.

I would huddle near the kitchen door, listening to them, feeling as if angels were singing in our house. What voices! What melodies! I learned some of them by heart that way, and could sing along in an undertone. I'm sure even the furniture absorbed some of those melodies.

Oncle Leibel was always very glad when I came, and he would greet me with a fixed ritual.

"Mach azoy," he would say, meaning "go like this" — "I'm going to take you to Heaven." I would hold my arms the way he showed me, folded tightly against my middle, and when I was ready, he would grab me above the elbows and swing me up high until I was next to the big chandelier in the dining room. "Oncle Leibel," I would scream, half in fear and half in delight, and he would hoist me even higher. In another second I would hit the ceiling. "Oncle Leibel! Oncle Leibel! Put me down!" I would scream, kicking my feet in their clean patent-leather shoes.

Everyone would laugh, and Oncle Leibel would carefully lower me to the floor, and once I was safely on solid ground, I would laugh too.

Oncle Leibel would smile. You could see he loved little children that he could lift up almost to the ceiling, until they screamed with delight.

But once I was sitting on the rug, playing with my cousins while all the big people ate Tante Rivka's best butter cake, I would think to myself that even though my uncle always smiled at me and loved to make me laugh, still, there was something very sad in his eyes, something that all the smiles in the world couldn't chase away.

But I didn't know what it was, or why it was there.

My mother had ten siblings, and my father had seven. I should have been surrounded by a whole tribe of relatives. But out of all those relatives, I had only this one uncle in Antwerp, Oncle Leibel, the husband of my father's sister Rivka. (There was also his sister Rachel, who had made *aliyah* to Eretz Yisrael before the war.) That one uncle had stood here, in this open square that now sprouted grass, where I was standing with fifty Israeli graduate students.

This uncle had lost a wife and three children, and here he had stood, after his whole world was destroyed.

The students all looked again at the *Appellplatz* of Majdanek and thought that I've known people who were in all these horrific places… how could it be?

I addressed the group:

"It was the morning of the holiday of Shavuos, and they stood here, lined up in rows, for a long time. Here, a place where Death itself had its arms spread out, ready to collect you, with no need to send its angel looking for you. In Majdanek, the people fell right into death's arms, one after the other, with *Shema Yisrael* on their lips. My uncle was here, in this place where you might have a few months to live, until they were finished sorting through the possessions of the dead and using your labor to help things along. It was a place without hope, without life, a place where even the living were already dead inside, but their souls were still stuck in their barely-living bodies because there wasn't any space free for them to die in yet. And now, on Shavuos, they stood here in rows as if all their will to live had been taken from them, and among them was my uncle, tall, young, and knowing he had nothing left. No parents and no brothers, no little sisters and no friends, no home, no youth. But he had one thing that was inside him, and this was something no Nazi officer could take from him. He had his faith, the Divine spark within him.

"The camp commander knew it was a Jewish holiday, and in honor of the day, he wanted to degrade them a bit more than usual. So he began barking exercise commands at them: "Hands up! Hands Down! Forward bend! Stand straight! Deep knee bend! Jump! Stop!" The abuse was more psychological than physical. They did harder work than this at Majdanek, but this sort of abuse, for no reason and no purpose, is harder to endure. After a while, the officer got tired of the game.

"He left the prisoners standing at attention, and after shouting that anyone who moved would be shot, he went off to drink some coffee, or just to sit in a warm room. My uncle was here, and in the midst of that humiliation and pain, he remembered what day it was. 'Today we received the Torah,' he mused. 'We became the Chosen People…' And there, under the rising smoke of the crematorium, standing at humiliating attention to nothing, he was carried back to the Gerrer *shtiebel* in Warsaw, and the special Gerrer melody of Akdamos, with its joyous marching rhythm, came to his lips. On the ground he saw a scrap of paper. He bent down and picked it up to cover his bare head, and softly began to sing the sublime *piyut* of the day.

"The words and the melody flashed out of him like flames, touching and igniting the other men around him, who stood in tense, subjugated silence. And suddenly for them, too, it was Shavuos, and they, too, were part of the Chosen People, and they, too, had something within that could not be taken from them. And the circle of flame spread out, taking hold of everyone in its path.

"More and more men began to sing along softly, and the strength of the marching melody grew. 'Today is Shavuos, brothers!'

it said. 'We have the Torah, and no lowly Nazi can take it from us!' The words came back to all of them from somewhere. From the shul they once had, from the normal life they once led. They still stood at attention, but the heart in them was renewed. The melody washed over them like waves, and they knew that the holy Torah was theirs alone, forever.

"Here stood my uncle, the *baal tefillah* of Antwerp, one man who vanquished the Nazi oppressor for one moment and led all his comrades with him to victory."

CHAPTER 15

Lizhensk — "Aderaba, Tein Belibeinu..."

BEFORE WE CAME TO Lizhensk, it came to us. On the way there, the trip leaders spoke about great tzaddikim, about the meaning of prayer, the significance of a gravesite, about *segulos*, miracles, and faith. The effect was like lifting a curtain of preconceived and entrenched notions to reveal a pristine hall where one could truly listen and conduct a dialogue, untainted by pre-programmed reactions.

The questions came spontaneously. "Why would I let a Rebbe decide for me what I should do? Isn't he a human being just like me? So how should he know what's best for me?"

"What's the point about praying at a gravesite? The tzaddik passed away; that's it. What is left of him in this plot of earth?"

"Why do the *Chossidim* keep themselves separate from mainstream society? And why do Chassidic women have to hide themselves at home all the time?"

"Why is the position of Rebbe handed down to the Rebbe's son, like a royal dynasty? Why couldn't my husband, for example, become a Rebbe someday?"

"Why do there have to be so many Chassidic courts, named after all these obscure little towns in Ukraine? What's the matter with having one Rebbe who's good at working miracles?"

The rabbi leading the tour answered the questions in a calm, confident manner that relaxed the students' raised hackles and created an atmosphere of receptivity. The answers they'd received were so intriguing that by now they were looking forward to being there, at the resting place of the tzaddik Reb Elimelech of Lizhensk, if only to get a little taste of the special spiritual relationship between a tzaddik and his followers.

And that is how Lizhensk came out and touched their hearts before their feet stepped there.

The rabbi told the group about the day the *Chossidim* of Reb Elimelech of Lizhensk came to inform him that a rival Chassidic court had been established nearby. They saw it as an affront to the honor of their Rebbe and a threat to the vitality of their group, as some of their members were attracted to the new *Chossidus*.

Reb Elimelech lifted his holy eyes. "A rival *Chossidus*? *Chossidim* packing up and leaving? *Aderaba* (On the contrary)..."

And that day, Reb Elimelech composed the famous prayer, "*Aderaba*... On the contrary, inspire our hearts to see each other's best qualities... And let no hatred of one another arise within us, G-d forbid..."

The girls were amazed by the story. In the dog-eat-dog world they knew, there were no stories like that. There was no one who prayed that people should see only each other's good qualities, and not, G-d forbid, their shortcomings...

The musical accompaniment began to play, and they all tried to sing the printed words that seemed so unreal: "*Aderaba, tein belibeinu...*"

The song rose like a wave, carried higher and higher by its touching words, and it shot up to a crescendo with the words, "And strengthen us in love, in love toward You... for it is known to You that we strive to give You only satisfaction and pleasure..."

A wonderful surprise awaited us in Lizhensk. The staff had prepared a *tisch* for us, with the tour leader taking the role of the Rebbe.

The girls were enchanted by the atmosphere. It was as if

they'd been carried back a hundred years to a shtetl, with *Chossidim* who traveled by train to be with their Rebbe for an authentic *tisch*. There were even trays of herring and crackers on the table, and little cups of liqueur for a *l'chaim*.

The Chassidic music, together with the liqueur, got into their bones, engendering a powerful longing for an experience of genuine joy, heightened awareness, and pure, solid faith. And perhaps the music gave the most eloquent answer to their questions, telling them without words what *Chossidus* is all about.

There was something I wanted to say. I felt an almost overwhelming urge to say it, and at the same time a voice inside was warning me not to go there. The urge kept rising, like a wave hitting the beach and being pushed back out to sea again and again. The water was so warm and cleansing; I so wanted to let it wash over me and through me.... Finally, I surrendered. The wave was too big; I could only close my eyes and let it engulf me.

Antwerp

Without a sound, I tiptoed into Mottel's room. I wanted to slip something into his suitcase, something to remind him of his little sister Chana while he was far away.

I couldn't think of anything to give him aside from the letter that shook in my hands. Mama had already stuffed in so many things that Mottel said he was afraid the plane would fall if she added any more weight to the bag. But of course Mama went right on stuffing things in...

Any moment Mottel might come in, and that would put an end to my surprise.

From the shelf facing me, Mottel's model airplanes looked down with annoying indifference. "Don't you care at all?" I felt like scolding them. "All those hours Mottel spent gluing you together so precisely, with so much love, while I sat on the rug watching, quiet as a mouse and curious as a bird — all that means nothing to you?"

The model planes had nothing to say. They were as perfect as my brother, but they would stay here on the shelf in their static perfection, while my brother Mottel would soon be flying away.

I remember those days, when Mottel would come home, his eyes glowing like two flames, with some chemicals he'd bought in the pharmacy. He'd read in his chemistry book about some reaction, and he just had to try it out for himself. He looked as if the chemical reaction were already taking place inside him, leaving no room for anything else. He would hardly even eat on days like those. Papa and Mama would smile tolerantly, knowing that for Mottel, the test tubes, flasks, and chemicals were like beloved pets.

Mama allowed him to experiment, but only in the basement. All she needed was a hydrogen explosion in the bedroom, and clouds of smoke in the living room….

Mottel always reminded me of the alchemists of medieval times, who, in the stories, always seemed to make their greatest discoveries in dim, chilly cellars, between broken furniture and jars of preserved fruits and pickles.

And now, my adored big brother was going away to Eretz Yisrael to learn in yeshiva, leaving his model planes and his test tubes orphaned, and a little sister who would miss him desperately.

He'd given us a farewell concert the day before. It was unplanned, but we were all there, drawn by the enchantment of the music. Mottel was playing a piece by Boccherini on his violin, so beautifully that Boccherini himself would have been proud. Sometimes people passing by in the street would stop for a moment under our windows to listen, for no one could hear Mottel's playing without feeling something stir in their heart, releasing an elusive, inexplicable mix of sadness and joy.

His violin teacher had come around that week to speak with Mama and Papa. He couldn't believe that his rising young star was going to leave it all behind for a yeshiva in Israel.

"But he's a musical genius," the teacher implored, almost in tears. "He's well on his way to the Brussels Philharmonic… you don't realize what a treasure you have here…"

"We do realize it," my parents told him, trying their best to placate him. "But this treasure wants to study Torah in a yeshiva."

The elderly teacher turned to Mottel. "At least take your violin with you," he pleaded, "so you can keep on practicing until you return home."

But Mottel decided not to take the violin. If he took it, he wouldn't be able to dedicate himself fully to Torah. So yesterday, he'd given a farewell performance and then gently placed the instrument in its case. As the last echoes faded, he smiled shyly at us and said, "We'll meet again at Pesach time."

And now, tears come to my eyes as Boccherini's melody runs through my head, and all the love, pride, and longing of that moment reappear, like a memento too intangible to be given, beside a closed suitcase.

CHAPTER 16

I Knew a Chossid

"THERE WAS A *CHOSSID* I knew," I said to the girls. "A real *chossid*. In the first years after the war, he didn't have a *shtreimel* or a long black coat. But on the inside, there wasn't a drop of blood in him that wasn't *Chossidish*. He was my father.

"My father had an only son, my only brother, one living branch of the Horowitz family after the conflagration that burned the whole forest down.

"My father gave him everything; he wanted him to have a happy childhood and every opportunity to grow. He sent him to yeshiva in Eretz Yisrael even though he and my mother would miss him terribly, because it was the best place for him to learn. We, his three sisters, felt the same way toward him; as the only son, he was special, and he filled us with love and pride.

"He got married in Eretz Yisrael, and soon he had a little son of his own. But then something went wrong. We didn't know what. My husband and I were a new couple ourselves, and nobody wanted to worry us. 'He's not feeling well,' my parents would tell us. 'There's an infection in his blood.' Somehow the infection never seemed to go away, and when the truth eventually came out, it was as bad as could be — leukemia.

"My beloved brother had leukemia, and at that time, decades

ago, there wasn't much the medical profession could do about it. My parents took a direct flight from Antwerp and arrived in Israel frantic with worry. They were there to do anything for their precious son. He mustn't suffer... he mustn't. He couldn't die... he couldn't. He had a young wife and a baby. And they were there to help in every possible way. They asked the doctors not to tell 'the boy' the real facts about his condition. Why distress him like that? 'The boy' had long since left his childhood behind. He was worried about his parents, and he asked the doctors not to tell them the exact truth about his condition. Why cause them needless distress? Both sides kept up the 'infection' pretense very well. For almost two years he had the disease, and it slowly consumed him. But then it loosened its biting grip, and it looked as though he was starting to recover. And just at that time, his wife gave birth to twins. Twin boys! 'He's got to survive now,' everyone said. The *bris* was unforgettable, an intense mix of happiness and crying, hope, fear, and prayer. But despite it all, he was soon back in the hospital.

"My parents came again to be with him, hiding their tears and believing to the end that a miracle could happen. And one day, this only son, who had three babies at home, was taken to G-d, and there weren't enough tears in the world to weep for him."

I wanted to cry now, as we stood by the grave of Reb Elimelech, to cry for my only brother who left this world while still in the bloom of youth, and I never saw him again. He was my best friend, and he was so young. But then I saw all these young women looking at me, and I didn't want to cause them pain with my crying, so for the moment I chased the tears away and pushed them into the place inside where I always keep them.

And with the tears safely tucked away, I continued: "My father was a *chossid* of the Beis Yisroel.* The Beis Yisroel was the

---

*Chassidic Rebbes (and other famous rabbis as well) are often known by

Gerrer Rebbe of the postwar generation, and he saved the Jews who survived. They would come, stripped of everything Jewish that had been theirs before the war, cut off from their faith, from the Torah, feeling that it had all died within them. The Beis Yisroel healed their hearts. He didn't criticize or admonish; he didn't show surprise or ask questions, and he certainly didn't preach. He just put soothing balm on their wounds and loved them. To one, he'd give an apple, to another, a bottle of wine. He listened to their pain and heard the screams of their souls that they were unable to release. He warmed hearts that had almost frozen to death and made a safe space for emotions that had nearly decayed from long repression. People would come and come back again and again, like lost moths on a moonless night, drawn to a warm flame. They came, and they stayed to soak up the Rebbe's love and be warmed by his words. The Beis Yisroel didn't think about the grand Chassidic court that had once been and was now gone; he didn't try to rebuild it or to recruit more *Chossidim*. He simply loved those who came, and they came.

"My father also came to him. He came on Shavuos to the Gerrer *beis midrash* in Jerusalem, just two days after getting up from shivah for his only son. His tears hadn't yet dried and the image of his child in his last agonizing days still lingered in his heart, but it was a holiday, a day of joy, and he was there next to the *bimah*. Yet he missed his precious son terribly, and his tears of longing could have filled the whole *beis midrash*.

"After davening, the *Chossidim* danced joyously, singing "*Uvo'u chulom biv'ris yachad...*"* The Rebbe gestured to Papa to come and

---

the names of the works of Torah thought that they authored. *Beis Yisroel* is the book authored by Rebbe Yisroel Alter of Ger.

*"And they all came together in a covenant; 'We will do and we will hear,' they said as one." These words, sung on Shavuos, are an excerpt from the Shabbos song *Yom Shabboson*.

dance and Papa obeyed. And suddenly, he was truly dancing, fueled by an inner flame. For it wasn't his feet that were moving him, it was his soul. It was a dance of joy, of thanks, and of faith. It was a true dance, and Papa was a true *chossid*.

"He danced, and when the dance ended, he said, 'Master of the Universe, you gave me a child for twenty-six years. For twenty-six happy years, you gave me *nachas*. For twenty-six years I had a wonderful, sweet, exceptionally fine boy.

"'I thank You for leaving him sons to carry on his name. I thank You, G-d, and I never question You, never. Even in Auschwitz I didn't question You, and I don't ask questions now, either.'

"And this," I said to the girls, as tears rose in my eyes and theirs, "this is what it is to be a *chossid*."

CHAPTER 17

Pictures of Life

On the bus, all the girls clamor to see the pictures of my brother as a child, as a young man, as a young father dandling a baby on his knee, and at the *bris* of his twins, wrapped in a *tallis* and weeping.

My father is in the pictures, too. "That's your father?!" they ask again and again, as if they mean to say, "This is the one who was with the Gerrer Rebbe on Shavuos? This is the one who lost his only son, and he could still smile? This is the one who worked so hard to get into Yeshivas Chachmei Lublin, and then never got the chance to go there because of the war... but seventy years later he went and made a *siyum* there? Is that him? Really?"

Afterwards, they ask me if I have any more pictures. "Pictures? Of what?" I ask innocently.

"Of your family," they say, looking at me accusingly, as if I'd seated them at a table laden with delicacies, and then snatched their plates away after they'd taken only two bites.

"Pictures of my family? Who would want to look at those?"

"We would!"

So I take out pictures. Pictures of my children when they were little, and pictures of them when they were big. This is Yocheved and this is Chaya, and this... and this... Here they are at their wedding... and this is at her son's bar mitzvah... and this baby is their daughter, and here she's about eight years old... and these three are that couple's children, and this girl with the bow in her hair and a tooth missing is my granddaughter from Vienna... and these three freckled boys on the monkey bars are her brothers. Oh, and this baby, too...

I maneuver among the pictures, telling my audience who is whose sibling and whose child, cataloging all the smiling faces. But nobody really cares who's the oldest and who's the youngest, or whose bar mitzvah was in Bnei Brak....

The names and the data don't matter to them. They're looking at something intangible that runs like a thread through all the pictures of happy, hugging people. They're looking at the story of a large family that is... a family.

"Really?" Neta asks me, flicking her long, light hair to one side. "Are you really like that?" She points to a bar mitzvah picture, as if she wants to touch the laughter in it with her hand.

"Like what?" I ask.

"Like... together. Everyone talking with everyone else and laughing with them, everyone friends... like this." She holds the picture in her hand, and there is yearning in her voice.

"I have only one brother," she says. "And he hasn't spoken to my parents in two years." She tells the story quickly, as if to get it over with as fast as possible. "For two years he's been wandering around in Goa, and nobody knows what he's been up to. My parents are out of their minds with worry, but he's incommunicado. Once he even said to them, 'Consider me dead.' And they cried for a week... so I stayed." Neta's blue eyes are full of so much pain that I can't contain it.

"I couldn't go away like my brother did. I have to be there for them, to try to make them happy. Someone has to be around to come and visit them, and talk to them on the phone. But somehow, I don't know how, they always have a way of making me want to cut off contact. But then something pulls me back to them again. I always want to escape, yet I have to be the good daughter."

Everyone is listening to Neta, looking at her soft, angelic features. The pain she's suddenly revealed seems more familiar to them than my pictures, which are such a novelty.

"My mother is about your age," says Shaked, appraising me with her eyes, "and I really do have a great relationship with her. My sister, my mother, and I are almost inseparable. I even asked if I could take my mother along on this trip. But still, when I think about her, with only two grandchildren, and you with..." — she waves a hand over the spread of pictures — "over a hundred, I guess, I can't help but think she's really missed out on something in life."

Suddenly, they all start talking about the family they have or never had. About their desire to feel what it's like to be part of a really big family, with lots of nephews, nieces, brothers and sisters and laughing in the kitchen, a good fight now and then, and birthday parties all through the year.

"I thought I was about to start a family of my own," Yif'at says to me privately, after all the chatter dies down. "I was already imagining myself in a white gown, and in my own home, and with a little, curly-haired baby.

"My dream was so close to coming true. At least, that's what I thought. I was almost ready to order invitations. And then... suddenly, I woke up, and it was nothing but a dream, because I had no one to make it a reality with me. The reality was that I was alone, as alone as could be.

"I thought we were already engaged. But he thought..." Her voice suddenly breaks. "He thought differently....

"I thought there was such a thing as a genuine relationship. Such a thing as family, faithfulness, and happiness."

For a moment, Yif'at is quiet, overwhelmed by the pain.

"But he thought there was only himself, and his self-serving interest of the moment. When I tried to tell him about my dream, he said there was no hurry, we had plenty of time... and when the time was up, he left....

"And now I'm alone." She gazes out the window, twenty-eight years old, still young, yet feeling old, desperately wanting the kind of happiness my pictures portray, and searching in vain for someone willing to share her dream.

CHAPTER 18

Maybe Bubbe and Zeide Will Come

RECOLLECTIONS FROM my sister Tzili:

For half an hour every day, we weren't allowed to breathe. That was the regular time each weekday when Papa would turn on the big, wooden radio that stood on the floor on four legs, and we had to be absolutely silent.

No matter what we were in the middle of, everything stopped, and silence fell all through the house. Even our fine, carved furniture let out not a creak. It was an unworldly sort of silence that seemed to have been created for this time alone.

Only one voice spoke into this silent void: "Kol Tzion laGolah," said the radio announcer. "The Voice of Zion to the Diaspora. The Search Bureau for Missing Relatives Program."

This was the one time of day when we mustn't even breathe, and also the one time of day when Papa and Mama didn't try to smile. Every day, disappointment sharpened its knife and stabbed them in the heart once again — no new relatives had been found. There was an air of suspense as the radio was turned on, and the pain was palpable as it was turned off. And this happened day after day.

Afterwards, the silence was folded up and put away, as if that anticipation had never filled our living room, pushing everything else out… and we went back to the normal rhythm of our lives. As if there was no terrible secret that nobody would talk about, as if the curtain hadn't been briefly pulled aside, revealing Gehinnom… as if nothing had happened.

We went right back to being normal children who play with toy soldiers or pretty dolls, Monopoly or cards with our friends. Regular kids who do homework and then organize their schoolbags for tomorrow, kids who remember they have an English quiz tomorrow and review the material one more time, because they have to get good grades… they simply have to.

They need to get good marks in every single subject, even in arts and crafts and gym, to make their parents happy. No, not just to please them, not just to give them nachas, but literally to make them happy. No one ever told us. There was a place inside of us that simply knew it: you mustn't ever cause Papa and Mama any trouble or sorrow, or disappoint them. You mustn't ever cause them worry or pain, and certainly you mustn't ever come home late from spending time with friends, or tell them that your math lessons are too hard. We were there to make sure they were happy and content. Surely every child in the world knew that. Wasn't it obvious?

Papa and Mama had a vinyl phonograph record. One day I broke it. I did it on purpose. I wanted Papa and Mama to stop being sad, so I broke the record with the man speaking in Yiddish, the one that always brought tears to Mama's eyes. I asked Papa once what the man was saying. Papa told me it was a testimony. Just a testimony. Why should my precious parents have to be sad because of some voice on a record, giving a testimony? A week later, Mama asked who broke the record. I came to her and told her I did it.

"But why did you break it?" she asked. She didn't understand.

"So that you and Papa wouldn't be sad," I told her happily.

If the radio program would only find them some relatives, Papa and Mama could be very happy, I thought.

Once, I asked Mama where my grandparents were. She said there'd been a war, and the Germans had taken them. The

Germans took them because there was a war? Well, it was about time they gave them back! How long were the Germans going to keep their family waiting?

I remember seeing an elderly woman in the street and thinking, "Maybe that's my grandmother. Maybe she came back from the Germans, but she doesn't know who I am. Maybe she hasn't heard she has a granddaughter Tzili."

A few months before that, some people came knocking on our door. They asked if they could come in, and they started asking Papa about his family; they wanted to know which Horowitz we were. Papa and Mama became very excited, and sat with them in the living room for a long time. After a long session of 'Jewish geography', it turned out that these people were distant relatives of ours from Holland. If Papa and Mama had won the lottery, they couldn't have been happier, and from that day on our visitors were called "Oncle" and "Tante," and we wrote to them regularly.

After that, I started hoping that maybe Bubbe and Zeide would come knocking on our door, and we would all be so excited. Mama would be ecstatic, and Papa would be very, very happy too. We would show them all our things, and they would give us candy. I knew that grandmas gave candy, because I'd read about it in books. Oh, how I wished they would come knocking at our door!

My mother was once asked, what was her message for life?

The question was asked by a group of young women who met her and were captivated by her. It was a simple, touchingly sincere question. They weren't looking for a slogan or a byword, but an answer as honest as the question.

Almost everyone who meets my mother wants to bring something of her specialness into their own life. Some spark of this woman who remained so queenly and noble despite the

Gehinnom she'd been through, this woman who is such a delight to be with, and who gives of herself to everyone, although everything was taken away from her.

My mother's answer to the girls was the simple, unequivocal truth. Her message for life was the message life had sent her: "Appreciate your family," she said. "That's all.

"Appreciate your family, value them, live life with them. It doesn't matter how big or small, how well-educated or simple your family is — they're your family! Appreciate that you have them, and don't lose the simple happiness of that experience that is closest to every person — family!"

My mother had no family to envelop her in its warmth. She had no parents to go to when she needed a shoulder to lean on, no sisters to share with. She was left with nothing and no one, and the little, precious family she raised with Papa was her only comfort in that chill of loneliness and pain.

And on that narrow road between a world that is lost and gone, and a present existence of studio apartments, terse messaging, mass media, and endless cynicism, people search for the warmth of family, but it evaporates even before the heart touches it.

"Value them..." My mother's words pulse through my heart as I gaze at the pictures scattered among the girls. "Appreciate them! You didn't lose them in an extermination camp, G-d forbid, and they live half an hour away from you. So what are you waiting for? Embrace them and don't let go. Fight to stay close to them, and don't lose them over foolishness like who gave and how much, who said this or that. Just appreciate that you have them...."

Finally all the pictures are passed back to me, and as I put them away in my bag, I feel as if I'm packing away the fond dreams of young women who want families, who hope that one day, they too will have lots of pictures like these.

CHAPTER 19

The Forest of the Children: Zbylitowska Góra

THE GROUND IN THE forest is freezing cold, just like me. But nobody comes to cover it. Even the snow clings to the tree branches, falling no farther, as if it doesn't want to touch that blood-drenched earth.

As the rabbi leading the tour describes how little children and infants were slaughtered en masse, here in this terrible forest, we all feel just as exposed as that bare earth, and the warmest fur couldn't take away the chill that grips us.

Almost all the girls have been here before. They recognize the picture of the doll on the memorial plaque, and the little toys thrown here in heartrending pain. They've seen the fences around the huge, seemingly bottomless pit that swallowed up thousands of little children, and the other pit where the mothers were buried — the mothers who couldn't save their tortured, screaming babies.

Almost everyone in the group has been here, eight or ten years ago, or at least they've seen the pictures their friends brought back. But this time it's different. Then, the effervescence of teenagers in hoodies surrounded them. Now, a violin brings out the melodies of the Jewish heart in exile.

Just listening to the rabbi's explanations makes these students feel as if they're on another planet, breathing an unfamiliar atmosphere. The pain seems so much closer now, as if they can reach out and touch it. Shir is feeling it more than the others; in fact, she looks as if she were about to suffocate.

Shir is the only student in the group who is a mother already. She's left her husband and little ones at home to come on this trip; that's how important it was to her to have this experience — precisely because she is raising children. Her husband gallantly encouraged her to go, taking all the complex logistics of diapering and feeding upon himself and promising her that everything would be all right. "I see it means a lot to you," he said when they discussed it, "so don't worry about a thing, just do it. And if I can't find the baby wipes, my mother will come over and help me."

And now Shir is standing here, beside the burial pit of thousands of tiny bodies, and she can't contain it. She has to go back.

I feel for her. I identify with the tears that flow unchecked down her cheeks. "The children," she sobs. "The children… the children…" She is unable to get another word out, and she walks out of that terrible place, back to the bus, where she might find a safe, sane refuge from this horror, where her mind might return to the present.

And the rest of us are left in that terrible place, the place where the children went on their last day, and the mothers with them. What mother would leave her children and run away? What mother wouldn't stay with her baby up until the very last moment?

And how much could a woman with a baby in her arms fight back against an armed enemy?

When the accursed war was over, and the world shook off the blood, there were no more mothers and no more babies. The survivors were mainly lone young adults, bereft of parents and the entire life they'd known. They had no mother to give them a guiding hand. The mothers buried here took their knowledge and experience with them. They took the womanly intuition and wisdom handed down from mother to daughter over thousands of years, and after every bullet found its target, the survivors were left in a silent void.

How, then, could they raise families of their own?

Who would teach them what to say to a child who doesn't want to go to bed? Who would explain how to speak with a girl who is starting to turn into a woman? Who would show them how to calm a screaming baby, and who would recommend the right time to start him on solid food?

Who would comfort and encourage them after the baby kept them up every night for a week? Who would reassure them that all babies are like that, and that they'd get through it? Who would come to visit, to pinch the toddler's cheek and say, "She's so adorable. You're doing such a good job raising her."

I was born in a place where all the mothers had spent their adolescence behind barbed wire. Instead of teenage noshing, they wasted away on a slice of stale bread and half a plate of thin soup made of half-rotten vegetables. Instead of school, they were educated with whips and truncheons. Instead of music, the sound of gunfire filled their ears. After the war, they pulled themselves together as best they could, and they got married without a mother to bless them with the words their mothers and grandmothers had whispered to their daughters before walking them to the *chuppah*.

And in that place of lone survivors, they raised children, children who were sick sometimes, and naughty sometimes, and who sometimes asked endless questions, and sometimes woke up at night afraid. And who was there to tell them how to manage?

Shir will soon go home and continue being a devoted mother. The pain and anguish she feels today will pass. The rest of us, too, will go back to our lives. But those women, then, had nowhere to return to. And the realization comes to me that along with the babies and mothers who were murdered, a whole world of wisdom was murdered as well, a whole encyclopedia of priceless trivia — parenting tips, methods of stain removal, how to keep cupboards organized, simple recipes for a hearty pea soup or a soft yeast cake. All of it was slain and buried in these forest pits. Yet my mother had started a family in that vacuum.

"When my older sister was born," I say to the girls around me, "her life was in danger because of a blood type incompatibility. And this was just three years after the Gehinnom my parents had been through. Just two and a half years stood between a starved, emaciated, barely alive young girl, and a young mother with a baby in her arms. And now the doctor on duty, who could do little to help, was telling her with no great sensitivity, 'If the baby lasts the night, then you'll know the danger is past.' And he turned and left. I can't imagine the night my parents spent, so young and so alone, waiting to see if their day-old baby, who symbolized all their hope and comfort, would live.

"The baby lived. G-d was there with them, although they had no one else. And we had a happy childhood." I myself was amazed at those last words even as I said them, no less than my audience.

"But Chana, how could that be?!"

Tanya, with her charming candor, is asking on behalf of them all. The facts I was presenting just don't mesh. I keep telling them I had a happy childhood — but with a background story like that? How could a young couple who'd both suffered inconceivable abuse, and never had trauma therapy, possibly go on to raise a happy family?

"G-d helped my parents… I don't know what else to tell you. There is no other explanation."

"How did G-d help?" Tanya insisted on a clear explanation.

"He always has His messengers," I said. "Hashem doesn't abandon people; He always gives them the strength and the tools to make up for whatever was taken from them. And challenges are always tailor-made and measured to fit perfectly. No one in Hashem's world will be left holding remnants that are too big to handle; someone will always come along to help fold them up. I knew some of those helpers in Antwerp… some of those Heaven-sent people who helped to raise the young parents."

CHAPTER 20

Holland and the Sea

Scheveningen, 1960

Morning, as always, comes early.

I hear the sound of milk trickling into the pot, and the gentle thump of porcelain cups on an ironed tablecloth. Mama is in the kitchen, heating milk for our breakfast. And that means it's seven o'clock.

I snuggle deeper between the stiffly starched white sheets, retreating into that drowsy zone between dreaming and waking. Somewhere far in the background, I hear my brother's voice. He's always the first one up, and he gets eight things done by the time I rouse myself. I know that in one more minute, my snooze time will be up and I'll really have to be on my feet.

As usual, I can't find my hat, and five precious minutes go by as I search feverishly, accompanied by the requisite sermon from my sister. At home, it's more orderly and calm; there's a proper place for everything, and I don't keep losing things every fifteen minutes. But at home, there's no beach, and here there is, and for that alone it's worth putting up with my sister's scolding.

At seven-thirty, we're ready to go. The sun is hardly shining, and it's so chilly outside that we're shivering even under our coats.

The street is empty, quiet, and very clean. At every window there are flowers... lots of flowers. That is the second-nicest thing about Holland. But the nicest thing is the beach.

I put my hands in my pockets. It's so cold that I can't believe it's summer. In a few hours it will be warm, and the sunlight will dance on the water. Mama will collect all our coats and pile them up neatly next to our boots, and she'll let us run around on the beach in our short clothes. But right now we're getting goose bumps from the wind, and it isn't a bit bothered by the coats we're wearing.

Mama hurries us along. At seven in the morning the air at the beach is healthiest, so of course we have to be there, and there's no point in arguing about it.

Fish is good for you, too. Around noon, when the beach is full of all the beautiful sand palaces and turrets we'll build there, and the tide comes in to fill our canals with water, we'll suddenly feel such hunger pangs, you'd think we'd never eaten in our lives.

And that's when we'll go with Mama to the fish store by the sea to look for some fresh, tasty, kosher fish. Mama brings her own knife, and the fishmonger will use it to clean and prepare our fish for cooking. After that, we'll go and buy potatoes, which is much more fun than buying fish. The potatoes are so small, and we love throwing them into the machine that goes round and round, where they bounce around noisily until they come out cleanly peeled.

All of our food is very healthful. Mama is very particular about that, and I'm glad. I love the soups she makes with lots of vegetables in them, and the cheese she makes at home, and for sure I love the sweet jams and compotes she prepares. We all like those so much that Papa brings her big crates of ripe fruit every week so that every morning we can have bread with jam and cheese.

I just wish that Mama would let us have fresh bread.

But even when it comes fresh and still warm from the bakery, she puts it away for a day. "Fresh-baked bread isn't healthful," she says. "And white bread isn't healthful either, certainly not."

One time at Debbie's house, I ate some white bread with chocolate spread. It was yummy, like having a whole meal of sweets, but I didn't say a word about it to Mama. If something isn't healthy, we just don't eat it, there's nothing to discuss.

Mama knows best what's healthy and what isn't. Whenever we go to the doctor, she asks him a lot of questions. The doctor knows everything, he has so many books and charts. For example, when Mama asks him how many hours I should sleep, he takes out a chart and asks her again how old I am. And then he tells Mama I should sleep ten and a half hours, or nine and a quarter, and I know that from now on, that is exactly how it will be, and I mean exactly.

The doctor tells Mama what's good for children to eat, and how to keep them from catching cold, how often she should replace the rug, and how to bathe a baby.

Mama listens to him carefully, and you can see that she's taking notes in her head, so she'll be sure never to do anything against his instructions.

I think I'm lucky she's like that.

And it's a good thing she remembers so well what he tells her. This way, when I'm a mother myself, I won't have to ask him, which is good because he'll be very old by then, but mainly because I can ask Mama. Mama knows best.

I have so many thoughts in my head that I don't even notice how far we've walked… and here we are at the shore already.

I feel like the sea is winking at us with its beautiful blue eyes. "Hi there!" it seems to say. "Here are the children who come every morning to open the sea!"

CHAPTER 21

The Curtain Is Thrust Aside

IN THE HOTEL ROOM, the pillow is soft and puffy, and the quiet out in the corridor is as perfect as the precisely-fitted sheets. The cold, banished by an air-conditioner humming monotonously, waits outside, disappointed.

But inside me, it's noisy as a crowded city street, and the quiet surroundings only make more space for the noise to take over my whole being. Now that I'm alone, it all comes to visit me — Warsaw, the wonderful young women in our group, Tiktin, and the tears we shed in the forest.

"I wasn't supposed to be here," I say to myself in the tone of someone lying awake, counting sheep. Involuntarily, the memory comes back to me, the memory of that day when I discovered my parents' terrible secret.

I discovered it through a back door, and it was more terrible that you could imagine.

It was like a fault line running underground, beneath the solid foundation of our happy life, just waiting to break through to the surface and overturn everything.

It should have been obvious all along that a day would come when we'd be forced to pull aside the curtain we'd kept carefully closed all those years. It should have been obvious that we couldn't go on forever thinking our house ended there, and there were no secret chambers beyond that curtain, nothing but a few bits of childhood trivia that Papa would bring out from behind there to entertain us once in a while.

It was as if we'd been living in a pleasant bubble that inevitably had to burst, sooner or later. And burst it did.

One day, a woman sent by Beit HaTefutzot, the Museum of the Jewish People in Tel Aviv, came to our happy home. The State of Israel had made supreme efforts to reach out to every survivor and to record his or her testimony in order to preserve the memory of the Holocaust for posterity.

The woman came and explained to Papa and Mama what her purpose was, and after they consented — with great difficulty — she spent several hours interviewing each of them in depth and professionally videotaping their detailed testimonies.

Reopening those profound wounds had a devastating effect on my parents.

I knew that their wartime experiences had been documented; I'd even encouraged them to cooperate with the museum. We children were all adults at that point, and we knew that our parents had grown up in Poland and that they'd been teenagers when the war broke out. We realized that this meant they must have either hidden somehow from the Nazis or spent some time in the camps — there weren't that many options, after all. We strung together a few words we'd overheard together with the history we knew, but we didn't know exactly how they had survived or where they had spent those years. And we never showed much curiosity, because deep inside we felt we couldn't deal with the facts. But now, we had the whole story, wrapped up in two big videocassettes.

"Chana," my sister said to me one day, "you have to hear Papa and Mama's testimonies."

"No! No! I don't have to!" I protested, wanting to burrow back into a world of dolls and games, as if I were a little girl in Antwerp hearing the grownups mention the *lager* and convincing myself that they didn't mean *those* camps... not the ones they talked about in those terrible books that were kept behind a rope in the library. Of course not — things like that had nothing to do with my lovely, cheerful parents.

But I wasn't a little girl. I had children of my own, quite big children, and there was no place to retreat to. The videotapes were sitting in my house, like tons of lead weighing on my heart. I knew that I had to watch them... but not today, of course. Today I had to take my older daughter to her dentist appointment, and I also had to buy shoes for my little son. Not today.

The next day I couldn't watch them either. The piles of laundry waiting to be washed and sorted were threatening to take over the house, and I desperately needed to organize things before my cleaning lady arrived, which would be any minute now.

On Tuesday I was too busy again, and on Wednesday I was too tired. On Thursday, *baruch Hashem* it was time to start preparing for Shabbos, and on Sunday? The videocassettes had already waited this long; they could wait a little longer.

They waited — wrapped, silent, and very frightening. I didn't want to see them, although I knew I really had no choice. I was afraid of what I'd encounter, but I knew I must find the courage. I wanted to stretch out my hand to my parents' past, but in my heart I hoped that somehow, my hand would never reach it.

My life was good. I had children in school, one already in high school, a nice apartment with the fresh mountain air of Jerusalem wafting in at the windows, the melodious sound of my husband's learning from the living room, and the soft breathing of my baby daughter from her crib. Why should I let a hurricane in? Why let it snatch away our serenity? I didn't have a good enough answer, and the tapes waited another week. Weeks turned into months, and I was still grasping the edge of that curtain, holding it tightly closed, lest the wind come and blow it aside, revealing what I felt unable to face.

Rosh Chodesh Av came and found me still procrastinating.

My deadline had arrived, and I knew it. Each passing day seemed longer and more painful, and I realized that nothing could be worse than feeling the constant presence of those tapes, like a ticking time bomb in the closet.

I was no longer a little girl who read books under a blanket with a flashlight. I knew that the Holocaust wasn't a distant horror like the Inquisition, and I knew that my parents had been there, in Poland, somehow evading the death sentence that hovered over them.

I wasn't an innocent child anymore, and I couldn't keep clinging to false innocence. "*Lager*" meant a concentration camp, a death camp; it meant Auschwitz. And my parents had been there. But the videotapes were still in the closet.

"That's it — no more excuses!" I said to myself. And I went and rented a videocassette player.

The device was much heavier than its physical weight. It was weighted with my fear. It was two days before Tishah B'Av. The laundry hampers were full and overflowing,* and there was little to do but feel the void left by the loss of Jerusalem of old. I made sure all the children had left the house for their summer day camps, and nevertheless I locked the door as an added precaution… Then I took the first videocassette, pushed it into the slot, and with a shaking hand I pressed the "play" button.

"Here it comes," I said to myself. "There's nowhere to run, Chana." I felt as though I'd entered a dark, narrow tunnel with no option of going back, but only forward, into the terrible darkness. Irregular stripes crackled across the screen, and then my father appeared in black and white. My beloved Papa, with a gray face, began to speak.

This wasn't the Papa I had known, not the strong, affectionate

---

*As a sign of mourning for the destruction of the Temple, laundering is not done during the days leading up to Tishah B'Av.

Papa who hugged us, lifted us high in the air and let us jump all over him when he came home. This was a different Papa, not the busy, energetic community activist. This was someone who had been there, with Gehinnom wide open before his eyes, living an inch away from death when his life had hardly begun. This was someone who didn't have to hide behind masks anymore, someone who could finally reveal what was inside him. He could do it now; the children weren't listening....

I sat there for hours, staring with huge eyes at the screen, horrified, yet unable to move a muscle, seeing and hearing what my eyes and ears couldn't bear, wanting only to whisper, "Papa! Oy, Papa!"

For six hours, he spoke. At the end, he spoke about the life he rebuilt, about the happy ending that we were part of. But I wasn't there. I was somewhere else. My world had fallen apart.

CHAPTER 22

A New World

THE CHILDREN CAME HOME from day camp, wanted something to eat, and asked me questions. Somebody was crying, and somebody wanted me to get something down from the closet shelf. I don't know how I functioned the rest of that day, or what exactly I said or did. I must have been running on automatic pilot.

The curtain that had been closed all my life had suddenly been thrust aside. The secret I'd been shielded from had been revealed, and it had caught me unprepared.

The next day, I did it all over again. I locked the door after making sure they were all gone, and with a pounding heart and sweating hands, I pushed the second videocassette into the slot — my mother's testimony. Again, I closed my eyes at first, and then opened them. "Is this really my aristocratic, beautiful mother, always so put-together and refined? Did you really go through all that, Mama? No... it's not possible!"

Mama was there for us all the time, making life beautiful, giving us everything she'd been deprived of: a happy childhood and a flourishing adolescence.

Mama had been a tender, delicate child, and her memories were so nightmarish, so inconceivable. "My dear mother," I said to myself, "are you really telling these stories? Is this the only youth you had?!"

My tears blurred the final subtitles and skewed the image on the screen.

Tishah B'Av came, and I was already filled to the brim with sadness. There was no way I could contain any more. I was in shock, consumed by a holocaust of my own. Suddenly I understood that I was — and always had been — the daughter of Holocaust survivors. Something in my life was changing. Something had already changed, irreversibly.

For the first time in my life, I had broken the agreement we had kept so carefully all these years. The unwritten, unspoken agreement to keep the curtain closed, never to discuss what lay behind it, not even to think there was anything behind it. The agreement we knew by heart, although no one ever told us about it. Don't ask us, and we won't tell you; we've put a coating of smooth glass on your lives — don't break it! Live in your happy, shining world, and our world will remain shrouded in silence. That's the only way we can give you a normal, happy life. Women chatted with their neighbors as they hung the laundry out to dry, children ran on the sidewalk, somewhere in the building a baby cried, and the telephone rang: Hi, it's my friend, wanting that chocolate cake recipe....

I felt I no longer belonged to that normal, everyday world, and I didn't know how to go on from where I now was. Everything within me — my whole personality and outlook on life — had been built on a foundation of trusting innocence, and now that whole foundation had cracked and collapsed under me. In my eyes, my parents had always been the strong ones, the ones in control, and now I'd found out how they'd been subjugated and tortured, how they'd survived and hung on by their fingernails to a semblance of normal living.

Suddenly, so many things were falling into place. So many little things I'd chosen to ignore — whispered words, expressions on my parents' faces, code words and looks exchanged between them — were now forming a clear picture. And it was a terrible, tragic picture.

The videos I'd watched were flaming inside me, and I had to do something before they consumed me.

In time, I learned that those flames could serve a wonderful purpose.

The shell protecting my innocent self had been struck by a lightning bolt and incinerated. But that lightning had also ignited something, fueling a new potential, setting in motion wheels that I'd never even known were there inside me. And I was soon to discover that my new world, built on the ruins of the old, was many times more beautiful, bright, and powerful.

"Now that I've been pushed out of my shelter and thrown into my parents' memories," I said to myself, "I can either sink or swim. I might as well learn to swim...." And I began learning to swim in those murky waters.

A craving for knowledge, almost a physical hunger, took hold of me. I wanted the facts and figures. Who was in which ghetto, which camp, which *aktion*? When? For how long? I wanted descriptions: how was all this done? And above all, why?

The questions surrounded me, pressured me, and demanded answers — many, many answers.

I found myself attending one lecture after another, soaking up knowledge. I cut out ads for continuing education courses on the Holocaust and filled up my calendar with dates, times, and places.

I became acquainted with the people behind the projects dedicated to teaching the public about the Holocaust and memorializing the victims, and I felt that I'd discovered a new world. It was no longer just a story of destruction; there was empowerment to be found there, as well.

Rebbetzin Esther Farbstein, the acclaimed Holocaust historian, became my personal guide and spiritual mentor. She knew how to dig up the historical facts, to peel away the coats of falsehood that had stuck to them over the years and to present the truth accurately, however unpopular it might be. She knew how to debunk myths colored by the sentiments of one sector or another of Jewish society and replace them with a legacy to be genuinely proud of. And so I chose her to teach me the truth I now craved, and became her very devoted student.

New books began filling the shelf of my night table. Since I was twelve, when I used to sneak forbidden books out of the library and read them by flashlight under my blanket, I hadn't touched a Holocaust book. Now I was reading them once again, not as forbidden tales of horror, but in a mature effort to connect with what was, after all, a major part of my own history. I also began asking my parents questions. They weren't exactly eager to discuss that segment of their lives, but they realized that I knew, and the jig was up. From their point of view, nothing had really changed. All they wanted was to get on with their lives, just as they'd been doing all along.

I was very careful with my questions, like someone trying to remove a brick from the bottom row and praying that the whole building wouldn't fall. I didn't confront my parents directly about their personal experiences, but when an opportunity arose, I would slip in a question about some factual detail, to fill in the gaps in my knowledge. "Was it really like that in the Lodz ghetto?" I would ask, or "Is it true that the commander of Auschwitz had such-and-such a habit?"

Every time I asked, I silently prayed that I might gradually dissolve the rock-solid wall that surrounded them, and my prayers were answered.

CHAPTER 23

War Clouds

THE NEXT STOP ON our itinerary was Tarnow. And there, I crossed paths at last with my father.

The father I'd known since my birth in Antwerp was a gentleman in a fine, perfectly tailored suit. He had that special European polish, and everyone who met him was taken with his charm.

My father had a twinkle in his eye and a smile full of joy. My father was tall and strong, and he always let us jump onto his lap when he came home from work in the evening. But the father I met in Tarnow had a different sort of eyes, eyes with a deeper expression, eyes that saw more, and his voice had a taped sound, slightly metallic and jumpy. I didn't really know this father, and I tried somehow to bring him together with the image of the Papa I'd always known… but never quite managed it.

In my mind, I was with him now in Tarnow, where the horrors had first caught up with him, taken him by the throat and sunk their claws into him. But really it had all begun earlier, while he was still in Krakow, his hometown.

For historical accuracy, the war broke out early in the morning of Friday, September 1, 1939. But for him, a fifteen-year-old youth, war was not yet a living reality. It was eight in the morning when he stood outside the shul, holding his tefillin bag and listening to the men debating. It was no secret that Hitler had risen to power in Germany and was running a dictatorship there. Everyone also knew that he was covetously eyeing the land of his weak neighbor to the east. Papa knew it, too. He read the news every day, and he viewed the whole situation rather pessimistically.

But the adults around him were clinging to the hope that Hitler would never get away with invading Poland. England and France were stronger than Germany. "If Germany starts a war, it will be crushed in two days," said the men gathered by the *shtiebel*. "There's no reason to panic."

Papa's father wasn't so sanguine. He would have taken the whole family to Eretz Yisrael before now, but he couldn't get visas. The British Mandate government was granting the precious "certificates" very sparingly, and only the fortunate few were able to wangle them. The American government wasn't much more welcoming. The Statue of Liberty lifted her lamp beside the golden door, but it was open only a crack.

Ten days before the warplanes crossed the skies of Krakow, posters had gone up in the streets announcing general conscription for army service and ordering all citizens to darken their windows due to the fear of impending war. The atmosphere was heating up against the optimists, but it made no practical difference —there was nowhere to run to.

Already now, the men could hear the planes and the explosions in the distance as they prayed in shul. They had no inkling of what was really happening, and they went calmly home to their breakfasts. Only at ten o'clock did the news reach them that the Germans had invaded Poland, and the Polish army was frantically trying to pull itself together and get organized for a war that was already in full swing. It didn't have a chance.

That night, Papa's family sat down as usual to their Shabbos meal, and the war that had begun was still just a topic of conversation. But in the morning, the first refugees arrived, their faces gray with fright. It was all happening too fast. On Sunday, the men all started rushing eastward, toward the Russian border. According to rumors going around, the Germans wouldn't harm women and children, but the men were in danger, so Papa and his brothers fled with their father, running eighty kilometers on foot. Train service had stopped, and all the good horses had been commandeered by the Polish army in its pathetic attempts at defense. But the mad dash for the border was useless; the Germans were already there. They had conquered Poland with incredible speed, and all the fleeing men were like mice desperately running on a wheel, going nowhere. Poland was one big firetrap. Papa and his father and brothers hid in a cellar in a little village near Tarnow. The bombs were falling directly on the houses, and on the terrified people running for cover. As they crouched in the cellar, the houses above them were bursting into flames. There was no point in seeking refuge far from home, and they decided to return to Krakow.

They traveled back with a Polish wagon driver, amid the fire and smoke and the bullets of the German snipers shooting at the long lines of people seeking refuge. The Germans took aim at their wagon too, but by a miracle, the bullets missed them. That was their first taste of the war.

But the Krakow they returned to had changed overnight. It was no longer the city that had stood, splendid and serene, for a thousand years, the beautiful city of polished red stone and pointed turrets. Now it was like a captive princess. Its shops were closed, commerce was halted. Jews walked about in dread, and the Judenrat, which had been set up with German efficiency, was already taking Jews away for forced labor. The Nazis were strutting about in the streets, selecting random victims for beatings, especially Jews with beards.

Yet, fluffy clouds of optimism still hung about the shuls, stubbornly refusing to dissipate, even as the abuse escalated, and harsh voices, shouting in German, filled the air.

"We'll get through this," people said to one another. "We've been through lots of hard times in our history; we just need to be strong."

But when the reports reached them from Melitz, the clouds of optimism turned black. There was no longer a shred of hope to cling to.

In Melitz, the Germans had gathered all the Jews in the main shul. There were innocent children there, and blameless elders. There were mothers and babies. They all crowded into the shul, as they were ordered to do by the conquering army. And when they were all inside, the Nazis locked the doors and set fire to the building. All the Jews inside were burned alive.

When Papa heard of this, he began dreaming of escape. By that time the Jewish shops had been looted, and it was dangerous just to step out into the street. His dreams of escape grew more intense, but there was no one to make them come true.

He had a brother, Yisrael Yitzchak, who went out to bring food to Jews who were starving in the ghetto, which was a death trap for the poor. The Nazis caught him in the middle of his errand of mercy, and they beat him and tore out half of his beard. He managed to flee to Lemberg, and from there he moved on to Kletzk, and then to Baranovitch. Baranovitch was his last stop. From there, he was taken to his death in 1942. May Hashem avenge his blood.

A year after the war broke out, my father's family was taken from their home in Krakow to nearby Tarnow, where a large area had been fenced in — the ghetto.

CHAPTER 24

The Tarnow Ghetto

PAPA AND HIS FAMILY found themselves imprisoned in a place that made slum life look luxurious.

It was a place where dozens of people were crammed into one dilapidated apartment. People who until yesterday had a home, a lovely family, a nice income, perhaps even a grand piano in the living room, now had nothing but a moldy mattress in a room not their own.

Every day, new notices went up out in the street — stark white posters with black letters. The people in the ghetto didn't want to read them. They didn't want to know about the latest decree; they didn't want to go out on the street at all. The Angel of Death was out there.

But they needed to know. And they had to go out, early every morning, to the hard work they'd been assigned to, otherwise they would get no food rations. At nightfall they would return with their knees buckling under them, to read another horrifying notice, to stand in line for the bowl of thin soup that was given in return for their day of grueling labor, and to hope they would make it back safely to the narrow strip of floor that was now their home.

They didn't necessarily come back. The Nazis would often attack people on the ghetto streets, pogrom style. They would shoot people indiscriminately. Anyone with a classically Jewish appearance was their most likely prey.

I stand there, trying to picture my father as a sixteen-year-old, between childhood and manhood, going out to work all day, without a break, in a paint shop, and coming back in the evening with food vouchers in hand. He wasn't thinking of his pain and hunger, of the demeaning labor or his stolen freedom; he would run back to the ghetto room to see if his parents were all right, to find out if they'd eaten anything that day. As a worker, he was eligible for meager food vouchers, which he would share with them.

They weren't old or frail, these grandparents I never knew. They were the strong, energetic parents of eight teenage children. One son was already married. A bright future seemed to await them. They had a shop that sold imported tropical fruit; only the well-off families could afford to treat themselves to fruit from Horowitz's. They had status in the community, a nice home, a maid to help with the chores, and a thousand dreams. They were about my age, I suddenly realize… and they never got any older.

For two years, life in Tarnow went on that way, hanging by a thread. Each day they would wake up to see if it was still hanging, or if their time was up…. Meanwhile, my father was growing up, and instead of spending those critical years studying Torah with other boys, opening a package of homemade cookies that just arrived, and going out late at night for deep conversations, he was spending his days at forced labor in a paint shop, and living in dread every moment.

But one day, even that narrow strip of life was taken from them.

Tarnow lies spread out before me. The trip leader's voice passes over me like a cold wind. The whole group blends into one colorful blur, and I sit down heavily on a damp rock, trying to imagine that day, right here, in the month of Sivan, 1942.

I picture German officers on black motorcycles, and those

of higher rank in long black Mercedes cars, rumbling into the big town square. Hundreds of soldiers in green jackets and high boots, assembling machine guns. The ghetto is encircled with barbed wire, and a sense of evil foreboding fills the air. Everyone senses that today's *aktion* will be worse than any that preceded it, but they cannot guess how much worse.

In the morning, tens of thousands of Jews, in the choked apartments and bunkers of the ghetto, were awakened by the blaring of loudspeakers. Everyone was ordered to come to the school building and bring their documents with them.

Once again, as they did whenever such orders were issued, Papa's family debated whether to obey or to hide. Should they voluntarily hand themselves over to the Nazis, not knowing what was planned for them, or hide and take the risk of being shot on the spot if discovered?

Still almost a complete family, they decided to comply with the orders, and they joined the other Jews streaming toward the school building.

There, they were divided up. Some Jews had their documents stamped with the letter K, and the documents of others were stamped with the image of an eagle, the symbol of the Nazi regime. No one knew the meaning of the mysterious "K." But the Nazi symbol surely indicated some sort of usefulness to the regime — in other words, life, for the present at least. Papa looked at the face of the Nazi at the head of the line, who was sorting them into these two categories. There was something very cruel in his expression, and he was giving a lot more Ks than eagles. Cautiously, Papa slipped out of line and joined another line. When his turn came, he said he was a house painter and answered questions about his workplace. The Nazi scrutinized him for a moment and then stamped his papers with an eagle.

The sorting process was over. Those whose documents bore the eagle symbol were now "free" to return to the ghetto. All the rest were detained in the locked school building all that day and night. Papa, a seventeen-year-old boy, came back alone to his empty room in the ghetto, wondering what would happen to his parents.

The answer came the next morning, when the rattle of machine guns was heard from the town square. Ten thousand Jews were there. Some were taken to the forest outside the town, where they were shot directly into the mass graves, and others were kept there in the marketplace, and the Nazis shot them down where they stood, helpless and defenseless.

Ten thousand Jews were shot in one day. The air shook with the rattle of machine gun fire, and the blood flowed from the town square and down the streets of Tarnow. The stream of blood reached Papa, too, as he made his way back from work. Was this the blood of his parents?

After the *aktion*, the Nazis spread out over the ghetto, looking for families in hiding, or people without work papers, fleeing from death. Anyone they found was shot down on the spot, sharing the fate of those who had come to the school building. In the course of a week, thirty thousand Jews were murdered. Papa never saw his parents again. May Hashem avenge their blood and the blood of all the Jews of the ghetto.

Papa dragged his feet back to the ghetto. His parents were gone, and their burial place is unknown. He never even had a grave to visit, a place to express the terrible grief that filled his being.

CHAPTER 25

Miracles in the Ghetto

Erev Rosh Hashanah, 1942

The Tarnow ghetto was rapidly becoming more spacious. The German *aktions* were systematically decimating the population, leaving frozen silence behind as the wind carried away the smell of gunpowder.

Families were shrinking: children's voices were heard no more, and all the mature adults were disappearing. And still there was a new *aktion* from time to time, as the Nazi bloodlust was insatiable.

It was the day before Rosh Hashanah, and Papa noticed that the Nazi soldiers and the Jewish policemen of the Judenrat were busy preparing for something. It looked as though they were preparing to surround the ghetto hermetically, and that could mean only one thing: another *aktion* — probably a particularly lethal one — was planned.

Moving swiftly and silently, Papa sneaked into the cellar under Uncle Hollander's paint shop. Others joined him. They all realized it was better to hide than to obey a Nazi order to assemble outside. Perhaps by the grace of G-d they would be fortunate, and the danger would pass.

They spent Rosh Hashanah in the dark cellar. A sumptuous

holiday meal was not served. There was no shofar, no Torah reading, no stirring melodies. Could they even remember what it was like to pray in shul on Rosh Hashanah? Yet surely their silent prayers to be written in the Book of Life were heartfelt like never before.

And then the door to the shop was flung open with one hard kick. The basement of a Jewish shop really wasn't the best choice of hiding place. The Nazis would routinely burst into the shops, find the door to the basement, line up whoever was hiding there, and shoot them down on the spot.

The Jews huddled together, not daring to breathe as they heard the voices overhead growing louder. This was it. The Nazis were looking for them. How could they fail to find them? But then Papa heard a voice he would remember for the rest of his life, the voice of the Pole who accompanied the German soldiers. "There's nothing to look for here!" he said to them. "This is just a paint shop, nobody comes in here."

The shouting and banging on the cellar door stopped. Heavy footsteps creaked over the floor above their heads, grew fainter, and ceased as the front door was closed. At least for now, they had not been erased from the Book of Life. The Nazis were gone.

A second miracle happened one night after curfew. Papa had gone out to get some food for those who were still with him in the ghetto. With a carton of food on his back, he suddenly found himself a few steps away from a Polish policeman with a ruthless expression and a loaded pistol. Papa's blood froze. He was out after curfew, and he was smuggling food. Those were clear violations of the law of the ghetto. The police guard could have shot him dead and had no problem accounting for it. But the policeman walked right by, without a glance in Papa's direction. Somehow, he'd been stricken with a kind of selective blindness, and he simply didn't see the young man with the carton on his back. Once again, Papa had been chosen for life.

And then there was the time, shortly before the ghetto was emptied of its last Jewish inhabitants, when once again, German voices blared from the loudspeakers, summoning all residents to the town square. They were to sort themselves into groups according to the company they worked for. Papa was working at that time laying tracks for Ostbahn, a railway company, his sister Rivka was a seamstress in Madritsch's shop, his sister Chana also worked, and his brother Avraham Leib had joined the Judenrat of the ghetto, hoping and praying to be spared.

The Nazis were running about feverishly, calling out the workers' names from their lists, and lining them up to board trucks which were going to take them to work — or so they were told.

Papa stepped into line with the Ostbahn group. Suddenly he noticed that the Boyaner Rebbe of Krakow was also in their group. The Rebbe was elderly and very much revered, and somehow, someone had gotten worker's papers for him. In a flash, Papa grasped what was really happening: the Boyaner Rebbe was not being taken to work. There was no chance of that. He, and the whole group, were being taken to their deaths.*

Papa's eyes darted around, looking for somewhere to run to, and his glance fell on the doorway to a factory, close by. A Jewish policeman was guarding it. Papa watched him, and the moment he wasn't looking, Papa slipped through the entrance and hid inside. That Jewish policeman had become his personal guard. It never occurred to the Nazis to search a place where the door was guarded.

Out in the town square, the soldiers continued shouting, holding their lists, and pushing people into the trucks with their rifle butts, until the trucks rumbled away, leaving an ominous silence behind. Afterwards he would learn that the transport went straight to the gas chambers in Auschwitz, with no selection or

*This was the last testimony concerning the Rebbe.

examination. Touching himself to verify that he really was still alive, Papa crept out of his hiding place. The day would come when he would return here and recite a blessing, thanking Hashem for the miracle that was done for him in this place.

Many days would come when Papa would say that he didn't survive the Holocaust. Him? Survive? That simply wasn't possible; no one could *survive*. But Someone Above was watching over him and preserved his life.

After the Holocaust, the Belzer Rebbe said that anyone who was saved from that inferno had two angels watching over him. Surely those angels were there for my father. They looked him in the eye and told him, "You will live." It was a Heavenly mandate, almost forced upon him: "You will live!"

"I wasn't a big *chevreman*," Papa said years later. "I had no special talent for thinking on my feet or talking my way out of tight spots. I wasn't physically stronger than average, and I didn't have the charisma that opens doors for some people. I was just a young boy, a bit shy, who'd never done anything very bold or heroic. To my right and to my left, family members were being cut down like wheat. Fire was blazing all around me; machine guns were thundering; the Nazis were swarming everywhere and killing my people wholesale. But Hashem picked me up by the scruff of my neck every time and kept me alive. He placed two angels at my sides, He put the right words into my mouth, He led my feet into hiding places and kept my pursuers out. I didn't do a thing, it was all Hashem..."

Time and again, he would reiterate: "I didn't 'survive.' It was purely the Hand of Hashem that kept me alive."

And I, his daughter, who had pushed that curtain aside so fearfully, was astonished to discover what a bright light shone through the dreadful darkness of those days.

The girls start walking through the paved streets of Tarnow. I follow behind them ponderously. "Did my grandparents' blood flow right here where I'm stepping?" I wonder, hardly able to put one foot in front of the other. "Did my father pass this way, astounded at the miracle that saved his life, when he came out of his hiding place in the factory?"

Tarnow has gotten into my bones; I can actually feel the ache. I want to say goodbye to my father's family. I want to find the woman who was my grandmother and the man who was my grandfather, I want to find my father's brothers and sisters, his cousins and his friends, I want to find all ten thousand Jews who were here and disappeared, and now, in their place, walks a group of young Israeli women in colorful coats and expensive boots, with cell phones in their bags and pompoms on their hats.... I want to tell these girls the story of Tarnow, about the cramped, disease-ridden apartments, about the blood flowing in the streets, about the black-on-white notices that no one wanted to read... but I'm afraid they won't be able to understand it here, on a modern street with an electronic sign flashing behind me, displaying an ad for men's suits, and a group of tourists clicking cameras. And then I remember the story of Kopush, and I know that this is the story I'm going to tell them, here in Tarnow.

CHAPTER 26

Kopush: A Little Boy in the Ghetto

KOPUSH WAS A LITTLE blond boy in the Tarnow ghetto, with intelligent, warm eyes and a personality that made everyone love him. His mother, a young woman named Frydzia, would go out every morning to forced labor as a seamstress that earned her a meager daily ration, leaving him in the care of somebody or other in the ghetto. Her husband had been taken away somewhere in one of those long trucks, and Kopush knew that one day his Papa would return.

When she came home in the evening, bone-tired, she would take back her treasure. She would hug him with all the love in the world, and Kopush would always tell her how nice his ghetto "family" was, and how they'd found a slice of apple or bread for him.

As the ghetto population dwindled, Frydzia realized that Kopush's current living arrangements were too precarious. There had already been one *aktion* in which most of the ghetto children had been taken away, and by now she knew quite well that they hadn't been taken for a vacation in the mountains. One morning, after the efforts of a wide network of friends on Kopush's behalf, she bundled him up in a knapsack, telling him that from now on, he had a new name. Nobody would know he was a Jew, and he would have a lady taking care of him like Mama.

Of course he must never speak Yiddish anymore, only Polish. And all this was only until the war ended; she would come then and take him home again. Kopush was no ordinary child, he was a ghetto child, and he understood even more than what his mother told him. He was obedient and quiet as she closed the bag and it was hoisted onto the strong back of a man who took him out of the ghetto. He remained motionless in the bag as it was laid down on the sidewalk, waiting to be picked up by the Polish woman who had agreed to take the child in as one of her own, in return for a suitable payment.

Frydzia returned to the ghetto that evening after another exhausting day, and this time, no little boy jumped into her arms, covered her face with kisses, and told her that he'd gotten a little extra soup that day from his ghetto "aunts and uncles." But that empty feeling was easier to bear when she told herself that Kopush was now out of harm's way, and his chances of surviving the war were good.

Before many days had passed, the knapsack, complete with its human contents, was back in the ghetto. The Polish woman had changed her mind; she felt the risk was too great. The sudden appearance of a cute little blond boy in her house had aroused too much curiosity among her neighbors. She was very sorry.

Kopush was overjoyed to be back with his mother, and with all the many friends who loved him. He had no playmates his own age anymore, but all the adults in the ghetto were his good friends. The adults were worried, though. How were they going to hide a child in a place where there weren't supposed to be any children left? Sometimes he was taken in the knapsack to the factory where his mother worked, and sometimes he stayed in the ghetto with one of his mother's friends, keeping out of sight and enjoying whatever dubious treats they could find for him... until one day, rumors of a child in the ghetto reached the ears of the Nazi commander.

He was incredulous. "A child?! A Jewish child, living in the ghetto?! I want him brought here this minute!"

But the child had vanished. All the men who were sent out to comb the ghetto in search of him, as if he were the number one enemy of the Reich, came back emptyhanded. The commander then told them to bring the boy's mother and all of her apartment mates. He would deal with them personally....

This group of friends had all been students of Sarah Schenirer in the original Bais Yaakov school in Krakow, until they were deported to the ghetto. My Aunt Rivka, Papa's sister, was there, and there was one girl who was engaged. The commander was the terror of Tarnow. His face was as savage as a wild animal's. He had them all brought into one room, where he informed them dryly that unless the child was handed over within the next hour, they would all be executed. His gaze lingered on the boy's mother, Frydzia Sternfeld, as if to say, "We'll start with you, of course!" But the girls refused to say a word, and their silence was more thunderous than all the screams of their captors. The commander left the room, promising to return in an hour to hear their answer.

The ghetto was abuzz with the dreadful news. Fathers and mothers of the girls, and the young man engaged to marry one of them, stood at the window, pleading with them not to lose their lives for a little boy, when it was uncertain in any case what would become of him. Perhaps the commander would have compassion on the child? There was still a chance he might live, whereas they were going to certain death with their obstinate silence. But the girls remained adamant, despite all their pleas. Not one of them could bring herself to hand over little Kopush, so strong was their bond with him.

I pause and gaze at the girls sitting before me on a cold, stone bench in Tarnow, listening in absolute silence. Are they capable of containing the world of the ghetto, where such dilemmas were at the center of life, and not just something to read about in a suspense thriller? Can they identify at all with my aunt as a girl years younger than themselves, trapped in the office of a notoriously ruthless Nazi officer, facing imminent death in her determination not to betray the little golden-haired boy who only yesterday had sat on her lap in a shabby apartment, showing her the little wooden boat someone in the ghetto had carved for him?

The voices outside the room were growing hysterical. Emotionally charged arguments were breaking out, but the five young women inside were entrenched in their resolve not to hand over the little child with the pure eyes, come what may.

The commander returned and found them unswayed by his threats. He ordered Frydzia Sternfeld to come with him. She followed him calmly. A horse-drawn carriage was waiting outside, driven by a Jew whose miserable fate was to take the wicked commander wherever he wished to go. The young mother stepped lightly into the carriage, and they rode to the Jewish cemetery. With German courtesy, the commander helped the young lady to alight from the carriage and instructed her to stand there, please. A single shot split the air, and the soul of Kopush's mother rose to the Heavens.

When the young men of the ghetto heard what had happened, they wasted no time. A youth was sent urgently to the Boyaner Rebbe, who gave a clear halachic ruling: Since their lives were in immediate danger, while the threat to the child's life was in doubt, Jewish law required them to bring him out of hiding with no further delay. The courier ran back to deliver the Rebbe's message to the girls. For a moment, they were dumbstruck. The sacrifice they had offered was still on the altar in front of them. But the rabbi had given his ruling, and this was G-d's will. There was nothing more to say. One of the girls whispered something to Avraham Leib, Papa's brother, and moments later he came rushing back with Kopush in his arms. The little boy had no way of knowing that his mother was no longer among the living. But the other young women were now free to go.

The commander beckoned to the child and seated him on his lap. On his lap.... The hand that had held the pistol steady and pulled the trigger minutes ago, was now patting the head of the murdered woman's little boy. "What's your name?" he asked playfully, and ordered one of the soldiers to bring him something sweet for the child.

Later, Kopush was taken to the Jewish orphans' home. The Nazi commander would visit him there now and then, bringing him little gifts and making sure he was all right.

In one of the final *aktion*s, the orphans' home was also emptied, and all the children there were taken to their deaths. Kopush's innocent soul ascended on high, and he was reunited with the mother who awaited him there.

The tears in my eyes also sparkle on the cheeks of the young women facing me. On the hill in Tarnow, big patches of snow cover the wilted grass, and sad strains of music arise from the houses behind us. The sky is gray, as usual, and in the relentless cold around us, we lose our sense of time.

My father knew Kopush. My father was the youth who ran to ask the Rebbe what the girls must do.

Through that innocent little boy, could we understand what Tarnow was all about?

CHAPTER 27

Tarnow: Judenrein

THE BUS ROLLS ALONG on the asphalt, and the road seems to move backward under the wheels.

Tanya offers Rotem a meat sandwich she bought at the gas station. But Rotem shrugs her shoulders in an Israeli gesture of refusal and resumes gazing out the window.

"Hey, Rotem!" Tanya says to her friend's back. "What happened? Did someone take your place overnight?"

Rotem turns from the window. Her face is pale; her eyes are big. She pulls her long hair out of her scarf's embrace, and with her eyes, she asks Tanya, "What it is you want, actually?"

"Wasn't it you yesterday who said she was craving a meat sandwich? Or did I have such a vivid dream last night that I went and spent ten zlotys at the gas station?"

"A meat sandwich?" Rotem looks at the clear plastic wrapper with the Polish words on the label as if it were an old shoe or a piece of moldy bread.

"Please, Tanya," she says. "Don't show me *basar lavan* sandwiches."

"Why?" Tanya is hurt. What is the matter with her friend all of a sudden, and why is she being so tactless? "Since when are you so careful about eating kosher — especially here? This isn't Israel, after all... What's with you today?"

Tanya turns the wrapped sandwich in her hands, not understanding what's so bad about it. Her own home country isn't far from here, and nothing about the weather, the local people, or the culture of insincere smiles bothers her. But she loves Rotem, so she searches in her bag for something else she can give her. She finds a mint candy with Hebrew lettering and offers it to Rotem with a conciliatory smile. Rotem accepts it with thanks and slowly peels off the wrapper, but the pallor hasn't left her cheeks, and her eyes still look unusually wide.

"Suddenly I care more about kashrut," she says apologetically to Tanya and to me. "I don't know why, exactly. I felt like this yesterday, too, when we stopped at the kiosk. Just looking at that Polish food kind of makes my stomach hurt. I don't know what's in it, I just feel repelled by non-kosher food all of a sudden.

"And don't scare me with any comments about how I'm turning religious," she adds.

The three of us fall silent. I'm not trying to scare anyone, really I'm not. But Tanya and Rotem are both trying to take in what Rotem said. And for me, this is a sacred moment, when a person chooses to take a step forward, even if it's leading toward the unknown, just because it is a step forward....

The bus keeps going as if its wheels don't want to stop, but I feel that it's all happening too fast. Are we really going to be in Auschwitz so soon? Couldn't we slow down a little? Must we see these evergreen trees all the way, on a carpet of snow?

"You know," Rotem says suddenly, as if the whole previous exchange hadn't occurred, "you didn't tell us what happened to your father after the Tarnow ghetto was closed..."

"My father..." I stop to take a deep breath, and I'm drawn back to the jumpy videotape of Papa's testimony. Again, it takes an effort to replace the image of the big, strong man I always loved with a half-starved teenage boy from the Tarnow ghetto. "He was saved from the last and most terrible *aktion*, when all the deportees were sent straight to the gas chambers of Auschwitz, and most of them died on the way there. His sister Chana was among them, may Hashem avenge her blood…

"My father found himself in an empty ghetto, with articles of clothing and other odds and ends scattered here and there in the apartments, and silence echoing from the walls. The Jews were gone… The Nazis were rounding up everyone they found hiding in the bunkers or the attics and lining them up to be killed.

"Amon Göth, the monstrous commander of the nearby Plaszow concentration camp, was supervising the liquidation with demonic intensity.

"He decreed life for the group of young women who worked as seamstresses in Madritsch's factory. They sewed coats there for the German army, and the conditions were a little more bearable. My father's sister Rivka was one of those seamstresses. Although most of her sewing experience came from sewing wardrobes for her dolls out of small fabric remnants, she managed to represent herself as an experienced and knowledgeable seamstress and find an island of refuge in that raging sea of death…

"My father was there when Amon Göth, with a smoking pistol in his hand, cleared out the ghetto. Even after three years of Nazi occupation, in which he thought he'd seen it all, that day saw new heights of cruelty. Some of the seamstresses were young mothers, carrying living treasures in their knapsacks and hoping to find safety for them in the shelter of Madritsch's workshops. But Amon Göth could not allow that… the little children who lay quietly in the bags were not included in the license to live he had so graciously given. These mothers had committed a terrible crime! They had tried to sneak babies past him! He took all the women with knapsacks out of the line and stood them at the edge of the square, with the sun beating down on them and terror beating in their hearts.

"Eventually the babies, who had learned at a shockingly early age to keep quiet and still, grew too thirsty to refrain from crying. One by one, the mothers took the knapsacks off their backs to give their babies a little water to drink. Come what may, the babies were thirsty.

"Amon Göth finished his selection. All the women with knapsacks were on one side. And right there in the square, he himself shot the mothers, sending a bullet through each of their knapsacks as well. My father heard those shots. Who knows how often he heard them again, in his dreams and awake, throughout his life?

"Afterwards he was sent to Szebnie, where another selection took place. Again, a large portion of the Jews were pushed onto crowded trucks. And then an uproar suddenly broke out. A group of people started yelling that they worked for the wood building company, and they weren't supposed to be on the trucks.

"The soldier in charge checked their papers and authorized everyone with documents testifying that they were wood builders to stand apart from the others. My father had no such document, and two Ukrainian Nazi collaborators pushed him roughly onto a truck. At that moment he knew that the Angel of Death was waiting for those trucks.

"At the last minute, when the Ukrainians were distracted for a couple of seconds, Papa jumped down and mingled with the wood builders. His brother Avraham Leib missed the chance to jump and remained on the truck...

"The truck rumbled away, headed for the mass graves in the forest, leaving behind a huge cloud of dust, a dreadful silence, and the final memory of Avraham Leib's hand waving goodbye, and his voice splitting the whole world: 'See you in the *Oilem HaEmes*!'"

Once more, Papa was saved. In the month of Elul, 1943, he found himself performing backbreaking labor as part of a building crew, under inhuman conditions. The holidays passed like a nightmare, the cold was unbearable, and in the whole region, the ghettos were desolate. Tarnow was declared Judenrein.

CHAPTER 28

Fireworks

All morning we worked on the beach like industrious ants, building our amazing boat. Mottel, Tzili, and I shaped it from the outside, the Pinkusewitz children designed the interior, and Esty was the baby we put inside to make sure it was big enough… Our marvelous boat had everything — seats with footrests, a storage compartment, and a very fancy steering wheel. We decorated the boat with beautiful shells and a few crepe paper flowers, and all the children on the beach came to see the wonder we'd created.

Not even the richest people in Holland had ever seen anything so splendid. But in the afternoon, as the sun slowly moved across the sky, it brought the sea with it, carrying the water right into our beautiful boat and sinking it, without a word of apology.

We waved goodbye to the grains of sand, now washed away, that had been our boat, and we promised it that tomorrow we would come back and build it again. And we went away happy, full of satisfaction and hungry as people should be when they've worked hard all morning.

Mama spread out a nice tablecloth in the shade and handed out fruit to all of us. We had peaches, apples, and a bag of raw, peeled baby carrots. We ate it all up, almost forgetting that this was only an appetizer before lunch.

After lunch, we went to the big tulip park and played with our peashooters. Our ammunition was little green berries that we picked from bushes in the park, and we would have contests to see who could shoot them the farthest.

I was always losing the jumpy little berries, and my supply would run out before the contest was over. While I was out picking more, Mottel would win. He could always shoot the farthest…

I would get upset about never winning the game, but when Mama handed out tea biscuits with jam for an afternoon snack, I would forget all my resentment and go back to loving everyone and everything.

After supper came the night. Behind the sheer curtain in my room, the windowpane turned black. It seems to me I was having a dream about a boat full of green berries, and Mottel was sailing over the waves in it. But the dream ended in the middle with a loud bang — fireworks!

I cowered in fright, hearing the explosions come one after the other, seeing the flashes of bright red, blue, and yellow fill my room. Fear held me in its cold arms, and I tried to escape its grasp, retreating deeper under my blanket until it covered me completely.

I couldn't understand what was so fascinating and lovely about fireworks, and what was the matter with the Dutch people who were so excited by them. All I wanted was for them to stop. I was a big girl, as Mama and Papa were always telling me, but the fireworks were bigger than me.

The blanket wasn't helping. The explosions came right through it, and even the blue-white light was flashing right in my face. So finally I got up, searched the floor for my slippers with trembling feet, and pattered over the wooden floorboards as fast as I could. "Boom! Boom!" the sky thundered, and the walls of the house were no protection against the fiery flashes that poured in. "Boom! Boom!" I flew like an arrow to my parents' room, where my father's bed waited for me, big, heavy, and safe.

With shaking hands, I knocked gently at their door and waited desperately for permission. And as soon as I heard the "yes, yes" I burst through the door and jumped under Papa's blanket, knowing that nothing bad could happen to me there. Now, feeling calm and safe, I don't hear the booms anymore. But it wouldn't matter if I heard them now. Later, Mama would come and find me rolled up in the blanket, and she would carry me in my sleep to my own bed. In the morning I would ask myself, like every other time, "Was all that a dream?"

But right now I was here, and Papa's blanket was protecting me... my kind, strong Papa, who was bigger than all the fireworks in the world.

Papa didn't come home to us every day. Holland wasn't a few stops away on the tram. We were on summer vacation, but Papa still had his work at the bourse. Mama traveled with us and with our relatives to Holland, and Papa would come only at the weekend.

Every week I waited, longing to hear his voice and see his smile. When he arrived at last, and I heard his voice by the front door, my heart would pound with excitement. "Chana'le!" he would cry, holding out his arms to me, and I could hardly speak; I was so afraid that tears would come out instead of words. I would jump up and let him catch me, snuggling into his jacket, inhaling the familiar smell of his clothing, and thinking how good it was to have him home again. No, no, this was no time for crying...

CHAPTER 29

Destination: Auschwitz

FROM SZEBNIE, PAPA WAS transported to Auschwitz, in an open freight car, in the middle of that Polish winter. He didn't know where the train was going. He and the rest of the passengers watched the passing landscape fearfully. The train passed by Plaszow, and for a moment, a tinge of hope washed over them: perhaps they were going to join the work force at the Plaszow labor camp. But the train didn't stop. Loaded with its human freight, it chugged on toward Upper Silesia, taking that tinge of hope with it. The monotonous clickety-clack of the wheels beat a steady rhythm, slowly heightening their dread, bringing it to a crescendo as the inescapable realization hit them — they were going to Auschwitz, to a place that had one meaning for them: the crematorium. Extermination.

The Polish fields now gave way to forests, and the Jews who understood the meaning of this journey tried to think of ways to escape. It was impossible. Any Jew who jumped off the train would quickly be shot by the SS men standing guard on the roofs of the cars, and even if they escaped the bullets, they were pretty sure to encounter some Pole who would gladly hand them over to the Germans for a bag of sugar.

Papa stayed on the train. A little boy wriggled over to him and asked for a cube of sugar. Papa gave it to him, looking in amazement at his final act of kindness in this world, knowing that it was time to look death in the face.

He didn't cry, he didn't scream, and he didn't lose his head. He didn't look for a way to escape, and he didn't cry out the names of his loved ones. He had nothing. His home was long gone, and his parents had disappeared from his life. The yeshiva, his friends, the ghetto, the forest… suddenly it all turned into a blur, and he was immersed in the infinite peace of eternity.

There were no longer any barking dogs around him, no rubber truncheons whistling through the air, no voices screaming in German.

There was no longer anything to lose or anything to give. He had nothing, and he had everything. He could let go, and enter into his inner being. His body was now a mere outer garment, soon to be stripped away. Even the piece of sugar he'd given away to the little boy was no longer with him. He was in communion with the Divine soul that dwelt within all the outer shells, which were now removed. At that moment, when the corridor between two worlds was so short, with death just hours away, he was drawn into the deepest freedom a person can experience — freedom of the mind, freedom of thought. To the endless ocean of the inmost soul, to that place where there is infinite love which no one can take away — freedom of the soul from the body's dominion.

Papa felt his soul breaking free within him, cutting the treacherous railroad tracks, rising over the heads of the Nazi snipers on the roofs, riding on air beyond the gas chambers, the death, and the crematorium that awaited him. He was wholly in the embrace of eternity, on the threshold of meeting his G-d face to face. That was the moment when he began to sing *Nishmas Kol Chai* under his breath, in a voice full of yearning. At that moment, G-d's infinite beauty was revealed, and nothing else was meaningful enough to remove his attention from offering thanksgiving.

Now, I reach into my bag and take out that *tefillah*. I don't see the girls' eyes fixed on me; I'm not here; I am there with Papa in that moment of perfect surrender: "If our mouth were filled with song like the sea, and our tongue with joyous song like its teeming waves, and our lips with praise like the expanse of the sky, and our eyes shining like the sun and the moon, and our arms spread like the eagles of the heavens, and our feet as light as gazelles, we would not be able to thank You enough...

"Until now Your mercies have aided us, and Your kindness has not abandoned us... therefore, the organs that You placed within us, and the spirit and soul that You blew into our nostrils...."

Papa's face was like a flame, and tears of *deveikus* rose into his eyes. He felt no sorrow or pain, no fear of death or suffering; his soul was given over to G-d's hands, lifted above the sky.

Snow fell on the open freight cars, wrapping the people trapped inside in an unbearable blanket of white freshness. Day and night the train chugged indifferently toward Auschwitz, and Papa's prayer was lifted above it. Its letters flew into the air: "Let them thank, bless, and praise... and sanctify and declare the sovereignty of Your Name, our King...

The train moved forward persistently, and Papa was not a passenger in it, but a presence hovering high over it, only his body occupying its place in the crowded car...

At last, the train slowed to a stop, and the people were hustled off amid shouts, blows, and barks, and ordered to stand in line for selection. Papa stood confidently before the tall Nazi, ready to hand over his life *al kiddush Hashem*, fearless and happy to have the privilege of being killed for his Jewishness. The Nazi quickly looked him up and down — and directed him to the right.

He was hurried to the showers. And the showerheads spewed not poison gas, but plain water. Papa saw that once again his life had miraculously been spared. At that moment, the feeling of perfect and serene resignation to death left him, giving way to a fierce desire to live. To live, at any price!

From that moment on, it stood steadily before his eyes — his own will and testimony in letters of fire. From near-death, he had returned to the living, and he would do anything, anything to live!

CHAPTER 30

The Call of the Shofar

We aren't eager to get off the heated bus and fall straight into the arms of the icy wind that blows over the most dreadful place in the world, shooting sharp needles of cold into our faces. Seeking refuge from the sound of the wind that whirls in our ears, we keep pulling our hats and scarves over our faces, but we cannot fight that wind.

A row of low, depressing barracks is spread out before our eyes. Some of them have collapsed, and the remains of a broken chimney are sticking out of the ground. An old barbed-wire fence is rusted and disintegrating, but its iron barbs still pierce our hearts.

I wonder if my father could ever have foreseen this moment. His daughter, flying back to this cursed land with a group of young, liberated Israeli women, walking freely on this spot and telling his story! "My father was here," I tell the girls, after all the explanations are given and all the questions asked, and the wind, like a wild animal intent on its prey, shows no sign of relenting.

His barrack block was one of these. I start walking along the row and counting: "One, two, three, four, five, six, seven."

Here is where my father spent his nights in Auschwitz.

I speak to the girls, trying to evoke in their imaginations the image of Papa as an eighteen-year-old, sent to paint gas pipes to prevent them from rusting. The cold cut into his bones, just as it is doing to us right now, but my father didn't have a fleece-lined coat and fur-trimmed boots. He wore clumsy wooden shoes and a thin prisoner's uniform, and his body was barely sustained on inhuman rations. Every half hour he escaped to the warmth of the industrial furnace in the workshop, to keep from freezing. In the morning he received a small slice of bread, stale and riddled with wood shavings. The afternoon meal was "soup" — a few wilted herbs cooked in water, and that was it until the next day. Papa knew he couldn't last long on that diet. He must get hold of some more food. He managed to rustle up a can of paint, and he would offer his services as a painter to the camp officers, painting their quarters for a slice of bread.

He had to put in his regular day's work in addition to his second job, but he had no choice. Without that extra bread, death was only a matter of time.

Morning roll call was before dawn. The prisoners would sleep fitfully, crowded onto hard, filthy boards that lined the walls like shelves. The barracks were very cold, and the threadbare blankets the camp provided were never enough. But still, any sleep they could catch was a respite from the torture they experienced in all their waking hours

And then the gong would sound, abruptly ending that short spell of peace. The men had to get up immediately and hurry to shower in ice-cold water, find their shoes and get their swollen feet into them, and rush out to line up for roll call. To be late for roll call meant death!

After roll call, and a cup of hot, moldy water called by the presumptuous name "coffee," they would be marched out to work. It was a long march, several kilometers, but they had to keep up the pace and the rhythmic step despite the snow, the biting cold, and the gnawing hunger.

They cried. A group of prisoners, dragging their frozen feet in the terrible cold to do ceaseless labor, day after day. No future lay ahead but more of the same, no end in sight… except for death.

The *kapo*, their foreman, was a Jew. He was touched by their tears; he cried with them. "*Kinderlach*," he would say to them, "if only I could do more to help you! I wish I could make it easier! But I'll tell you what: close your eyes for a moment, and imagine the time quickly passing. Ten hours from now, all this is over and we're lying on our bunks again. It's only for ten hours, and the time is getting shorter and shorter. Every step is shortening the way. Your afternoon soup is getting closer and closer, and after that you get to rest for the night."

Somehow, the sparse comfort he offered kept them going. After they'd marched for half an hour, the *kapo* would say, "In nine and a half hours, we'll be in the barracks again. Picture that moment, when you'll have a bowl of hot soup, in less than nine and a half hours… even less."

The *kapo* was a prisoner like them. He had no bread to give them, but he didn't hold back his kindness and concern, and knowing that someone cared was more strengthening than bread.

When the painting project came to an end, Papa and the rest of his crew were sent to carry huge, heavy gas pipes. The work was too strenuous for him, and even the merciful *kapo* and his guided imagery couldn't make it bearable. About a fifth of the crew members had already fallen from the ranks, and Papa knew that he, too, would soon join them if things went on this way.

The *kapo* found a moment when no one was listening. "Come to me tonight," he whispered to Papa. "I want to show you something."

Papa crept out of his bunk in the darkness and found the *kapo*. In complete silence, the *kapo* taught him the locksmith's craft. In the shadows, he showed Papa how to assemble and disassemble a lock, and with a few private lessons, he saved Papa's life. Now Papa had a valuable skill, and when the camp commanders heard of it, they were quick to take advantage of it. For Papa, it meant a respite from the grueling labor that would have killed him.

The year was 1944, and new transports were arriving at the camp. These Jews weren't from the ghettos, they were from Hungary. The destruction of Hungarian Jewry had begun without warning, and trains were bringing thousands every day. They arrived reeling with shock. Just days before, they'd been living normally, and suddenly — here they were, in a nightmare.

For Papa, it was a chance to get word of events outside the camp. He had lost track of the calendar, and now, one of the Hungarian Jews informed him that the month was Elul.

His new friend, Nisan Leizer, shared his thoughts with Papa. "Rosh Hashanah is coming," he said quietly as they lay in their bunk. "We have to get hold of a shofar."

A shofar! The boards beneath them almost laughed out loud. It was 1944. The death machine was spewing smoke. Their lives hung by a spider's thread. Every morning, new corpses were carried out to roll call. But those two young men wanted only a shofar. No more and no less.

CHAPTER 31

Beyond the Sky of Auschwitz

WITH SHAKING HANDS, PAPA gave his blanket to a Pole in exchange for the horn of an animal. His blanket! In Auschwitz, he gave up his blanket and conducted business with it, although the act was punishable by death.

The horn was unprocessed and not hollow. But Papa had his locksmith's toolkit. Every night, he would sit on his wooden bunk in the dark and hollow out a little bit of the horn, and then go back to sleep for whatever was left of the night until he was jarred awake by strident scream of the predawn bell.

It took a few weeks, but by Rosh Hashanah, the horn was ready. They had a shofar.

Nisan Leizer's shofar blasts split the air of Auschwitz that Rosh Hashanah morning. Could the sound of the shofar in any grand synagogue match those muffled blasts? Could anything pierce the heavens like those blasts? Was there a shofar in the world more precious than that roughly-hollowed horn, bought with a blanket and so many hours of lost sleep? Those blasts were the cries of two pure, burning hearts. The shofar blasts of Auschwitz.

A week passed after the two days of Rosh Hashanah, and then came Yom Kippur eve. The Nazis delayed the afternoon meal on purpose, intent on torturing the men as much as possible. They would wait until sunset, and only then would they hand out the bread. Papa managed to swallow a few crumbs for his pre-fast meal, and then, as the holy day began, he stopped. No matter what, he was going to fast. No Nazi could take away the freedom of his faith, his freedom to heed G-d's command.

In the morning, there was roll call as usual, in the usual frigid square. There was the usual screaming, the truncheons and whips swinging wildly, and the usual cup of moldy water and slice of bread taken into a black hole of hunger that could never be filled. Papa closed his fist over the bread and kept his hand at his side. "It's Yom Kippur!" he said softly to himself.

The friend standing next to him noticed that something was different. "What's with you?" he asked impatiently. "Hurry up with the bread, we have to get going." Papa moved away a bit, heading stealthily for the barracks, where he meant to hide the bread until he came back for it after dark. "Where do you think you're going?" his friend asked, pulling the sleeve of Papa's thin tunic. "If you don't get into line right now, you'll be in big trouble...."

But Papa kept going. He slipped into the barracks and hid the bread. He couldn't keep it with him and risk being overcome by his terrible hunger. He wanted to fast. The bread would stay here.

His friend followed him and stood by the door to the barracks, thunderstruck. "What?! You're fasting!? Yom Kippur? You can't fast! You have to eat to stay alive! You could die from fasting, and we swore to live!" He stared at the emaciated body in front of him, at the sunken cheeks and the skin stretched over the bones, but the eyes were shining with confident determination. Papa was going to fast, no matter what!

Trembling all over with worry, fear, and anger, Papa's friend quickly pulled him back out to the *Apellplatz*. "Do you see the sky?" he asked rhetorically. "The sky is always gray in Auschwitz. Clouds of smoke block out the heavens. The smoke of human remains, the smoke of souls leaving this world. Can you smell the burning bodies? Do you see the crematorium churning out smoke even now?" His voice rose, hoarse and passionate. "Look up, can you see the heavens? Can you find someone there who cares about your Yom Kippur fast? Find him for me!! Find him for me, here in Auschwitz!"

Papa spent the rest of the day in silence, surrounded by silence. Twelve hours of work without a morsel of bread or a spoonful of soup, twelve hours outdoors without a drop of water. Evening finally came, and at last Papa was back in his bunk. The night was black, and the stars were very distant. The smoke of the crematorium continued to steal into the barracks. His hands fumbling with exhaustion, Papa found the dry bread he'd hidden away in the morning. He had put himself to the ultimate test and prevailed; now he could break the fast. He recited the blessing and ate some bread, and then took some time out to speak with his Creator.

He had no words for that conversation.

I know the words my father said to G-d that night after Yom Kippur, and I want to sing them to the girls — girls from Tel Aviv and Ra'anana who live their lives under the blue sky and wake up every morning to comfort and plenty. Tears crowd in among the words until there's no more space, and then they must stream out. I stand right here where my father said these words, in the first row of Block Seven, and the words are still etched in those wooden walls.

I say them very slowly at first, as if I were taking diamonds out of a little box one by one and displaying each one's dazzling brilliance. Then I begin to sing them, and by the end, I am crying them.

"Habet miShamayim ur'eh, ki hayinu la'ag vakeles bagoyim... Look down from Heaven and see how we were made a laughingstock among the nations. We were thought of as a flock to be led to the slaughter, to kill and to wipe out, to be struck and put to shame...

"Habet miShamayim ur'eh, ki hayinu la'ag vakeles bagoyim... uvechol zos Shimcha lo shachachnu... And despite in all, we have not forgotten Your Name..."

Six men were crammed into one freezing-cold, wooden bunk, without a blanket or a mattress. Their bones looked disjointed, and the lice crawled where they liked. Papa had been in that hell for over five years already, with death right before his eyes every day, yet he still held the bread in his hand after the fast of Yom Kippur and solemnly promised his Creator, "We have not forgotten Your Name." Although You have hidden Your face and it may seem You are nowhere to be found, we have not forgotten You. Although the smoke fills the sky, and our parents are gone, and the cries of little children still echo, and we endure ceaseless humiliation...

My eyes are closed, and I continue singing, *"Uvechol zos Shimcha lo shachachnu...* And despite in all, we have not forgotten Your Name..."

We have not forgotten You. Please, do not forget us....

The girls aren't making a sound. They're hardly breathing. I don't want to let go of this moment. Slowly, I open my eyes. I see their faces. Every face is streaked with tears.

I take a breath and say, "HaKadosh Baruch Hu has not forgotten us, girls. Here we are, *Am Yisrael, chai vekayam*!

"My father didn't know then how the story would end. Then, the sky was black and starless, and he sat on a wooden board with a thin slice of stale bread, saved for after Yom Kippur. But he believed..."

And they cried even more.

CHAPTER 32

A Moment of Eternity

PAPA HAD A FRIEND in the camp, a fellow his own age by the name of Gesundheit.

On the outside, Gesundheit must have looked like all the rest, with his head and beard shaved and a row of numbers on his arm, and dressed in a baggy, striped prisoner's uniform. But on the inside, he was one of those people made of flaming fire, a fire that nothing could extinguish.

One day he managed to smuggle a treasure into the camp — a pair of tefillin that one of the Hungarian Jews had brought with him to Auschwitz, on the last trip of his life. The intrepid Gesundheit dug a secret pit outside the barracks and concealed the tefillin there. Every morning, he would somehow find a fleeting moment to put them on between roll call and the march to work — although in fact no time was given.

Papa and Gesundheit were kindred spirits. They were made of the same flaming fire that refused to be crushed out. And Papa was in on the secret.

I lift my head and look around me. Somewhere within a few meters from here the pit was dug, and it held two small objects as dangerous as hand grenades.

Papa would steal over to the pit every morning, quickly scan the area to make sure no Nazi was there, and hastily tie the tefillin to his head and his arm, winding the leather strap down to his hand and reveling, if only for a few seconds, in G-d's closeness.

Soon other men in the camp, Jews who were beaten and starved, men who had lost their Jewish appearance but not the glowing Jewish spark in their souls, were also putting on the tefillin. Word had passed in whispers from one Jew to the next: "There's a pair of tefillin hidden in the yard!" And those men put the tefillin on, laughing in the face of death, for no one could defeat them at that moment of courage and inner freedom.

For eight months, Papa put on tefillin in Auschwitz. Then the war ended, and he hid that sublime daily moment, together with his horrific memories, in a locked safe, hermetically sealed to make sure nothing would leak out into his new life. None of that must touch his children and their peals of happy laughter.

Papa had his own tefillin now, and he would carry them to the *shtiebel* each morning. He would put them on with a beautiful *aron kodesh* in the background, amid a peaceful crowd of congregants. When he took them off, he placed them calmly in the nook of polished wood in front of his seat. No one could imagine that years ago, he would look left and right and hastily conceal a pair of smuggled tefillin in a pit of earth. His past was locked away, and no one ever broke into the safe.

Years passed, the children grew up and married, and grandchildren began to fill the world with their tender young voices. The grandchildren grew, and then it was the bar mitzvah day of the eldest grandson. Mama and Papa flew to Israel and sat down excitedly in the upholstered chairs of the Wagschal hall in Bnei Brak.

Papa was full of emotion, and when he laid eyes on the bar mitzvah boy in his new clothes, a boy who had just started laying tefillin on his entry into manhood, he remembered the tefillin in Auschwitz, and he stood up and told the story to all the assembled family and friends. It was the first time they'd ever heard him tell a story from "there," and the whole hall fell silent.

"I remember when I was eighteen years old," he related. "Every morning I would run and put on tefillin quickly, quickly. I could see the chimney of the crematorium from where I stood, belching out thick, black smoke. And there I was, with tefillin on my head and arm. I knew that if any Nazi were to pass by at that moment, my life was worth no more than a pebble on the ground." Papa let out a sigh. He was carried back in memory to the unpaved grounds of Auschwitz, to the urgent calls of his friends and the dreadful screaming in German.... "But I knew more than that. I knew that beyond that thick smoke and that terrible smell, there was a G-d! And I would talk to Him, I would say, 'I know You are here, I know it. And for You I am putting on tefillin. For You, I'm risking my life.'"

Stunned, we all quietly wiped away tears. It was as if someone had suddenly turned out the lights in the bright hall and projected pictures of another world on the walls.

After Papa finished speaking, we tried to return to the chicken and potatoes on our plates, back to the big smiles of a family celebrating a bar mitzvah. Glowing lights shone on little girls in long party dresses and on the polished floor. It was a very nice party, but somehow the youth behind the wooden barracks of Auschwitz, shivering with hunger and cold as he laid tefillin, clinging tightly to his Creator for that too-brief moment, was still there with us.

There was a sequel to the story. Many years later, while attending the World Economic Forum in Davos, Switzerland, Papa went to daven Shacharis, and someone was asking to lead the prayers. "I have a yahrzeit today," the man explained, taking a neatly folded yarmulke out of his pocket and putting it on. Papa listened as the stranger led the prayers and was astounded. It was the prayer of someone who had been in another world.

After davening, Papa went up to him, extended a hand in

greeting, and asked whom he had the pleasure of meeting. "I am Elie Wiesel," the man replied.

Papa told him a little about himself, and soon they were deep in conversation, talking of things that others, who had never been where they had been and seen what they had seen, could never conceive of... things that words could not describe. But the same images were before the eyes of them both: the barracks... the hard bunks... the death all around that had somehow spared them....

And the tefillin. Somehow it came out that both of them had put on that same pair of tefillin, hidden in that little pit in the cold earth of Auschwitz. They had both belonged to the same secret club of men who laughed at death and risked all to keep the eternal flame of their spirit alive.

Their tears flowed, and Papa said to his new friend, "You know, I often wonder if it was the merit of putting my life on the line to lay those tefillin that stood by me, if that was the reason I got out of there alive and live in health and happiness today, surrounded by a large family, and have the pleasure of seeing them all on the straight path of their ancestors."

Elie Wiesel thought for a moment, took a deep breath, and laying a bashful hand on his temporary yarmulke, he said, "The merit of those tefillin has stood by me, to bring me back to my G-d in my old age. I'm coming back home now..."

Eight months of quick, stolen moments putting on tefillin in Auschwitz, had added up to eternity.

CHAPTER 33

Shehecheyanu

FINALLY, THE SNOW BEGINS to fall, as if it were waiting especially for us, a group so quintessentially Israeli, so unaccustomed to the cold. It is going to teach us the meaning of snow in Auschwitz-Birkenau.

The snow doesn't fall quietly or majestically the way it does in storybooks. It falls upon us violently, savagely, slapping, punching, and kicking. It spins around us in a roaring wind and shoots thousands of frozen arrows at our faces. This is a real storm, and it is so cold, even our thoughts are frozen in place.

It isn't lovely at all, and white roofs look nothing like a picture postcard. The cold is unbearable, and we can think of nothing else. We want to leave the barracks and continue on, but who can step out there? The wind sprays us with frozen nails, mocking our thick coats and penetrating them with ease.

We're in a kind of helpless shock, that state of mind where the whole group just wants to be somewhere else. We all want to close our eyes and feel padded and protected again in the shelter of our heated bus, with a big paper cup of hot coffee.

But we are here, in Auschwitz-Birkenau, in a place where people were held captive behind electrified fences, at the mercy of two-legged beasts every hour of the day. This same snow fell on them, too, and they didn't arrive on a heated tour bus, nor were they going to get back onto one shortly.

"Hey, girls!" I call, trying to raise my voice above the howl of the wind. "Let's all try to think about the thousands of Jews who stood here for roll call at dawn," I suddenly say, without planning to at all. It just comes out, because suddenly I'm thinking of my father. Papa, so strong and kind… my smiling, happy Papa… and I feel a tear, warm for half a second, on my frozen cheek.

"My father was here," I say, "together with thousands of other young men, and they stood here in snow just like this for hours. For hours! Can we comprehend that? They couldn't even pull their little hats down over their ears, and anyone who was caught with a blanket under his uniform was shot.

"Come," I urge the girls, "let's all hold hands and run! We'll draw strength and warmth from each other, and together we'll break through this storm!"

We all join gloved hands, and as one unit, full of strength, we burst out into the raging blizzard, singing with all our might, feeling that every one of us has more strength than she ever imagined. Because the mind and heart are so much bigger than the body…

Finally, panting from the cold and shaking from the exertion, a bunch of walking icicles, we fall somehow through the doors of the museum. There we begin to thaw a bit and ask ourselves if we really need any guided explanations here, after running through a storm like that.

Suddenly we begin to have an inkling of what it meant to be imprisoned here, taking cold showers, sleeping on bare wooden shelves in barracks with one stove in the middle that was never lit. It all falls into place, becoming a little too clear, in fact. There is only one thing left for me to tell the group — I'll tell them about the *succah*.

After Yom Kippur, Papa's friend Gesundheit took him aside

secretly. He remembered that Papa had learned in *cheder*, and he'd probably learned the laws of Succos in the Mishnah. Gesundheit needed him to check something for him now, and tell him if it was kosher. "Come and see what I built," he said under his breath. "Does this comply with all the laws of a *succah*?"

"Did you say a *succah*?" Papa was thunderstruck. Here, where people had no past and no future, where apathy was the prevailing state of mind because sensitivity wasn't conducive to survival, building a *succah* was like landing a spaceship from the moon.

He followed Gesundheit rather skeptically, wondering if his friend was turning delusional or seeing hallucinations of a *succah*. He wouldn't be the first to lose his mind here... it was one thing to hide a small pair of tefillin — but a *succah*?

But on the other hand, this was Gesundheit. Quietly, he led Papa to a spot not far from the barracks. And there, Papa beheld a low, ramshackle structure of rough-hewn wood, hardly distinguishable from the pile of wood that had been there all along. He measured it with his eyes and noted how it was roofed. Yes, it could be called a *succah*. "It's kosher," he said in amazement. "And I want to be in it on Yom Tov night."

Gesundheit had done it again.

On the first night of Succos, the two youths stood in front of the *succah*, eager to crouch down and get inside. But in order to fulfill the minimal requirement of "dwelling in the *succah*," they had to consume a meal consisting of a *kezayis* of bread, at least, in the *succah* that night. And only Gesundheit had bread. Papa had finished his afternoon ration, and he would get no more until the morning.

The full moon, marking the midpoint of the Hebrew month, glowed above them. Two young Jews needed bread, not because they were starving (although of course they were), but because they wanted to recite a blessing in the *succah*.

Gesundheit divided his bread in two and handed half of it to

Papa. Half of the sustenance that kept him barely alive. And the two of them crept into the *succah* in absolute silence. With tears choking their voices, they whispered the blessings: on the bread, and on the commandment "to sit in the *succah*."

Many years later, a beautiful, spacious *succah* stood in Jerusalem. Its walls were lined with fresh white fabric and hung with sparkling decorations. From its windows, one could look down on the Western Wall. It belonged to Gesundheit, the man who built a *succah* under the chimneys of Auschwitz, never dreaming that one day a cool Jerusalem breeze would be blowing in his *succah* over a sumptuously set table. "Come and visit," he would say to Papa, who was living in Bnei Brak by then. "Come and drink a *l'chaim* with me in my *succah*. You were with me when I crawled into a tiny hovel of a *succah* in Auschwitz, you shared a piece of bread with me that night, and we said the *brachah* on the mitzvah. I want you to be with me when I thank G-d for bringing me here and giving me the beautiful *succah* I have now."

Many days afterward, Papa would talk, at last, of the biggest *nisayon* of all. It wasn't that they had a *succah* there, under the Nazis' noses. It wasn't sneaking out of the barracks, risking their lives to fulfill a mitzvah. It wasn't Gesundheit's *nisayon* when he had to decide whether to give half of his bread to his friend, or Papa's *nisayon* when he had to decide whether to accept the gift. No... the biggest *nisayon* was crouching in that tiny *succah* and reciting the joyous blessing, "*Shehecheyanu, vekiyemanu, vehigi'anu lazman hazeh* — Blessed are You... Who has given us life, and preserved us, and enabled us to reach this time!"

Their hearts wanted to cry out, "To reach this time?! This place?! Where our people are murdered in gas chambers and burned in furnaces, where children scream in agony and terror... a place where there is no pity. Is it even permissible to say a *brachah* on the fact that we are here today?"

"It was no simple matter," Papa told us. "It required more

strength than anything I'd ever done, and it was harder than any physical exertion could be. I closed my eyes and felt that getting out each word was like quarrying stone. *Shehecheyanu* — yes, I am alive! *Vekiyemanu* — yes, You have preserved me! You have done miracles to save me! *Vehigi'anu lazman hazeh* — yes, even now, at this terrible time You are still here, and I still believe in You, and because it is Your will, I am sitting in a *succah,* against all odds!"

The snow is still falling hard. People in the museum are saying they can't remember any other storm like this. Our bus is turning white out there in the wind. Soon we'll be inside, leaning back on upholstered seats, and they'll hand out something hot, and the storm will be framed by the windows of the bus.... The storm lets up a bit, and the girls trudge out to the bus, leaving footprints in the snow. I leave my footprints here too, on the snowy ground of Auschwitz-Birkenau, trying to follow the steps of those who walked here, those much greater than I. I leave my feelings here and my thoughts, and all the tears that should have been cried long ago for Papa's sake.

But suddenly I see his comforting gaze, as if he were looking at me through the snow. He seems to smile and say, "Chana'le, *mein kind,* it wasn't I who was here. There's no possible way I could have survived it. I was surrounded by a shell of *emunah* that protected me and gave me the strength to endure, you'll never know how much. It was all *emunah,* Chana'le... *emunah* and more *emunah*...."

Afterward, on the bus, we all feel overloaded, as if we've packed a suitcase to the bulging point, and it's about to split open. It's all running around in my head, and Neta, sweetheart that she is, comes to sit next to me and talk with me a bit. Unconsciously, I start humming a tune to myself. "What's that you're singing?" Neta asks me.

"Oh, it's a song I heard recently," I say. "Sometimes I think my father must have written it."

V'afilu bahastarah	*Even when concealed*
sheb'toch hahastarah	*within the concealment,*
b'vadai gam sham nimtza Hashem Yisbarach.	*even there, Hashem, Blessed be He, is surely present.*
Gam me'achorei	*Even behind*
had'varim hakashim ha'ovrim aleicha	*the hardest things that befall you, [says Hashem,]*
Ani omeid…	*I am there…*
Ani omeid…	*I am there…*
Ani omeid…	*I am there…*

CHAPTER 34

A Picture of Papa

THE HOTEL RECEIVED US with a warm, comforting embrace. The rooms and corridors were heated, and the dining hall was almost steaming.

We remove our coats and unwind our scarves, but Auschwitz is still frozen inside us, refusing to thaw. The barracks and guard booths linger before our eyes, the stories and the feelings whirl around in our hearts, and somehow, even the delicious, thick soup is hard to swallow.

Shilat takes a chair and squeezes in between me and Rotem. We move our place settings slightly to make room for her, but then Sapir and Yif'at also join us, and then Dana. Again and again we move our plates and shift our chairs, until I'm surrounded by a tightly packed group that wants to hear "a little more about your father… Chana, do you have something more to tell us?"

More about my father? Are you serious? I could sit here day and night and hardly begin. My father's story could fill volumes, with a new chapter for every day.

Dana asks to see a picture. She has a very gentle voice, and when she speaks, everyone stops and listens, not wanting to interrupt that soft melody.

I haven't heard much from Dana on this trip. She always

stood close to the speakers and listened wide-eyed, with her hands in her pockets, absorbing every word deep into her core. Now she would like to see a picture, and I look around, wondering where I left my bag before we all started shifting our places, or if I even brought it down with me from my room at all. But anyway, I've already shown them pictures of my father, haven't I?

No, says Dana, not the same pictures they've already seen. She wants to see a picture from that time, from after the liberation or before it, a picture of him in his twenties.

In his twenties?! No, I have no pictures from that long ago. All the pictures I have with me are from recent family occasions. There are pictures of Papa and Mama right after the liberation, actually, but it never occurred to me to bring those old, black-and-white pictures, what on earth for? Meanwhile, I've found my bag and start searching through the pictures... maybe I do have one of those old ones, after all?

"I need to put a face to the stories you told," Dana explains, a bit apologetically and very eagerly. "I need to see his eyes, what was in them at that time... to understand how all that could have really been...

"Not that I think it didn't really happen, but because I know it did happen, and I want to understand how... what sort of boy was he? Who brought him up to be like that? How did he climb to the top of the mountain with his bare hands? And where did he get the strength to reach the heights every time, when they were barely alive?"

"My father was from a family of Alexander *Chossidim,*" I say quietly, allowing my plate of soup to fill the air with coils of steam. "And somehow, the flame of Gur touched and ignited him, and he found his place there. And that was when he met Matisyahu Gelman. Matisyahu, or Mattis, as everyone called him, was a very talented young man, with a razor-sharp mind and a lot of charisma. He was born into a family of Viennese

Jews who were well on their way to assimilation. He went to school at the famous Akademisches Gymnasium, and his teachers envisioned a brilliant intellectual future for him. But one day, after Rav Meir Shapiro visited the city, Mattis dropped out of academic life and left it all behind, to the disappointment of his family and friends. He had discovered Judaism, and he dove into it with all his talent and enthusiasm. He wasn't just a *baal teshuvah*, he had turned into a new person overnight, and his whole previous life was burned in the fire that blazed from him. Mattis became a flaming Chassidic torch. He soon became one of the prominent figures in the Gerrer Rebbe's court, and the young *Chossidim* formed a group around him like bees swarming around a hive.

"In Mattis's *chavurah*, all property was shared. The boys would leave their hats and coats in the vestibule of the *beis midrash* when they came in, and when they left they would put on any hat or coat that came to hand. Whatever food they brought was also shared equally. Torah study was the fire this tribe gathered around, and they dedicated themselves to spiritual achievements. They would work on character improvement, setting uncompromising goals for themselves. That was the environment my father came from," I explain to the girls. "Material things were nothing but props, providing a setting for learning and spiritual growth."

There was a song in Yiddish that they used to sing:

The Song of the Mattisovitches

א פייער זאל ברענען
און קיין רויך זאל נישט גיין
דאס קען נאר א חסיד אליין
אובער דעם אליין איז כדאי
איז כדאי א חסיד צו זיין

אלעס איז דיין
או גארנישט איז מיין
דאס קען נאר א חסיד פערשטיין
וואס ביי דער וועלט איז שיין
זאל ביי דיר זיין געמיין
דאס פארשטייט נאר א חסיד אליין

A fire may burn
Without any smoke —
This, only a *chossid* can grasp
And for this alone it is worth it,
It's worth it, a *chossid* to be

Everything is yours
Nothing is mine —
This, only a *chossid* can fathom
What the world thinks is lovely
You will find worthless
This, a *chossid* alone understands

When the Nazis took all that away from my father, when they tore his parents, his brothers, and his sisters from him, and put him to forced labor while suffering from cold and starvation for nearly six years, when they slowly sucked the life out of him until he was thrown onto a pile of corpses in Bergen-Belsen, there was one thing they didn't know: they could never take his spirit away from him, no matter what they did.

Papa wasn't there to greet the liberators when they arrived at Auschwitz. As the Soviet army approached, the Nazis evacuated most of the prisoners, forcing them to march westward to German territory. Papa was in one of those Death Marches. When he arrived in Buchenwald, he was at death's door, but despite it all, he was chosen for life.

Purim fell two months before the liberation. The dead were piled in heaps at the roadsides. Gloom hovered in the air; the prisoners all felt that their end was near. Yes, the liberators were on their way, but death was coming faster.

As they passed a bombed-out house, Papa noticed a saccharin tablet on the ground. He picked it up and handed it to his friend Hershel Protzel as *mishloach manos*. That must have been the smallest *mishloach manos* ever given. Hershel extended a bony hand and accepted the gift. Then he handed it back — his *mishloach manos* to Papa.

"*A freilichen Purim*!" they wished each other. And then they both cried.

But even as their tears fell, they added, "Next year, we should be *zoicheh* to be by the Rebbe on Purim!" They still remained with something that no one could take away from them.

With a gentle touch, Dana presses my hand. Like shining beads, tears hang from her eyelashes and then drop to her smooth cheeks.

"You'll find me a picture of your father, and send it to me," she pleads. "I need it very badly....

"Can you understand me?" She suddenly sighs and looks apologetically at the group around the table. "I need it as an amulet, like a compass in the desert, like a flashlight in a cave..."

The waiters collect our soup plates, and hot platters of rice come to the table, followed by potatoes, chicken, and vegetables. We all serve ourselves... all except Dana. She wants to talk about the compass she needs in the desert.

"I grew up in a religious home," she tells us, taking the opportunity to speak while we're all busy eating. "We had Shabbat, Kiddush, holidays, synagogue. I went to a religious high school, and I was even in Bnei Akiva. But once I started living away from home, it was all taken from me. I wasn't a sheltered religious girl anymore. I stopped wearing skirts, I gradually stopped keeping Shabbat, I even stopped caring about the holidays. They took all that away from me, and they gave me nothing in return. I was left cold and empty. I left home with something in my bag, but I ended up on my own, with nothing....

"It bothered me, but what could I do? Who could give me back what I'd lost? My whole crowd of friends was cynical, strong, confident, and always moving with the flow, and I was small and weak, too bashful to talk about boring, old-fashioned things... I felt like I was no match for them, and I just gave in...."

Even now, Dana's voice sounds injured. She takes quick breaths between her words, as if she's trying not to cry.

"I thought, that's just how it is," she says, almost in a whisper. "Young people can't withstand all that social pressure, and values are something for adults. The evenings out with the gang, the years in the army, and the friends in the singles' apartments took away all my sweet innocence, and I was swept away with the waves… I couldn't even see the shore.

"Now I'm in university, and I feel so far from my roots. Even the will to fight my way back seems out of my reach. But deep inside, it still hurts — all the time. And then I hear about your father. He was young like me, and he was swept up in waves like a tsunami, but he didn't let them put out his fire. I need a picture of him as he was then, I need to put it up on the wall somewhere in the dormitory suite so I can look into those eyes and know that if he could do it, maybe I can, too.

"If I have values deep inside, and I dream of having them back in my life again, I don't have to let anyone take them away from me. And no one will take them away from me…"

Dana's voice fades out, and I give her a loving hug. I just hug her, and don't say a word. What more is there to say?

CHAPTER 35

Laughter amid Tears

"CHANA, WHEN ARE WE going?" says Lihie, speaking not to me, but to the leader of today's outing, as she practically drowns her roll in chocolate spread. She's wearing a hat with a pompom on top and two braids of wool hanging down, and I wonder if she put on makeup this morning, or if she's just gotten her color back. Either way, she looks like a happy third grader.

They've prepared a lavish Israeli-style breakfast for us. I look around, and it seems as though the girls somehow found room in their suitcases for yesterday's experiences, and the night came and packed it all away neatly, sprinkling some comforting stardust over it all for good measure. Now they've woken up to a bright new morning, and they're all young and fresh again, well-dressed, helping themselves to what's left of the chocolate spread or moving along the buffet to find healthier offerings. To balance the meal, they nibble on freshly cut vegetables, and they look like any energetic young group that came to tour Poland and do some skiing, which is what they are about to do.

"For me, this day is going to be like an island of happiness in an ocean of tears," says Lihie. She's already on her second roll, and the way she's going at it, I suspect she'll be having a third, too.

"Hey, look at her," says Sapir, helping herself in an emphatic manner to the cheese and vegetables. "Is it the chocolate that's making her so poetic?"

"No, it's the ski trip. The pure white snow, the mountains. I've been dreaming of this day since before we left Israel… imagining myself flying down a mountainside with the wind whistling in my ears. Whooo……whoooo." Lihie spreads her arms out like wings, even putting down her roll in the enthusiasm of the moment.

We all laugh. Lihie's exuberant mood is getting contagious, and we start feeling that delightful anticipation.

"But isn't it strange?" Shir remarks, serenely drinking her coffee, occasionally dunking a tea biscuit, and letting her thoughts rise with the steam.

Shir is a serious type. She looks as though she's playing the teacher to Lihie's rambunctious third grader.

"Strange?! Are you kidding? What's strange about skiing? It's the most fun thing to do when you're abroad. And do you know how much snow there is on the mountains after yesterday's blizzard?"

"Yes, but on this trip? The March of the Living, Auschwitz, gas chambers… I feel it's a bit lacking in taste. Somehow it doesn't quite add up. How does skiing come into the picture? Who's in the mood for frivolity right now?"

"I am," says Rotem, playing with her fork and lightly stabbing the piece of omelet on her plate. "I feel I need a bit of release from all the crying. I need to laugh, to breathe freely and get back to a healthy state of mind."

"Tell it, girl!" says Sapir. "I hadn't thought of it, but you're right. I think we all need it."

We're in the dining hall, and the heating is keeping the place warm. But the view from the picture window is so white and sparkly that it gives the feeling of a wintry chill even here indoors.

Shir goes to get more biscuits to dunk in her coffee. "Well, maybe so," she says reservedly. "Maybe there's a need for release, but still, does it have to be done now? And here, on Polish soil, where it all happened?"

"Yes, here exactly," says Lihie, refusing to let Shir spoil her meal and her enjoyment. "What do you want? Can we go skiing in Tel Aviv? I want to ski right here!" she says, tapping her foot on the hotel's polished floor. "So could you loosen up a bit, Shir? Not everything has to be so philosophical, and if you keep digging so deep, we'll end up in the basement, and that won't be any fun. You come with me, and you'll see, it's going to be fabulous! Me and Shir are first in line to fly down the mountain," she announces for all to hear. "Who wants to go third?"

Again, everyone at the table laughs. A wave of excitement rolls over the group as one girl after another gives herself permission to have a good time today. Light chatter is heard over fresh or toasted rolls and omelets made to order, everything comes together to create a feeling that matches the snow sparkling in the sunlight, fresh and bright.

Some of the girls are continuing the discussion Shir began, and I, too, pause to ask myself what I think. And although I have no solid evidence, my intuition tells me that it's a good idea, this trip to Zakopane. We aren't here to celebrate death. This is a journey of the living, and it doesn't all have to be like a funeral. Part of life is to know when to put weeping aside.

Amid all the chatter, reflection, and half-cups of coffee growing cold, I come back to tell everyone that we'll be leaving shortly. "Don't forget to make sandwiches for lunch," I remind them, "and make sure you're wearing your warmest clothes. Come on, don't linger, or the bus will leave without you and you'll have to ski here in the dining hall."

The reality surpasses anything a postcard could depict — the mountains really seem to come right up to the bus windows, evoking admiring whistles from the girls.

We arrive in Zakopane, and the bus stops at the ski resort and ejects us all. Dressed like woolen mummies, we move awkwardly toward the cable car platform.

The cable car is pulled suddenly into the air, and we hold onto its walls as if that could slow it down. It's like being in a spaceship flying over a craggy, frozen landscape. Are we about to crash into that mountain?

But the view is incredible, and it vanquishes our fear. It doesn't take our breath away; it makes us breathe deeper, wanting to take it all in, to soothe our aching souls. We all have our faces at the windows, our eyes drinking in the scene, absorbing the beauty — snow-covered mountains, snow-covered trees, and snow-covered houses, outlined in white with surprising precision. The mountains of Poland.

And now we've arrived. Welcome to the mountaintop. The air is sharp, freezing cold, and it has the cleanest smell in the world, the smell of snow. The guides hand out bags of equipment. Each bag, numbered and labeled, contains a kit for a specific girl. Nefesh Yehudi is amazingly well organized. Before we left Israel, they took each girl's shoe size to ensure that there would be properly fitted ski boots for everyone. Now, the organizers call out names as they pass the kits, although their voices are hardly heard over the eager babble of the girls. "Here, this one is Rotem's! Where is she?" "Yif'at! I saw yours a moment ago..." "Shaked? Over on the left somewhere..." One by one, the ski kits find their way to their designated users, who hold them up triumphantly like flags. But instead of planting a conqueror's flag on the mountain peak, their task now is to get to the bottom of the mountain....

CHAPTER 36

Fifty Punches on the Ticket

AMID ALL THAT CHAOS, I stood aside. There was no bag prepared for me... the staff was supposedly too elderly for skiing, and no one had asked me my shoe size. But to me, it was inconceivable to pass up a chance to go skiing.

I went up to the woman in charge and asked if she happened to have an extra kit in size 39. "For you?" she asked, trying not to look surprised. "Well, yes, I do have... Certainly!" In a moment, I, too, was equipped with ski boots, poles, and a ticket for ten rides on the cable car that would take us back up the mountain after each trip down.

Excitedly, we took off our shoes, and put on the thick boots exultantly. Hopping, giggling, and leaning on each other for support, the girls went out to conquer the mountain.

Suddenly, a few girls noticed that I was there, too, with all my skiing gear. "Hi, Chana!" They looked at me quizzically, trying to avoid insulting me. Clearly, I wasn't supposed to be there. Skiing was dangerous for old folks like me. I might break a bone, *chas v'shalom*. But instead of saying that to my face, they delicately inquired if I really meant to ski down the mountainside with them. Much as they tried to hide their thoughts, there were about a million question marks hovering above their heads.

"Yes!" I replied, concealing a smile like someone with a little secret. "Why not? Come on, let's go down together!"

We held hands, a *segulah* against fear of heights that works at all ages. Then someone said, "On your mark... get set... go!" I dropped whosever hand I was holding, and away I flew. The mountain treated me like an old friend, and it skimmed smoothly backwards under my skis. The fresh wind patted my cheeks encouragingly. It was a very easy path, and in a few moments I was dropping with a soft thump at the bottom, expecting the girls to appear any second. Meanwhile, I reveled in the experience of skiing again after all these years. But the mountain behind me was still pure white, with nary a spot of moving color. "How strange," I thought. "What could have happened?"

I decided I'd better head back up. The attendant punched my ticket, and I climbed into the cable car for the upward trip to see what was going on there.

What was going on up there was more like a slapstick comedy than anything to do with skiing. Half of the girls were sprawled on the snow, and the other half were about to join them. Ski poles were flying, boots were stuck in the snow. Laughter competed with groans amid futile attempts to stand up, only to fall down again. Clumps of snow flew this way and that, and I stood there, wondering what on earth was the matter here.

"Hi, girls!" I said, trying to restore some semblance of order as I pulled girls up by their elbows, recovered ski poles that were half buried in the snow, and picked up an assortment of wooly hats gone astray.

"Come! Let's start over!" I encouraged them. The laughter slowly died down, and they beat the snow off their clothing. But when they tried to get up, I could see that the comedy was about to replay itself. They were trying to walk on the snow as if they were on a sunny street in Givatayim, and they hadn't the slightest idea what they were supposed to do with those sticks in their hands besides poking each other with them every time they fell down.

"All right," I said, resigning myself to the dismal reality, "let's start from the beginning." I explained how to use the ski poles, how to flex the feet while fastening the boots, how to do the basic skiing movement, and how to keep it going. A very quick mini-course. "You see?" I said, showing them two strides. "This is how you stand and push off. It's really simple!" I showed them again: one foot here, and then the other foot comes this way. Steady yourselves, and start right after me..."

Very obedient and full of desire to make it smoothly to the bottom, they tried. But once again I found myself alone, leaving them somewhere up there, convulsed with laughter and pain, rolling around or half buried in the snow, slipping, sliding, bumping, and calling out to me with cries of distress and hilarity that disappeared into the mountain air above me.

On the third try, they started throwing snowballs at me in playful irritation. "Where did you learn to ski so well, Chana? You've been keeping secrets from us! Were you the skiing champion of Belgium? Come on, tell us the truth!"

"The truth?" I laughed. "Yes, I was the skiing champion of Belgium. We were all the skiing champions of Belgium..."

"Come on — seriously. You're like a professional athlete. What have you been keeping from us?"

"I really am a pro at this," I told them when I returned to the top of the mountain for the sixth time. "I went to skiing school from first grade to fifth grade. Every year we learned new skills and started practicing for the next grade. We had the whole winter to do 'homework,' and we were good students, all the way through fifth grade.

"In fifth grade, our final project was on a ski path from one mountain to the next. We traced fancy figures in the snow, and they gave us beautiful diplomas."

"Skiing school? Is there really such a thing?" They searched my eyes for that glint that can nearly always be detected when someone is joking at other people's expense. "Are you serious?" they finally asked straight out.

"As serious as can be," I laughed, and the whole mountain laughed with me. I made another descent down the mountain, feeling like a solo performer.

When I'd used up all ten punches on my cable-car ticket and exhausted all my attempts to teach the girls the un-Israeli art of skiing, they handed their tickets over to me. Since it seemed there was no chance that they'd ever make it to the bottom without looking like the scapegoat that was sent down to Azazel, they preferred to build snowmen, to throw a few clumps of snow at me as I started down the path, and most of all, to cheer me on as I passed by and performed a few nice turns, leaving curly figures in the snow. Their applause accompanied me all the way to the foot of the mountain... and my ticket was punched for the forty-fifth time for the return trip upward.

By the fiftieth time, I was a young girl again, back in the Swiss Alps, with the snow falling ceaselessly and the air bitingly cold. And we were at the top of the mountain in Davos. It was as cold as could be, and as wonderful. So wonderful!

CHAPTER 37

Davos and a Coat, Too

TODAY, I GOT A *new coat! Mama found nice coats for all of us at the big store in the center of town, and the price was so low that she got excited and decided to buy them. "Such good coats, and such a bargain," she kept repeating, rubbing the material between her fingers until the saleslady politely took the last one and wrapped it.*

We came home with our hands full, very happy, and we couldn't do anything but walk around each other admiringly as we all tried on our new coats, until Mama called us to come and eat supper.

It isn't really that cold anymore; it feels more like spring than winter. I wish I could wear my new coat to school tomorrow and show it off to all my friends. But if it were cold, the coat wouldn't have been on sale, and then Mama wouldn't have bought it, because it's really a very expensive coat. I know, because I heard Mama telling Aunt Rivka.

So now my coat will have to wait in the closet, stored away until next winter, when the snow comes again and we go to Switzerland. Oh, how much fun that will be. Switzerland, and new coats, too!

We have winter vacation every year. And every year, we all go to Switzerland.

The rich people go to Arosa, to ski in the Alps, and they rent rooms in hotels there. They leave Antwerp, where the snow gets black, slushy, and slippery from everyone walking and driving on it, for Switzerland, where the snow is high, so fresh and sparkling.

We don't go to a hotel. It's very expensive to stay in a hotel, so we've never done that. But we do go skiing in Switzerland, and we enjoy it just as much as the richest people in the world. We come home with lots of pictures and stories, all about riding the cable cars and cutting perfect figures in the snow, just like them.

Papa and Mama rent an apartment in Davos. It's hardly even an apartment, really. The local people in Davos have tiny little guest apartments that they rent out to vacationers like us.

Mama packs all our things in our winter suitcases, and everything she knitted while sitting on the beach in the summer goes in. We jump around her like little dolls on springs, asking her every two minutes if it's time to go to the train station yet.

Mama doesn't get annoyed with us. She's calm and patient, and we can tell she's happy to see us all excited. That's what she wants — that we should be happy. And at exactly the right moment, we leave for the train station.

The porters help us load our luggage and we board the train. And we're off! Straight out of Belgium and into Switzerland, with clouds of steam swelling above us.

After a while we just have to open the windows to get a better view, even though it's cold — so cold that the bones in our faces start to freeze. That's when we really feel that we're in Switzerland, and by the time someone finds out where the wind is coming from and makes us close the window, we're almost frozen solid. Now we're just waiting to see the big sign that tells us we're at the Davos train station…

At the station we stop for hot tea. It's so hot, it burns our tongues. We feel our bones thawing one by one. The taste of the tea at the train station is the taste of vacation, and that's the taste of happiness. We're here, in Davos! Here for the mountains and the snow, and for all the good things that Papa and Mama give us.

We're not alone in Davos; there are at least ten other families here from Antwerp who rent guest apartments as we do, and go up to the Alps every day. Papa is the "mayor" of our little vacation community, and every morning the "town council" meets to discuss the weather and issue a decision: Is it too cold and cloudy to go up today? Shall we all head for the cable cars?

Oh, how we hope and pray the answer will be yes! I love riding the cable car almost as much as I love to ski. It's like being in a little plane that flies between the mountains.

But even if the council decides against the cable cars, Papa never keeps us in the house; we always go out skiing. It may be below freezing outside, and the cold may bite us like a hungry dog, but who cares? We can always walk up the mountain trail with Papa, singing the lively Gerrer marches he teaches us, poking our special walking sticks deep into the snow. It's always the same path, and always the same marches, until we reach the skiing area, and we can begin!

The wind whistles in your ears when you ski. It doesn't matter how warm your hat is, and how much love went into knitting it; the wind always whistles in your ears, louder than your screams of delight. At the end of the slope the whistling dies down. We land with a thump, shake off the snow, and laugh. Oh, how we laugh…

When the wind whistles, I always think it's yelling at us for not wearing a coat. "Who forgets to wear a coat in this weather?" it screeches. We're wearing a few layers of sweaters, all beautifully knit by Mama. Our top layer is knit with perfectly aligned stripes of blue and red. Mama really knows how to knit.

But the wind can't guess why we're not wearing coats. We didn't forget them. We just don't have any. Winter coats are very expensive, and Mama can't afford to buy them. So she knits and knits, and we wear one sweater on top of another, with Mama's warm love knitted into every stitch.

Who needs a coat? Who needs a resort hotel in Arosa? Mama doesn't have a fur coat, either, like some of my friends' mothers do. But what does it matter? Let the wind screech all it wants, we'll keep on laughing. And we really are warm. Our cheeks are so red with the white snow behind us, we look like cherries on whipped cream.

Next winter, we'll take the train to Switzerland again. We'll crowd in again with our cousins, and Papa will sit at the head of the town council again. But next year, I'll have a real coat! I can hardly believe it, and instead of preparing my schoolbag for tomorrow, I'm sitting here dreaming. Mama is calling me to come eat my supper, and in a moment my brother will come to get me. But think of it — next year, Davos and a coat, too!

CHAPTER 38

No Surprises

AS WE STROLLED ALONG Zakopane's main street, I was surrounded by a fan club. My fifty times down the ski slope had earned me more admiration than I'd ever had in my life. But instead of autographs, they asked for more stories.

So as we walked, I told them stories. The tourist shops, built of wood with a rustic look, framed my stories, and the dazzling white snow formed the background illustrations as I told them about a young girl, the Alps… and a blissful life.

After we'd been traveling to Davos every winter for a number of years, the mayor presented my father with a certificate, decorated in color and honoring him in calligraphic lettering as "the constant tourist." But Papa didn't know he would earn this distinction, and he would have come back again and again in any case.

By now you know that my parents didn't have much money. They started their life in Belgium with nothing but the clothes on their backs and a thousand dreams in their hearts. They had no parents to help them pay the rent or give them a washing machine to start out with. There were no uncles to buy them a nice set of china, or to get them a job in a friend's office. My father had nothing, and he was too honest for the moneymaking schemes that others around him were concocting. Papa and Mama could have passed up the yearly vacation in Davos, as it really didn't suit their budget, but they wanted to give us children, born against all odds, everything good in the world. If richer people's children went skiing, they wouldn't deprive us of that joy.

Every year, we went back to Davos, to the same little guest apartment and the same ski slopes.

Was it because my parents had such a deep-seated need to give us a life of stability, following an unchanging pattern? After all, they knew, and how well they knew, what it was like to have your life fall apart. They knew what it was to be thrust out of a happy, thriving routine, with every prospect of a fulfilling future, into a gaping hole of horror with no apparent meaning.

I only know that Papa and Mama did everything they could, and even went beyond their strength, to ensure that our lives would be secure, stable, and predictable.

If they could help it, nothing would come by surprise to tear us away from the happiness that encircled us. I'm sure that's what motivated Papa to go back every year to the same store to get walking sticks, the store with the giant teddy bear that held all the sticks in its embrace, and the same saleslady who knew he would come in like clockwork at winter vacation time.

Yes, it was all about a happy, predictable life for his precious children. But such a thought never entered our minds at the time. How could it, when we knew nothing of what our parents had suffered?

Now, in the colorful marketplace of Zakopane, with souvenirs and other pretty items on display all around, I'm so tired from my fifty trips down the slope that I wonder who has the energy to browse here.

But just when I was thinking that I couldn't be bothered with shopping, I saw the stone heart. It was hung on the wall outside the shop, and it was calling to me. The shop was picturesque, with open shutters at the window, painted a bright turquoise, and window boxes full of pink geraniums.

I went over to get a closer look, and it called to me even more. It would be perfect for my mother's kitchen, and the words on it said just what my heart felt. There was a price sticker on the back; all I had to do was hold out a crisp bill of Polish money to the smiling Polish woman at the till, and smile back at her until she gave me the change.

Meanwhile, my Israeli fans were trying to read the inscription. "It isn't in English," I said, squashing their attempts as I rolled the gift in a sheet of brown paper that the saleswoman had produced from somewhere at the back of the store. "It's in German."

"German? You can read German!? Chana, what else do you know?"

Not much, I tell them frankly. Nothing to get excited about. Every Belgian Jew starts hearing five or six languages from the day he's born, before he even leaves the hospital. German is similar to Yiddish, and the words etched on the heart are very simple.

"And they're classified information?" Rotem asks, with a mischievous gleam in her eyes, as if she were about to get state secrets out of me.

"No, not at all… just a few words of love for my mother. I think she'd like to have this in her kitchen."

"It's for your mother?" Now it's Tanya speaking, and as usual, there's something direct and candid in her manner. "You know, you've hardly told us anything about your mother. Wasn't she here during the Holocaust? Didn't you say she was born in Poland?"

"She was here," I say, almost in a whisper. And suddenly the paving stones seem to stretch under my feet, and I'm walking slowly. "She was thirteen when it began. She spent six years — her whole adolescence, the most significant years of her life — in the shadow of death, hunger, and fear. And you ask me if she was in the Holocaust?

"My mother," I start to say. But now, the picturesque shops are all wrong. They can't form a background to the story when I speak about Mama. All around us are displays of colorful costume jewelry, knickknacks made of wood or painted ceramic, and loud T-shirts for tourists. When I speak about Mama, it all seems to be pushed to the sides, out of the way. My mother...

Suddenly she appears in my mind's eye, like a radiant princess with eyes that hold all the goodness in the world. "Chana," she seems to tell me, "let the girls enjoy their shopping. This isn't the time to tell them my story."

I pause, letting my last words fade and vanish into the bright midday air. "This isn't the right time," I finally say to the group walking along with me in expectant silence. "The right moment will come, and I'll tell you my mother's story. But for now, what do you think of these banana earrings and pineapple pendants?" I ask, as a whole stall full of enamel fruit jewelry accosts us.

The girls hesitate for a moment, waiting to see if I'm really not going to tell the story now, and when they see that I really mean it, they bring their attention back to the merchandise, trying on jewelry and bags, fingering knickknacks, jumbling up the displays, ruffling the peddlers' nerves, and laughing a lot — warm laughter of pure enjoyment. And I say to myself, "Mama was right, as she always is."

No tears are shed today. We spend a thoroughly pleasant afternoon, and plenty of Polish money changes hands. The girls come away laden with trinkets. "Taking a bunch of girls shopping is a disaster," says Yif'at, plopping down on her seat in the bus with half of Zakopane in bags all around her. "One of these days I'm going to have to get brain surgery, and have them take out the lobe in charge of shopping. At this rate I'll be left with no money to live on!"

Later, though, in the quiet of the hotel as I arrange my purchases in my suitcase, I come across the little stone heart again. And I remember Tanya's eyes. "What? Wasn't your mother in the Holocaust? Didn't you say she was from Poland?"

My dear Mama, will I know what to say about you tomorrow? I could never find enough words to tell them what you suffered, or to describe your character. Will you forgive me for that? After all, you never had the words to talk about it, either. You kept silent, too, because you couldn't find a way to say it — and we never knew.

Antwerp, 1960

It's such a lucky thing that after Shabbos we have Sunday. I think Sunday comes just to comfort me because Shabbos is over. I can't imagine how I'd feel if I were to wake up the morning after Shabbos and suddenly find out that it was Monday, and I'd have to hurry out to school with my big, brown schoolbag.

Everything is bright and lovely in our house on Shabbos. We eat in the dining room, at the big, shiny table, spread with a stiffly starched and ironed white tablecloth. Papa turns on all the lights in the chandelier, and the light sparkles on the crystal drops and pours down on all of us. I set the table with the china that Mama and Papa bought once in Germany, with the wide gold stripe around every plate. * *I place a*

---

*My parents didn't boycott German-made goods. We had a good-quality German washing machine, and anything else that would serve our needs and provide good value for its cost, never mind where it was from. On the contrary, I think my parents must have felt that taking such a petty revenge on the Germans was absurd. What vengeance in this world could ever suffice? Who but G-d could possibly find a fitting punishment for Germany's crimes? Leave vengeance in His hands, and let the Jews who survived have a good washing machine. Let the Germans work for them, making quality products for them and their children. Of course, many thought differently, and they had every right to their feelings.

silver meat fork, and a smaller fork for fish, at each setting, along with a folded cloth napkin. It looks so elegant that I can pretend this is the main dining room in a prince's chateau.

On Shabbos afternoon, we go for our regular walk in "Cholent Park." That's a silly name for such a beautiful park, but all the Jews call it by that nickname, because we all go there after the Shabbos cholent.

There's a lake in the park, where proud swans swim, with lush green lawns all around it. We always meet families we know there, and I see lots of my friends from school. It's fun to meet in the park, dressed in our Shabbos clothes, together with our families. It's nothing like a school gathering. The grownups talk among themselves and let us girls talk and play together, until our mothers call us and say it's time to go home and rest.

The swans are Jewish. Everybody knows it. Even the goyim joke that it's true. It may sound strange, but it has to be so, because of all the bits of challah they eat. Every Jewish family brings a bag of leftover challah to feed to the swans. "But why don't the goyim bring their leftover bread?" I once asked my best friend Debbie. She didn't know, but her big sister said it was because the Jews don't throw away food, and it had something to do with the war.

The war? I wondered what connection there could be between the war and feeding challah to the swans. But I didn't want to let on that I didn't understand, so I just nodded and then changed the subject.

Today is Sunday, and I hear Papa's voice from the dinette where we eat our meals. Papa has the day off from work on Sunday. He eats with us and has time to listen to us and tell us stories, so every meal on Sunday is like a little family party.

At exactly one o'clock, just after we all sit down to eat, Papa turns on the radio, as he does every Sunday to catch up on the news. The radio announcer sounds excited. He's saying something about the Congo, speaking quickly in French with a lot of hard words that I don't really understand. That's all they've been talking about lately on the radio, that faraway Congo. Papa explained to me that it's a country in Africa ruled by the Belgians, and the African people there are rebelling against them. But we're not in Africa, we're here in Belgium, and I've never even seen anyone from Africa, except some pictures of black people I once saw in an encyclopedia at a friend's house.

So why are Papa and Mama so quiet and serious? Don't the people on the radio know that you're not supposed to spoil the mood on Sunday?

I guess they don't. Papa doesn't even notice that we're waiting to start the meal. He's talking fast to Mama in Yiddish, and she's asking him something. He shrugs his shoulders and doesn't answer. Mama asks him again, insistently. "What if Belgium doesn't agree?" she says. "What will be then?"

Papa sighs. "There might be a war," he says quietly.

"A war!?" Mama is whispering, but her whisper is like a scream of horror. "Nein!" she says. "Nein! Nein! There won't be a war! There won't!"

Her face is pale, her lips are trembling, and her voice sounds terrible. I've never heard her sound like that before. "Nein! There won't be a war!"

A thousand questions are running around in my head, hurting me, troubling me. What's going on? Why is Mama so upset? Maybe she's just afraid of wars? Does this have anything to do with the leftover challah we feed to the swans at Cholent Park? But how could it?

What a shame… and on Sunday of all days.

CHAPTER 39

A Little Girl in Pabianitz

THE BUS IS ON the way to Lodz, and my heart is in Pabianitz. We won't be going to Pabianitz; it isn't on our schedule. Next on the Nefesh Yehudi itinerary is the big city of Lodz, with its proud stone buildings. Lodz, the grand city where wealthy Jewish industrialists once lived and made fortunes from factories that produced textiles and smelted metals, the city where they owned entire residential streets, lived in palatial homes, and had silver Shabbos candlesticks a meter tall. But I don't want to go to Lodz, when I haven't yet been to Pabianitz.

Pabianitz is a suburb on the outskirts of Lodz. I try to imagine it as it was just seventy years ago. Clean, narrow sidewalks, well-tended gardens, overflowing with flowers, in front of pretty houses surrounded by carved wooden fences, and one little, golden-haired girl, wearing a high-collared muslin dress and white silk stockings. Her shoes rise above her ankles, laced up to the top, and a big white bow adorns her hair. She opens the door to the house with a slim arm, looks around with her blue eyes, and calls to her Mama in Yiddish. This girl was my mother.

My mother. A little girl in Pabianitz. The tenth of Rabbi and Rebbetzin Horowitz's* eleven children, in a family de-

*Horowitz was both my father's last name and my mother's maiden name. They were distantly related.

scended from Rav Yehonasan Eybeschutz. The house is full of life. Married siblings and their little children are constantly coming in and out. Embroidered curtains cover the windows, a big grandfather clock stands near the front door, and tempting aromas fill the air. Something good is always cooking on the kerosene stove. Only during late summer is the house silent and empty, patiently waiting for the family to return from its vacation in the mountains, and then once again cheerful voices fill the rooms of this lively, yet dignified, home.

My mother's mother was an only daughter, whose father had found a *talmid chacham* to be her husband — my grandfather, Rabbi Yitzchak Aryeh Horowitz. And just like in the stories, my great-grandfather housed the young couple in his own home and fed them and their children at his own table for eighteen years while the young Torah scholar sat engrossed in study, learning and analyzing the Gemara aloud in the traditional sing-song melody.

The Talmudic melody was like an echo of life itself in that big, happy Jewish home. The children woke up to it, and it accompanied their daily routine. It was the theme song of my mother's parental home in Pabianitz, and the chorus was repeated again and again: *"Zugt di heilige Gemore..."*

I would have loved to go there, to Pabianitz, and look for that house. The house where my mother's little nephews would come, with *kasket*s on their heads, *pe'os* alongside their cheeks, and white sailor suits in honor of Pesach, each taking his turn to stand up on his chair at the Seder and sing *Mah Nishtanah* — what makes this night different? The house where my mother would invite friends to come and play, and they would say, "Nadja, who bought you that beautiful doll with eyes that open and close just like real ones?" And she would answer, "My Zeide bought it for me. He buys us everything."

I would have liked to take just a peek, to meet her older brothers, her energetic sisters, and her mother, the only daughter, the princess who raised this little empire. They were my aunts, uncles, and cousins, my grandmother and grandfather… and I never knew a thing about them.

Until my mother was thirteen, flowers still bloomed in the front yard. But after that, nothing was ever the same again. The warm, lively family was trampled underfoot by the Nazi invaders, and suddenly the melody of their lives went off-key. Strange, shrill, threatening notes sounded in its stead.

The men were taken first. The young ones were kidnapped right from the streets, and if they stayed at home, the Nazis came looking for them. They had lists of all their names and addresses. The yeshivas were all closed, of course, and the *bochurim* all went underground and disappeared from the face of the earth.

My mother's family belonged to the Gerrer Chassidus, and their large house made an excellent place for an "underground" yeshiva. The *bochurim,* who were friends of her brothers, concealed themselves in one of the rooms and continued their learning, keeping as much as possible to their normal schedule. They knew every day might be their last chance, every day they could still learn Torah was a miracle, and they must use their time well. My mother served as their sentry. An innocent-looking young girl, she could watch from the window, and whenever she spotted German soldiers in the area, she would signal to the *bochurim.*

One day, despite all their precautions, it happened. The Nazi soldiers were already near the house when she spotted them. She gave the signal, and quick as lightning the boys slipped out through the windows and made a silent dash for their hiding places. All except one boy, whose name was Frankenthal. He couldn't get to the window quickly enough, so he got into the big wardrobe instead and hid behind the clothes. The Nazis burst into the house and conducted a search. They found him huddled there, pulled him out roughly, and went off triumphantly with their prey. His friends didn't hear from him again.

They all cried over him and his bitter fate, a life cut off in its youth. A somber mood descended on the house. My mother couldn't help feeling responsible, and she was tormenting herself with guilt. Why hadn't she given the signal faster? Maybe the *bochur* would have managed to get out in time if only she'd been more alert… and so on, endlessly.

For many days, his memory haunted them all, hovering over them like a dark shadow.

Years later, at the Zeilsheim DP camp after the war ended, where those who had lost everything but their lives were trying to recover their health, Mama suddenly heard someone calling her name. She ran toward the voice, breathless. Could it be that someone from her family had just arrived here? Dare she hope that one of her loved ones was still alive?

She stood facing a Chassidic young man who bore no resemblance to her brothers. Who was this? She stood looking at him for a moment, baffled. Suddenly, she recognized him and cried out in astonishment, "Frankenthal! Is it you?!"

Yes, it was Frankenthal. The only survivor among all those *bochurim*. The one they'd all mourned was the one who lived to tell of G-d's wondrous ways. He married and raised a family, and his son, Rabbi Yissachar Frankenthal, became mayor of Bnei Brak. My parents stayed in touch with Mr. Frankenthal until his last day, and he would often say to Mama, "From your house, I was taken out and put to… life!"

CHAPTER 40

Mesirus Nefesh for a Gemara

THE NAZIS DIDN'T STOP at taking only the young men; before long they were rounding up all the Jews. My mother's family was taken to the ghetto of Pabianitz. Each person was permitted to take a suitcase containing whatever was necessary for the family. A suitcase! For a family of fourteen people, and a houseful of possessions. How do you pack up your life into one suitcase? What do you leave behind, and for how long would they have to live out of a suitcase?

Mama was thirteen years old, but she and her younger brother were the "little ones" of the family. The older ones always knew better what should be done and how, so Mama and her little brother stood aside, looking on as chaos spread through the house and panic appeared in the eyes of their elders.

Her mother was beside herself. So many people were depending on her! She flitted among the kitchen cupboards and drawers, feverishly scanning their contents and desperately wondering which items to take. Time was running out, and the suitcase just wasn't big enough. She couldn't possibly fit in the china... and there was no point in taking the silver. Finally, she selected a potato masher, flourished it like a soldier claiming his plunder, and stuffed it into the suitcase.

To this day, the image of her mother holding up that pathetic potato masher is branded on Mama's memory, encapsulating the breakdown of the world she knew, a world where things made sense.

They were hustled out of the house as if it were an emergency, with no chance to pack up and store their things or to leave a letter. It was all so unreal. A wonderful welcome to the ghetto.

All that day, chaos prevailed. Suitcases and duffel bags, people, wagons, horses, and babies… all were shoved into the ghetto as if there weren't a moment to spare. The families were all looking for someplace where they could possibly live. But nothing was possible, nothing.

Little Nadja looked around her in dismay. The whole crowded space was pervaded with fear, so thick she could smell it. The one suitcase was full of an odd assortment of things, and nothing was as it should be. But worst of all was when her father cried, "Oy! I forgot my Gemore!" and they all froze in shock. Tatte had left his Gemara at home… and the curfew had already begun. No one could go back to the house for it now. And that was the moment when all his pent-up pain and anguish spilled out to the surface.

His precious Gemara, his very life's blood, was lying there on the table in the big house, on the starched tablecloth, back there where they'd left normal life behind for this insanity.

How could this have happened? Nothing in the world was more important than the *heilige Torah*.

Mama didn't stop to consider. To her, there was no question, there was only Tatte's anguish, and the Torah he needed — that they all needed — like water to drink. This miserable, crowded space, maybe even more than the comfortable house, needed to be filled with the melody of Tatte's learning. Somehow, Mama knew that once the Gemara was here, it wouldn't be quite so dark. Some of the bright, familiar light of home would come back to them.

Silently, Mama got up, tiptoed over the mattresses that covered the floor, and felt around for her shoes. It was ten o'clock; she should be sleeping by now, but instead, she crept out of the house, slipping past the soldiers patrolling the streets until she found herself at the boundary of the ghetto. The wall hadn't been built yet. Rows of soldiers, armed with rifles, marched back and forth, blocking anyone from going in or out.

But somehow, Mama got out, not even knowing the magnitude of the risk she was taking. And then, light on her feet as a gazelle, she ran through the familiar streets toward home. With a trembling hand she opened the door, which hadn't been locked, and entered the house, breathless. The house caressed her senses with its lingering fragrances, the feel of the soft rugs under her feet, and it filled her with longing — but there was no time for that now. The Gemara lay on the table, closed and waiting. Mama picked it up, and holding it close to her heart, hurried back to the ghetto. Once again, she found a way to escape the soldiers' notice and sneak past them, unaware of how much she was risking.

Mama found the apartment where her family was housed and went inside, to her father, holding the Gemara before her like a flag of victory.

The family stared at her, stunned. What was this? "Nadja," her parents wanted to know, "where did you get that from? You went home?! How on earth..."

Her father took the Gemara and put it down. He hugged her with all the love in the world, and then he gave her a light slap on the hand with all the love in the world.

Mama was a thin little slip of a girl, who was always being urged to finish her milk or her kasha, so she would be strong and have some flesh on her bones. And she, of all the children, had sneaked out of the ghetto and back in again, past merciless, armed guards! "It was wrong of you to endanger yourself like that," her father reprimanded her, with nothing but concern in his eyes. "The Gemara isn't more important than your life. Don't ever go out again without asking our permission..."

Mama stood there, silently accepting her parents' rebuke, her lovely blue eyes fixed on the floor. She didn't know how to explain it to them. But she knew inside that she couldn't have done differently. She simply had to go and get that Gemara.

That night, the singsong melody of her father's learning filled the house once more, carrying away their pain and sorrow, their fear and confusion on the soaring notes of "*Zogt di heilige Gemore....*" Their anxious breathing slowed down, and they deeply inhaled the words, the song of life that had followed them even here. And Mama knew that although she'd risked her life, she had brought her Tatte a gift of life.

CHAPTER 41

A Straw Shoe

AND THEN ONE DAY, they were all taken away.

Mama didn't understand much of what was happening around her. She knew they'd been forced out of their home and didn't have a proper house to live in, and the life they were leading in the ghetto bore no resemblance to anything she'd ever known before. When the ghetto residents were ordered to prepare for another relocation, she had no idea how much worse it could get.

Once again, they stuffed all that was left of their belongings into suitcases, or bundled them up in sheets. Once again, they prepared food and drink for the trip from whatever they could scrape up. And once again, they assembled in the designated square, knowing there was nowhere to run, and without the faintest idea why they had to do this.

That was the last time she saw her parents. There were no tearful goodbyes, no final embraces, no last requests or parental exhortations that she must never forget, because none of them was aware that these were their last moments together.

Mama certainly didn't know it when she and her younger brother were put on a tram.

It wasn't a long trip. Soon they found themselves in the nearby city of Lodz, in the poor, run-down part of town called

Baluty, in what was to be the most notorious of ghettos.

In one day, she cast off her identity as a child tied to the apron strings of the mother she so admired. Her mother wasn't there, nor was her father, nor were any of her older siblings, except one sister who lived in Lodz. She was no longer the "little one," with all the privileges and pampering that go with the position. She was thrown all at once into a sea of troubles, and she had no choice but to sink or swim.

Mama's sister Pesya with her little son had died in the ghetto of Pabianitz. Only Pesya's daughter Rutka was left, and she went with her young aunt and uncle, Nadja and Moishe, to live in the Lodz ghetto with their older sister Sorche and her children. Just for now, they told themselves. For the meantime, until they were brought to their parents, wherever they were waiting for them.

But their parents weren't waiting for them anywhere in this world. They were resting in Gan Eden, together with all the souls of the righteous. They'd been put on trucks and taken straight to Chelmno, where they'd been murdered with bestial cruelty. But how could the children have known that?

In Lodz, everyone worked. The ghetto was one huge factory, where thousands of small, undernourished hands were kept busy from dawn to dusk. Rumkowski, the Jewish ghetto commander, held that if the ghetto were productive enough, the Nazis wouldn't liquidate it. So everyone there had to work hard. Under terrible conditions and suffering continual hunger, they worked ceaselessly.

Sorche's job was registering documents, and Mama was put to work making straw overshoes for the German soldiers, to protect them from the cold Polish winters.

She would get up in the morning and hurry to work at the improvised factory. The straw would prick her hands and leave them sore and bleeding, and the wounds wouldn't heal, because the straw would prick the same places again and again. But she had no mother to run to, no one to bandage the wounds and kiss them away.

Mama sat there for long, long hours and endless days, pricked by straw from without, and hunger from within. Taking a break wasn't an option; the big coils of straw kept appearing to replace those already sewn into shoes, and no matter how many she made, her work was never finished. If we're productive, we'll survive, was the oft-repeated slogan, and there were no compromises.

"Many days have passed since then," I tell the girls who are walking with me in the quaint alleyways and wide streets of Lodz. "The ghetto was demolished down to the ground, and the Jews, productive though they were, were sent on to the concentration camps, to the death camps. Their protectors in the ghetto didn't save them, nor did all the hard work of those young children.

"Many years have passed," I tell the girls. "Look at this city, how it's come back to life, look at the beautiful houses that once belonged to Jews. The City Hall building used to be the home of a big Jewish philanthropist. My mother survived. Her ravaged hands healed, and eventually they stroked the heads of her own little children. They peeled, chopped, and cooked healthy meals, and when they weren't busy with housekeeping, they kept a pair of knitting needles merrily clicking, as if her hands led a life of their own.

"The straw was a distant, dead memory, and it was never spoken of. Until Yad Vashem opened its new museum complex."

The girls look at me the way people look at someone who reveals the end of the story, but still leaves them in suspense.

"Yad Vashem in Jerusalem?" Shaked asks. She is from Tel Aviv, and she's asking just to make sure, but what she really means to say is, how does Yad Vashem come into this?

"Yes, in Jerusalem. The opening of the new museum was announced in all the media, and when she heard about it, Mama called me right away. 'Chana,' she said, 'next time I come to visit, take me to the museum.'"

I wasn't enthusiastic. To my mind, taking Mama there was like taking a walk across an unmarked minefield, never knowing what might explode right under your feet. But Mama had asked me to go with her, so I went, forcing myself to keep my breath steady as we passed through the dim, somber hallways.

Suddenly, we came face to face with a straw overshoe. Yes, an original straw shoe, made in the ghetto, exactly like the ones Mama made. Who knows, maybe she'd even made this one.

Mama squeezed my arm. "Look!" she said, pointing at the silent glass case, and her voice trembled. "That shoe, with the straw... it's just like the ones I used to make... exactly..."

Silence fell in the little exhibit chamber. Mama had spoken to me quietly, but her words were said so tremulously that all the other visitors heard them and sensed that something momentous was happening.

A group of policemen stopped and turned toward Mama. They looked at her, and at the shoe she was pointing at. Here was a real-life drama! Quietly, they came over, the whole group, wanting to hear what this aristocratic lady had to say, this elderly woman who had once been a young girl, making shoes like these by hand in the Lodz ghetto. She told them a bit of her story, and they gazed at her in wonder. She wasn't a picture on the wall; she was standing before them, so alive, so lovely and refined. "You're her daughter?" they asked me in awed tones. "Your mother lived through that and then married and raised a family?"

Mama smiled at the policemen who stood in a semicircle around her, silent and astounded as she listed the names of all the children and grandchildren she'd been blessed with, the little girl left to fend for herself in the ghetto of Lodz.

It was a touching moment, and the men in uniform bowed their heads in respect before Mama. She and the straw shoe had met again under new circumstances. Her hands were no longer riddled and bleeding; they were full and overflowing with Hashem's blessing.

I end my story and return to the group of girls strolling through Lodz, and to Mama, a young girl in the ghetto, who never dreamed that one day, all that would be left of that dreadful existence would be a shoe in a glass case.

CHAPTER 42

A Spoonful of Flour, a Spoonful of Sugar

THERE WAS NO SCHOOL in the ghetto. Why should there be? School wasn't productive. So Mama found herself without teachers or classmates, lessons or homework. And certainly not school trips, summer activities, or youth enrichment programs. There was nothing in her life but straw shoes and hunger.

She was fourteen years old, and until now her path in life had been straight, well paved and well lit. Now, she was in the dark, stumbling among the brambles and hoping she wouldn't fall into the next pit in this treacherous path.

In Pabianitz, before this nightmare had begun, Mama had gone to a local Jewish school, and the rest of her education had come from home. That was all so distant now, so foggy.

Mama found one friend to save her from complete isolation, a charming girl around her age. Her brother Moishe however, did not approve of the friendship.

"She's a Communist," he told Mama. "She's not our type. She wasn't brought up the way we were."

When he said "we," he meant the whole Horowitz clan of learned, pious Chassidic Jews. Mama's little brother had been in *cheder* long enough to learn a thing or two, and it was clear to him that his parents wouldn't be pleased with the friend she'd chosen.

But Mama couldn't see what was bothering him. So the girl was a Communist — what did that matter? She jumped to her friend's defense.

"She's so good to everyone," Mama argued heatedly. "I see with my own eyes how she's always helping people, how unselfish she is, and I know what a true friend she is to me."

In the ghetto, a friend meant a slice of bread when you were faint with hunger. It meant another blanket when you were lying awake, shivering. A friend wasn't something you let go of easily. But still, Moshe's words struck a chord in her heart, and it resonated painfully. Her values meant a lot to her, too.

"Go to Bnos," her little brother urged her. "They meet every Friday night. You'll find good friends there."

Bnos was an organization of older girls who'd been to the Bais Yaakov schools in the big cities. Here in the ghetto, they had found each other and formed a new group. Mama hadn't gone to Bais Yaakov; there wasn't any in Pabianitz. Those girls were much older than she was, and she didn't know them. How could she go barging into one of their meetings?

But her wise little brother knew what to say to that: "I'm sure Tatte would be happy if he knew you went."

So when Friday night came, Mama went. She could hear them singing from the ghetto apartment where they gathered; it was a song from another world. Bashful and a bit scared, she went in, wondering what sort of reception she'd get from these big girls. But she needn't have worried. They quickly made a spot for her on the crowded floor, and welcomed her like an old friend. If friendship was a slice of bread, Bnos was a whole loaf.

Every girl there felt the warm embrace of the atmosphere they created together. It was so good to be part of a group that still bubbled with youth and optimism, despite the terror raging in the streets. Their songs wafted between the windows, and their eyes sparkled as they listened to each other's words of Torah, laughed together, and most of all, planned their good deeds for the poor and sick.

After Shabbos, they gathered again. Each girl was asked to bring one spoonful of flour, and one spoonful of sugar. No more, because there wasn't any more. It was all collected in a pot, and they cooked up a porridge of sorts for the orphaned children and the sick.

Mama would go to the meetings with tightly clenched fists, one full of flour and the other full of sugar, not letting a single precious speck escape. This was her offering on G-d's altar, a sacrifice brought willingly despite the maddening hunger. Despite it all, she was still able to give to others.

Elsewhere, girls her age were finishing grade school, organizing graduation pageants, getting insulted if they were only picked for a minor role, having their picture taken, signing autograph books, and wishing each other success in high school. But Mama never went to high school. She never even finished eighth grade.

CHAPTER 43

Another Picture for the Album

Antwerp, 1967

I'm tossing and turning now in my bed. Something woke me, and I don't know what it was. The house is as silent as an ocean floor without fish, and the darkness at my window is black and dense. What was that? I ask myself, looking over enviously at my older sister, who is sleeping peacefully.

I want to go back to sleep; I've had enough of all these butterflies fluttering around in my stomach and crowding into my lungs so I can hardly breathe. My white lace Shabbos dress is draped over a wooden chair, waiting for me. Last night it was perfectly ironed and looked so pretty, but now, in the dark, it looms like a threatening mass, filling me with waves of excitement and tension. Tomorrow is the last day of school. Mama prepared my white shoes and socks, and Papa asked if there was anything else we needed and reminded us to get up early, because the photographer was coming first thing in the morning.

I feel like a jar with something fermenting in it, as if my lid will fly off any minute.

In the morning the photographer will come, like every year on the last day of school, to perpetuate the memory of this little triumph, one more year of school completed, a good year, and with a good report card, too.

We'll draw the curtains all the way shut, and we'll move the plants aside. Mama and Papa will treat it like a grand, solemn occasion. They might even look a bit pale. At least, that's how they looked last year and the year before. I don't know why they always look that way on the last day of school. They make a very big deal about these pictures, and it's very important to them that we smile and look as nice as possible.

Even in my first picture, as a chubby baby in my little bathtub, which Mama filled with pretty towels, I was smiling. Mama had combed my downy baby hair into a stylish curl in front, and I was a little baby, born into a loving, happy home, with a photographer who came especially to photograph me. Why wouldn't I smile?

Wherever we went, they took pictures of us. Mama had her own little camera for snapshots, and she even had a small movie camera with no sound recording, a hi-tech marvel in those days. But on special occasions, we always found ourselves in front of the same professional photographer and his big machine. He would get inside it, and we would smooth our collars, straighten our posture, and smile. Click, and there was another picture, another record of happy times.

When I was born, a relative in Israel, from the branch of the family that made aliyah before the war, sent us a little photo album meant to document the baby's milestones. It had empty rectangles crossed diagonally with bands of glue to hold the pictures, and under each space was a caption in Hebrew, such as "What is My Name?" "My First Tooth," and "My Favorite Food," with lines left blank alongside each picture for the parents to fill in. Papa worked laboriously to fill in the text properly. After a while, he stopped adding the handwritten lines, but the album was faithfully filled with pictures to the last page — and in every picture, I'm smiling.

There was never any need to order extra copies of these pictures. There was nobody to send them to, or to bring them out and show them to, while they responded with admiring exclamations. The pictures were for Mama and Papa, and for us.

Tomorrow is the last day of school. I'm finishing sixth grade, and before long I'll be going to high school. The photographer will come to document the great moment, and the emotion in our living room will run so high that even the walls will feel it. If they could speak, they would say, "Ah, another year has passed, another year when all was well. What an achievement! What a blessing! Can you understand that at all, Chana?"

No, I couldn't understand it. My parents' feelings were too deep for me. Trying to understand was like stepping into a sparkling lake and suddenly finding myself immersed up to the neck.

I just wish I could go back to sleep! I just wish it would be morning already!

CHAPTER 44

Shidduchim in Poland

IT'S BEEN RAINING ALL MORNING. Now the clouds are breaking up — perfect for today's plans.

The trip leaders take us across a wide avenue to a sidewalk café, where we sit down at small tables, forming discussion groups.

"Oy, it's so cold!" I say, and what I really mean is, "I'm so nervous!" I've only led a discussion group once before in my life, and that was in Agudath Israel, when I was a teenager, unless you count all the discussions with my children at the supper table over the years.

And here I am with a group of young women who seem perfectly at ease, and Shaked, the de facto spokeswoman of the group, is saying, "We'd like to hear about your real life. What's it like raising a large family? Where do you put eight kids in a three-room apartment? How do you remember who likes what in his sandwich, and who has what club today after school? And most of all, we want you to tell us the inside story about arranged marriages. I mean, really, Chana — you meet a guy three times and then you marry him? What if you don't want to? And please don't tell us that never happens..."

They want the truth, they don't want me to gloss it over, and they have a thousand questions. "What do you do on a date? Do you have to talk only *divrei Torah*? Does the girl have to wear high heels? What if she doesn't want to go out with him? Is it true that the parents decide for her?"

The questions came like a flood, but the kind of flood that does no harm. It's the easiest thing in the world to talk about everyday life as it really is — having the children take turns with morning chores, bunk beds and triple trundle beds, jolly Shabbos meals, going over the teacher's weekly newsletter.... This is all that's needed to peel away layers of preconceived ideas and old stigmas that nobody put there on purpose; it's just that they've always been there.

"Did you get married through a *shidduch*?" they ask me suspiciously, and when I say, "Yes!" they find it hard to believe.

"All right. So tell us what it's like." Well, at least they believe me now. "They send a girl from Antwerp to Israel and tell her, 'Go to such-and-such an address; your bridegroom is waiting for you there'?"

I can't help laughing. "No, no! You are so funny!"

"Well, tell us, then."

But it's a long story, and our schedule is tight, and my cola is rapidly losing the last of its fizz. "Are you sure we have time?" I ask them.

"Yes, yes!" They're burning with curiosity. "Tell us, you've got to!"

I took a deep breath, and went back in time... I was nineteen, an energetic young woman, and busy as six people put together, somewhere in Antwerp....

Antwerp, 1973

The night would always come too early for me, and my little wall lamp worked overtime. The school year was ending, and we'd been studying for exams day and night. If I hadn't run out of ink for my fountain pen and been forced to go out and buy a new bottle, I probably wouldn't have seen sunlight all that week.

Schoolwork wasn't my whole life, though. I had friends and programs, Agudath Israel activities and summer camp, and the Bnos annual performance.

All the women and girls of the Antwerp Jewish community were invited to the performance. I approached the management of the big theater in town, and they agreed to lend us professionally made costumes. The tickets were quickly sold out, and everyone in the family could have recited my lines in their sleep.

I wanted my married sister Tzili to be there, too, and very much hoped she could come from Israel a few days ahead of time.

I loved it when they came to visit, a happy, smiling young couple that brought sunshine into the house every time they stepped over our threshold. I wasn't a little girl anymore; I was a young lady finishing high school, and I adored my first little nephew, a handsome baby in a big pram with high, spoked wheels, who held out his arms to anyone willing to take him out of there… and I was always more than willing.

And then they would fly home again, saying goodbye with hugs and tears, not knowing how hard it was for my parents to see them go.

They went back to their own affairs, and I went back to mine.

It never crossed my mind that my sister wasn't quite as innocent as I'd always thought. She wasn't just sitting quietly in her home in Israel, but was busily weaving a net that would capture me.

While I was running around merrily, meeting with friends and filling my days with all sorts of activities, she was sitting at home, crossing out the names of young men she didn't think were suitable for me.

She obtained the lists from the heads of the best yeshivas in Israel, and she sat, patient and industrious as a worker ant, reviewing the information she'd received, crossing out the candidates that didn't meet her criteria, and leaving only the names of the young men who seemed like potentially good matches for her temperamental sister with the high spiritual aspirations…. and especially those who wanted to live in Eretz Yisrael and would bring her little sister with them from the Belgian Diaspora… "He's a fantastic boy," she wrote to me, when she believed she'd found the right one at last.

"I've checked him out thoroughly, and you can rely on me," she wrote in her next letter, after she'd made inquiries and found him suitable in every way. "You must come and meet him."

She went on to tell me all the excellent information she'd found out about him. "Chana, he's perfect for you!" she enthused.

My parents read the letter over and over again. But I wasn't impressed. I didn't see marriage on my horizon yet. "There's nothing to talk about," I wrote to Tzili. "I'm not flying all the way to Israel to meet a boy, and anyway, Papa and Mama have to see him first."

First... as if I had anything in mind that would come second. I wasn't interested in meeting any young men at all. I was so young, and I had a whole summer camp to deal with.

I thought I'd managed to shake her off, and she'd stop pestering me now.

I'd been chosen to manage that year's summer camp. It didn't take place on a permanent campground, like the camps in America, but rather, in a different pastoral location every year. And although Europe is full of beautiful country settings of all sorts, we'd made the bold decision to have camp in Israel that year, where the air was still full of the heady optimism that followed the Six Day War. The flight was booked for the beginning of summer.

Camp took five exhilarating weeks. We traveled from north to south in open trucks, seated on two long benches that jumped with every bump on the road, until we saw the Sinai Peninsula spread out before us, orange, glowing, and breathtaking. The hot wind blew in our faces and harmonized with the songs we sang. We were intoxicated with our beautiful land, with the white sand of Sinai and the sapphire blue of the sea.

At Sharm el-Sheikh, we set up tents, and all the Belgian girls, accustomed to European comforts, slept happily on the hard ground, rolled up in sleeping bags, while mosquitoes hummed lullabies.

There was hardly anything to eat, as it was a shemittah year. We were almost living on bread and water, but the incredible view was enough to satisfy us.

When my sister heard about my travel plans, she wouldn't accept any more excuses. So, on one of the last evenings of camp, I mumbled something about stomach pains (and I wasn't making them up — they were real!) and sent the girls off on their own for the next leg of the tour.

Then I dragged myself back to our lodgings, put on high heels, buttoned up my Shabbos dress, and went to meet the boy who would become my husband. He was the first young man I ever met, and right from the start I knew he would be the last. The girls went back to Belgium without me, joking about their brave leader's stomach pains, and leaving me free to continue dating without pretexts.

Suddenly, my whole life changed. I found myself calling for my father to come quickly and meet the young man before I became engaged to him. My father came, was favorably impressed, and came back with the whole family for the Yamim Nora'im and Succos. And then came the surprise attack from Egypt, and the Yom Kippur War was upon us, putting all our plans on hold. When the "blackout" order was lifted at last, we celebrated our engagement and made it official.

I tell this whole story in brief to the girls around the table, as they lean forward hungrily to catch every word. "This is the truest story I can tell you about *shidduchim*, girls," I say, "the story of a young woman who feels sure of the choice she'd made, and is so happy with the first young man she's ever dated… and here is my family." The girls are dumbstruck now, as I spread the pictures on the table. "And every one of them got married through a *shidduch*."

CHAPTER 45

Mama's Vow

THE SILENCE OF THIS Jewish cemetery in Lodz speaks loud and clear.

The stones tell the sad story of the place. They tell it all the time, wearied by the years and by the people, but the story never gets tired. It remains alive and poignant.

It is a story of great wealth, splendor, security, and financial stability. Those are the first chapters, and you can feel it in the smooth, beautiful marble stones, see it in the imposing wall, and then have your picture taken beside the grand mausoleum of the Poznanski family, which looks like a miniature palace, and speaks of the zenith of Jewish life in Lodz, when textile magnates rode in fine carriages, women wore fur coats, and little girls had gold jewelry and fashionable dresses.

But then comes the end of the story, such a tragic ending that one cannot read it without crying.

The story is told by thousands of newer graves, unmarked by any stone, which were dug ceaselessly, every day, for the burial of the victims of plague and starvation in the Lodz ghetto. A whole horizon of hastily-dug graves, and a row of open pits, dug for those who were saved at the last minute.

The great, echoing silence is the closing chapter of the story, a silence that is broken at times by the footsteps of tourists, by the clicking of cameras, and by the recitation of a few *Tehillim*, and that's it, until the next visit.

In the cemetery's upscale *taharah* chamber, where the bodies of the deceased are cleansed and prepared for burial, I tell my mother's story:

When her parents were taken, Mama was left in the Lodz ghetto with her married sister Sorche and her younger brother Moishe. Sorche lived in the ghetto with her mother-in-law. Sorche's husband was an only child, born after twenty-five childless years of marriage. He was all his mother had in the world, and she couldn't be separated from him. And then one day, there was an *aktion*. The mother came home that evening and learned that her son had been taken away with the other men, to an unknown fate. The only son, whom she'd spent a quarter of a century praying for, was gone.

This was beyond the elderly woman's strength. She sank to the floor, before the eyes of her daughter-in-law, her little grandchildren, and Mama, who was then sixteen years old.

There was a commotion as people ran to bring water, wet towels, and whatever folk remedies were available. But all their attempts at resuscitation were in vain. The mother's heart was too weak to bear the terrible news, and she lay there on the cold ghetto floor, lifeless as a stone.

Sorche, still in shock from having her husband snatched away, now covered her mother-in-law's body with a sheet. As there was no man around who could help, she sent Mama to go and alert the Chevra Kaddisha.

Death was rampant in the ghetto, and the Chevra Kaddisha had its hands full to overflowing. No one was coming to collect the body. They hardly took notice of her. Mama had no choice but to pluck up her courage and speak up more assertively. "We have a dead woman in the house," she said.

"We'll come to bury her," they answered curtly. "But do the *taharah* in the meantime."

"Me? Do the *taharah*?"

"Yes, you." The man barely looked in her direction. Mama thought she would faint. She hardly knew what *taharah* was, and she had no idea how it was done. She, a little teenager, was supposed to perform the ritual cleansing of a deceased, elderly woman?

They told her, step by step, without preface, what she must do. "And then we'll come and bury her. You have to understand, child, there is no one else to do it."

And Mama, being Mama, went back to the apartment, biting her lips and holding back the waves of shock and horror that threatened to engulf her. She removed the sheet from the corpse and did as she'd been instructed. Her feelings were put aside, locked up in a safe. There was no place here for such luxuries now. And at that moment, Mama made a vow: If this horrific war ever came to an end, and if she should still be among the living, and life should return to normal, she vowed to volunteer to serve in a Chevra Kaddisha and perform this mitzvah of her own free will... if only that day would come, and she would be saved from this inferno...

It was a vow made from the tears she didn't cry. There was no time, no space for them at that moment.

Years later, Mama began living a normal life in Belgium. Carefully, she opened the safe, and there she found her vow. She went to the Chevra Kaddisha in Antwerp and asked to join as an occasional volunteer. They wouldn't even hear of it. "This is no place for you!" they told her firmly. "You're a young woman with little children!"

But Mama wouldn't be deterred. "I made a *neder*," she told them. "Back then, in Poland... I made a vow and I can't break it."

What could they say to that? They gave in, and once every few weeks, she went to help perform a *taharah*, thanking G-d for saving her, and remembering what she'd been through, which others could never understand. We children didn't know, of course. We only knew that once in a while, the phone would ring and a mysterious male voice would ask for Madame Horowitz. It was the man from the Chevra Kaddisha, but Mama never told us who it was, or where she was going.

We stand in the *taharah* chamber of the cemetery in Lodz, and I tell the girls this story.

We can almost see the young girl, timidly approaching the Chevra Kaddisha, looking around for someone who will listen to her. We can imagine this room, full of men who cannot cope with so much death. They mark each grave in some minimalist fashion and write down the details in a notebook. Finally they turn to her, rushed and distracted, and say, "Do the *taharah* in the meantime." In the ghetto of Lodz, death was the only thing that they had more of every day. And my mother was here.

My voice fades, there in the *taharah* chamber, and we walk away, shaken and deep in thought.

Outside the bus window, Lodz passes by. Lovely trees, squares with monuments, red brick houses, churches.

As we move away from the cemetery, I tell them about the dream.

"Did anyone go around without a dream when she was fifteen?"

The girls smile. Their teen years are not so long gone; they can still reach out and touch them. Their dreams were so big, and so full of air, that it's both easy and hard to remember them.

Who doesn't have dreams? Dreams of something great, of a future she yearns for, of an apex to reach.... People keep their dreams in a hidden place in their heart. They don't reveal them to others, for fear that they'll extinguish them before they ever catch fire, and take the air out of them before they float up to the skies.

When my mother was fifteen, she had a dream, too. It wasn't a dream of achieving fame, or of owning a beautiful home, or of a fabulous trip abroad.

In Mama's dream, there was nothing but a huge loaf of bread. A big, fragrant, fresh loaf like the ones she dimly remembered from the tiled brick oven in Pabianitz, from those distant days of her childhood. A great big loaf that you keep cutting slices from, and there's still plenty left. A loaf of bread that's enough for everyone... they can even have seconds and thirds and not use it up. That was Mama's great dream, and she relished it secretly and often. She dreamed of it in her fitful sleep, and it was the stuff of her daydreams as she worked — a big, endless loaf of bread.

The real ruler of the ghetto was hunger. It ran people's lives. It pinched them and hit them. It took over their thoughts, their feelings, and their dreams, and in the end it killed them, leaving them expiring on the streets, begging for a bit of food.

Two hundred thousand Jews were crowded into that ghetto, in that dilapidated part of town without running water, closed in as if in a sealed tin can.

In other ghettos there were stories of children who crept out at night to sell their mother's wedding ring for a sack of flour or beets. But in the Lodz ghetto, there was no getting past the wall. No one could climb over it or dig under it. It was closely guarded, the Judenrat kept order strictly, the Nazis would shoot at close range, and the Poles outside the wall weren't interested in selling any food. Seventy percent of Lodz's Polish citizens were ethnic Germans who supported the Nazi regime, and far be it from them not to hand over a hungry Jewish child to the authorities.

In Lodz, all the work was done within the ghetto walls. That closed off yet another way of obtaining food, which was sometimes available to Jews who lived in other ghettos and worked outside the walls.

Even Hans Biebow, the Nazi administrator of the ghetto, requested an increase in food rations for the ghetto inmates. He was profiting from their slave labor, and he realized that they couldn't be sustained on their current rations, but his request was denied. Trapped without adequate food and with no source of help from the outside, the ghetto population was dying of starvation.

Mama was alone. She woke up with hunger pangs every morning and lay down to sleep still craving food. She had no mother who would give her a bit of her own bread, and no father who might somehow organize a bit of extra food for her. Hunger was larger than life, and it gnawed at them constantly.

Sometimes their rations included paper-thin slices of horsemeat. Mama's brother Moishe would hand her his slice. "Take it, Nadja, this isn't for me," he would say. "This meat is *treif*."

"But you must eat it. It's a matter of life or death," she would insist. She was his big sister, and he was the little one, so thin he was nearly invisible. "No, I mustn't!" he would answer, his eyes flashing with an inner flame. "If Heaven has decreed that I should live, I can live without this revolting meat, and if it's been decreed that I should die, why shouldn't I die kosher and pure?"

There was nothing more she could say to him. He wouldn't eat the meat, even to save his life.

Both of them continued to hunger, with a hunger that went on day after day, year after year, and was never satisfied. And these were their teenage years, when they required more food to support their transition to adulthood. But there was no more to be had, no end in sight, and no way to cope but to retreat into dreams. One big, endless loaf of bread that could satisfy the hunger of both body and soul.

Years later, when I had children of my own, and I'd learned that Mama had been in that terrible ghetto, I asked her what it was like living in the shadow of hunger.

"We were hungry," she said. "Very hungry."

I waited for her to say more. I wanted to know how a sixteen-year-old girl could cope with such terrible hunger, without parents and with a younger brother to worry about. But Mama had nothing to add. "We were very hungry," she said simply. What more was there to say?

CHAPTER 46

Good Children

Antwerp, 1964

Today is Monday. It's cold and gray outside, but once in a while the sun shows its face between the clouds, as if it were a royal princess coming out to greet the cheering crowd.

I'm walking home from school with Faigy and Jeanette. Our brown leather schoolbags swing to the rhythm of our step, and my friends' cheeks are pink in the bright, cold air. Today we learned a new song in Hebrew, and we're trying to recall the lyrics, all about citrus groves, golden oranges, and blue skies.

We started learning Hebrew this year, and we roll the words on our tongues as if they were a new and surprising food. The teacher announced at the beginning of the year that all our kodesh classes would be conducted in Hebrew from now on, without a word of French, and we're all bravely trying to live up to the challenge.

Our secular subjects classes are actually in Flemish, not French, ever since fifth grade. The government wants Flemish to be the official language. But French is still the main language we speak with our friends, never mind what the government decided.

We know English well, too, and also Yiddish, of course, which we don't learn in school, but we hear it at home. All of our parents speak Yiddish at home, and that's the language we speak with them. That's how it is in Antwerp: we switch between five languages like walking into another room in the house, without even stopping to think about it.

Near my house, we stop to chat a little more before we part. "What day is it?" Faigy suddenly asks. "Oh," she remembers. "It's Monday. What do you have for dinner on Mondays?"

"On Mondays? Oy, Faigy, why do have to spoil things?" The sun disappears behind a cloud, a gray fog envelops me, Faigy goes on her way, and I climb the steps to our front door like a tired old elephant with a thorn in its foot. Why should I hurry if we're having steak?

Every Monday, we have steak. It doesn't matter what errands Mama has to do, or what mood we're in that day — the steak will be waiting for us on the table without fail.

I love our Sunday dinner. On Sunday we have chicken schnitzel, farfel, and a delicious, thick vegetable soup with lokshen, and nobody has to prod me to eat… On Wednesdays, though, we have beef liver with spinach and mashed potatoes.

Spinach isn't something that children like, and liver isn't, either. But food is something you eat, not something you love. Love is for your best friend in school and for Mama and Papa at home, but food you just eat, because you must, not because you love it. And on Wednesday you eat liver and spinach, because that's what we eat on Wednesday.

I wish it were Thursday, even though I know it's Monday and wishing won't change it. I always hurry home on Thursday, bypassing the long avenue and taking a shortcut, hopping like a bird all the way. Because on Thursdays, Mama makes a dairy meal. From outside the door I can already smell the fresh, creamy tomato soup with rice, and the fried sole with tiny potatoes that melt in your mouth. And for dessert, we always have sweet cheese blintzes! Oh, I wish it were Thursday.

But today is Monday, and we're having steak, and it's as large and tough as the sole of a man's shoe. We could chew it all day and never be finished chewing…. Mama sets up a little hand-cranked grinder and puts pieces of the steak through it, slowly turning the crank. Tiny bits of meat fall nonchalantly into the bowl of soup she's placed underneath. And now, after all that effort, and with plenty of good will, we can finish eating our steak. Good children have to eat everything on their plates, Mama always says, and we try very hard to be good children.

Papa looks on with a twinkle in his eye as Mama grinds the steak with gentle determination, and then he turns to her and whispers in Yiddish, "Let them be! They'll be all right! Roize used to say, 'A hungry child eats, and if a child doesn't eat, that means he isn't hungry.'"

Roize was a young girl who lived with Papa's family in Krakow before the war, something between a foster child and a servant. She had lots of wise Jewish sayings that Papa often quoted, and recalling those good old days always seemed to ignite a cheerful spark in him, as if he were transported back to that kitchen in Poland where you could see the mulberry tree right outside the window.

But Mama doesn't much care what Roize always said. She will sit with us patiently until we've finished that whole big steak, and only then will she begin washing the porcelain dishes. And as the bits of steak fall into the soup, Roize's wise sayings echo in the background. Before the war… before the war…. So there was a war, of course there was, but what was it all about, and what happened in the war?

Ah, but that wasn't a question that children asked. It wasn't a question that anyone asked. There was a war, and it was over. Why talk about it now? Now, all we have to do is finish up all our food. Good children don't leave healthy food on their plates.

CHAPTER 47

From Lodz to Auschwitz

EVENTUALLY, MY MOTHER WAS taken away from Lodz.

She didn't know where she was going. She was shoved into an overcrowded, stifling train car, holding hands with her niece Rutka, who was close to her own age, and trying to locate her older sister.

Outside, people were still being loaded onto the train. Everyone still left in the ghetto was there — tens of thousands, with sunken features and bony limbs. The survivors of shattered families. This was the last and biggest *aktion*, the final liquidation of the Lodz ghetto.

And still, they didn't know where the train was going, and what sad song the train wheels were playing on the iron tracks. For hour after miserable hour, pressed together unbearably, the Jews were trapped in the swaying, rattling train cars, moving steadily toward the unknown.

When the doors were opened at last, the light of day was frighteningly bright, illuminating the awful scene that met their eyes as they were hustled off the train. Men with shaved heads in striped prison uniforms, barking dogs, screaming, club-swinging Germans in polished boots, and lining up for selection on the unloading ramp.

This was the usual "welcome to Auschwitz" ceremony. Jews

throughout Poland had heard the horror stories about Auschwitz. But not in the hermetically sealed ghetto of Lodz. Mama didn't know what this place was. Auschwitz meant nothing to her. She and the rest of the Jews from the transport were completely bewildered.

Someone came over to her and Rutka — a shaven-headed man in a striped uniform. "Tell them you're seventeen," he said quietly, urgently, and quickly moved on. A Jew who came to save them at the very gates of Gehinnom…

They understood from the man's tone that his advice was not to be questioned. And so, when they stood before the Nazi doctor to be quickly assessed for their worth to the Reich, his lethal hand sent Sorche and her children to the left. Moishe, too, was deemed unfit and sent to the left. Only Mama and Rutka were directed to the right.

They clung to Sorche's hand and protested. "But we have to stay together!" they cried, wept, and pleaded.

They didn't know this was Auschwitz, and that the Angel of Death presided over the selection. They didn't know how dangerous it was to insist on staying together. But the soldier in charge of keeping order knew what to do. He shouted and hit, and Sorche was dragged away with the little ones to be sacrificed on the altar. The two remaining girls were led to the barracks. They had been chosen for life.

What happened next? How did those thousand young women feel when their mothers, husbands, or siblings were ripped away from them all at once? How did they feel when they were stripped of their possessions, the clothes on their backs, and their personal dignity? What were their thoughts when they smelled the smoke billowing from the crematorium?

These are questions that cannot be answered in words. No words have been created to describe such things. And anyone who wasn't there could never begin to know what it was like.

But they didn't take everything away from Mama. She still

had her niece Rutka, and Rutka still had Mama, and at that moment, an unbreakable bond of friendship was forged between the two.

She still had a hand to hold when the suffering overwhelmed her, and a shoulder to lean on. There was still a listening ear to whisper to at night, and eyes she could always look at and know they understood what she was saying, and she understood their story, too.

She had someone in the world to care about, someone who loved her and was there for her at the end of the day. It was the kind of friendship that gives you a reason, that gives you the strength, to go on living.

In those dark, turbid waters of grief, helplessness, dread, death, and despair, their friendship was like a boat with a taut, white sail, gleaming as it somehow stayed afloat.

CHAPTER 48

Tante Rutka from America

Antwerp, 1966

The delivery man from the laundry came today, so I hurry to get into my nightgown before anybody else. I love to unfold it and hear that little krechz, as if it were complaining because I'm spoiling all the nice, neat folds they made at the laundry.

It feels so good to wear a starched nightgown, with that special fragrance of fresh laundry.

"Isabelle's Laundry!" the delivery man says into the intercom when he arrives, his arms full of sheets, folded and piled in a tall bundle. I always run to the door to see how the jumbled bag of laundry we brought them comes back in a perfect pile, like smooth sheets of paper fresh from the printer.

Once every few weeks, Mama brings all our sheets, tablecloths, and nightclothes to the laundry, and when they're brought back to us, the house fills up with that familiar, pleasant smell. Then Mama makes the beds and puts the extra sheets away in the cupboards, and I get my delicious, fresh nightgown, starched and ironed, all ready for a night of sweet dreams.

Tonight, I choose to dream of America. I imagine myself boarding a real jet plane that crosses the sky like a big bird and lands in America. And then I go to meet Tante Rutka's family.

Tante Rutka's children are in all the pictures she sends, and they're mentioned in every letter she writes to Mama. We have whole picture albums of her family, but I've never seen any of them in person. Mama flew to America to see them last year, but I didn't. A plane ticket is expensive, and children don't just fly to America for a visit.

Mama always shows us the pictures, and she tells us a lot about what Tante Rutka writes in her letters. We know which one of the children just started school, and which one just got her first tooth, so we almost feel like we really know them all.

"Are they our cousins, like Pinkusewitz?" I once asked Mama, while we were picking out nice pictures to send to Tante Rutka.

*"No, no," Mama said with a smile. "Not first cousins. Rutka is my niece."**

---

*Rutka really was the only surviving relative Mama had after the war, and they shared a bond that only two girls who had gone through Gehinnom together, hand in hand, could appreciate.

They kept up a lively correspondence, each of them writing a long, detailed letter twice a week. And one day, when I was already a young married woman living in Israel, my father called me, very distraught. He had just gotten word that Rutka had died suddenly of a stroke. She was only forty-four. She had four children at home, and she did not live to see them married. It was Papa who received the message, but he couldn't bring himself to tell Mama; it would be taking too much away from her. Worst of all was that letters from Rutka continued to arrive that week, and Mama couldn't have dreamed that her niece had left this world just days ago. My sister Tzili was recruited to break the news, and she went on a surprise visit to Belgium. Mama was overjoyed; it wasn't every day that her eldest daughter visited from abroad. Tzili went out with Mama, looked for the right sort of place to break the news, tried to formulate the right words... and failed. There was no right place, no right words. She returned to Israel defeated. "I didn't manage to tell Mama," she said. It was my turn to try. I gathered up all my courage and flew to Belgium. Mama was thrilled; it wasn't every day that her married daughters missed her so much that they both flew in within such a short span of time. But I didn't manage to tell her, either. Rutka was part of Mama's very soul — how could I take a piece of her soul from her? In the end, Papa found the words and told her. Mama was shattered with grief. She and Papa stayed in touch with Rutka's children, treating them like their

"Your niece?! But Mama, isn't she your sister?"

"She's like a sister to me," Mama said, still smiling, but for a second, a shadow flickered across her eyes. And then she was happy again, and we continued going through the latest family pictures. And I knew I mustn't ask any more questions. What did it matter, anyway? Sister, niece... someday we would meet, and that was all that mattered. Maybe they would come to Belgium? No, I'd rather go and see them in America. What an exciting dream that would be, to fly to America in a jet plane!

---

own. They helped to marry them off, and made sure to keep up with the news of every grandchild that was born. To this day, we are one big family. Rutka's children and grandchildren are all *bnei Torah,* following in the way of their ancestors in Pabianitz, and they still send us their latest pictures, just as Rutka always did.

CHAPTER 49

A Roll and Herring

NOTHING AWAITED MAMA AND Rutka in Auschwitz. Not death, and not life. No work, and no slice of bread. Nothing but unbearable suspense.

They hadn't been given a meal since their arrival. They, and the rest of the women deemed fit to serve the Reich, were simply left in the barracks, waiting for the unknown. What was going to be done with them? Why weren't they giving them anything to eat? Were they going to kill them? Death crouched at the door the whole time, but didn't come in.

And then they were taken to Hamburg. They found themselves at the Hamburg-Sasel labor camp, where they were required to join work crews that were clearing away rubble and rebuilding houses destroyed by the Allied forces. Mama and Rutka were now two more out of thousands of starved women put to backbreaking labor.

But they were together, sharing the extremely hard, intensive work, the short hours of sleep, the harsh shouts of their taskmasters, the miserable rations that could never satisfy their hunger, and the knowledge that every day of life was another miracle, in this place where anything could be punishable by death, if disease or starvation didn't claim them first.

Their day began with the sharp cry of the wake-up alarm that propelled them from their bunks. Shivering under their shabby work dresses, the girls and women would run to the *Appellplatz* for the predawn roll call, as the prolonged screech of the alarm continued its assault on their ears.

Lining up for roll call was the same every day: standing at attention, motionless, for no reason other than to humiliate them and leave them open to any sort of sadistic abuse that struck the fancy of the commander, who strutted between the rows swinging his whip.

One morning, it was pouring rain, but they had to stand there as usual, in perfectly straight lines, with the rain beating on their faces, soaking their dresses, and chilling their emaciated bodies. Mama stood there, silently murmuring the Morning Blessings, as she did every day. She had no *siddur*, and davening the whole morning service was impossible; it belonged to another time, another world where life was normal. Here, there was nothing to life but staying alive for one more day. But every morning, Mama said *Birkos HaShachar* under the nose of the Nazi with the whip. No one could take the Divine spark of her soul from her, and that short segment of the daily prayers was a window through which its light shone.

That morning it was harder. It was very cold, and she was soaked through. The ground under their feet had turned to mud, but the commander went on as usual, up and down the rows, abusing the young women as if they weren't suffering enough.

Mama recited the blessings silently, and just when she came to the *brachah* of *"shelo asani goy,"* the Nazi passed by her. He was well protected from the rain in his long, heavy coat, his polished boots, his officer's cap, and his gloves. He had everything they didn't have. He embodied power and strength, while they were defenseless, weak, and exposed.

But Mama looked him in the eye, through the pouring rain, thinking for an extra moment about the *brachah* she was about to say. What a blessing not to be a gentile like that one, even with all his power, strength, and splendid uniform! Suddenly, fear left her, and she was filled with clarity.

The rain continued beating down on their heads, filling their dresses with water. But Mama was lifted above all that. She was above this Nazi, with his bloodthirsty eyes and his whip. She was drawing in all his strength. She felt nothing but scorn for him, and nothing but pride that she was not in his place, striking out at young, defenseless women. *"Baruch Atah Hashem… shelo asani goy."*

The terrible hunger that raged in the camp brought on an epidemic of typhus that ran wild through the barracks, snatching young women and leaving them to die in the absence of any proper medical care.

Mama caught the infection, too. Burning up with fever, writhing in pain, and half-conscious, she was taken to the infirmary. In the bed next to hers lay another girl, delirious with fever and mumbling unintelligibly. The high, uncontrolled fever caused strange delusions. Suddenly, the girl turned to Mama with glassy eyes and said clearly and eagerly, "Could you please get me a roll and some herring? I've just got to have it, a white roll and herring. Please!"

A white roll, and herring? She must have a very high fever and a lot of imagination to be asking for something like that. She might just as soon have asked for the moon.

Mama began to recover, which was a miracle, since she wasn't getting any medicine. She went back to Rutka and her other friends, weak and shaky, but out of danger. The strange request of the girl in the infirmary retreated to the back of her mind.

A few hours later, some items were thrown over the fence that separated their camp from the men's camp and landed on the ground near them. The men didn't have any better conditions than the women, but sometimes if a man managed to steal or barter for some extra food, the thought that his wife, sister, or daughter might be on the other side of the fence moved him to toss it over to the women's side. There were certain times of day when the Nazis weren't watching closely and the "mail delivery" took place.

Mama went over to the fence when she noticed the first items flying over, and suddenly a little bundle landed at her feet. She picked it up, opened it, and froze in disbelief. It was one white roll, and a little packet of herring.

The image of the girl in the infirmary rose up before her. She saw the pleading eyes, glassy pools of suffering.

According to the rules, she was supposed to share her prize with her closest friends. It was an unwritten, but sacred law. Everyone shared; that was the only way to survive. And her friends were looking at her expectantly. But Mama made a special appeal to them: "There's girl in the infirmary, and she asked me for a roll and herring today. And of all things, that's exactly what I found here! It might be her last request. We must give it to her!"

"You're not being rational," they told her, their eyes flashing hungry fire. "That girl is dying, and this food won't save her. But it could save us!"

But Mama didn't see it that way. How could it be that a roll and herring, of all things, had just fallen at her feet, if it wasn't meant for that poor, sick girl? "We wouldn't dream of asking for something like this," she said. "And we certainly would never expect to get it. But that girl, in her delirium, asked for precisely this. Her last request! How can we refuse?"

Mama won the argument. She went to the so-called infirmary, where the sick were left to get well miraculously or to die, and with trembling hands she offered the little meal to the dying girl. The girl took it in her hands, not sure whether it was real or part of a hallucination.

That was Mama.

One day, many years later, someone told Mama that Malka Wolf from Bnei Brak had sent regards. "Malka Wolf?" Mama scrolled through her memory, trying in vain to remember someone by that name. No, she didn't know any Malka Wolf. The regards must have been meant for someone else.

And then one day, Mama herself was in Bnei Brak, and a lady of impressive bearing came over to her. "I'm Malka Wolf," she said, almost choking with emotion. "Don't you recognize me?" Mama gazed at the woman's face for another moment, and suddenly, she recognized the eyes. Big, blue eyes... a high fever... Hamburg... delirium... a roll with herring.

"Is it you?!" Mama grabbed her by the shoulders, as if to verify that she wasn't seeing a ghost. "You mean you survived?!"

"Yes, it's me. I had *techiyas hameisim*. The shadow of death was closing in on me. I felt my life running short, like the last bit of sand in an hourglass. And then, suddenly, a hand reached out to me, breaking through that dark fog — a hand bringing me a roll and herring. I held that roll in my hands, and I felt new strength flowing into me. It came from knowing that someone had thought of me... someone saw me... someone heard my cry... someone cared... and suddenly I knew I could make it... I knew I deserved to live... and I began to get well.

"I don't know how you got that roll and herring. It was surely a miracle, and many more miracles got me through the rest of the war, and all this time I've been searching for you. I found out your name, but I didn't know where you were. And now, finally, I've found you!"

Mama's eyes were full of tears. "I was surely going to die that night," said Malka. "When you came to me with that little package, that was the turning point. I owe my life to you.

CHAPTER 50

Experiences with Trains

WE'RE ON A TRAIN platform in Lodz, and we've been asked to wait. The group ahead of us hasn't departed yet, and the trains are a bit behind schedule.

A group of Israeli high-school students is waiting to board the next train. Loud and boisterous, they're shouting to each other across the crowd and taking pictures of their friends, who return the favor and take pictures of them. Their teacher, a purposeful-looking woman, tries in vain to establish some order and decorum. She argues with three boys who are busily snapping "selfies," and scolds a few girls for chewing gum. The whole scene looks like an annual school trip to the north of Israel in the summer heat, with an Egged tour bus patiently waiting.

Our group looks on with forbearing smiles, keeping a distance to avoid getting into their pictures and being caught in the middle of all the shouting. No one says anything, but we all have a strong sense of the gap between them and us, the experience they are having versus ours. After they leave, we wait a little while longer, and the silence feels like a summary of what hasn't been said. Ours is such a different sort of trip....

An old, shabby, wooden-sided railroad car arrives to pick us up. In trains like this, Jews were taken to the last stop, to their final destination in this world. We crowd in, and everything is shut out. There is nothing to experience but a chilling realization that right here, packed in tightly with others desperate to live, someone's lungs tried to inhale the oxygen that was depleted, someone's eyes looked for a window that wasn't there, someone asked for a drink of water that was gone... Someone held a little baby, or the hand of a little girl, someone was next to her husband or her mother, and what? What did they feel?

The girls are having difficulty finding a place for themselves here. There is no room in this car, no room for anything; it is all packed with the people who were here, and their cries and their pain are still here all around us.

The rabbi tells the story of Azriel Dovid Fastag, a Modzitzer Chassid and a *chazzan,* who was in a packed, windowless train car like this, locked in, speeding toward death. Suddenly a melody came to him as if of its own accord, stealing into his heart and spreading through him like a great, powerful wave. Next came the words to the melody, the immortal words, *"Ani ma'amin be'emunah sheleimah b'vias haMashiach..."* *

Fastag began to sing the song in his beautiful voice, and others around him picked up the melody and joined him in singing. And then he made his last request: If anyone there ever had the chance to go to the Modzitzer Rebbe in America and convey this song to him, he promised that person half of his share in the World to Come. Two youths managed to break some planks in the roof of the car, escape, and jump off. One was killed in the fall, but the other survived. Eventually he made his way to Israel, where he met the Modzitzer Rebbe's son, and through him, conveyed the song to the Rebbe in New York.

Azriel Dovid Fastag was long in Gan Eden by that time, but

---

*From the Thirteen Principles of Faith: "I believe with perfect faith in the coming of the Messiah, and even though he may tarry, nevertheless I shall wait every day for him to come."

his song lives on to this day. When the Modzitzer Rebbe heard the song and the story behind it, he said, "When the Mashiach comes, we will all go out to greet him, singing this melody."

As the rabbi ends the story, music begins to play, softly at first. The violinist is playing the tune that was composed in a cattle car like this, on the way to Treblinka. The girls allow the music to engulf them. They become the strings on which it plays, lifting up, rising, and the ancient words pluck them, one by one: *"Ani ma'amin, ani ma'amin, ani ma-a-amin, be'emunah sheleimah, be'emunah sheleimah, b'vias haMashiach, b'vias haMashiach ani ma-a-amin…."*

With tears flowing from their eyes, the girls sing. There seems to be more space above us now, as if the song is lifting the roof of rough, unsanded boards. Nothing can stop it from rising up to the skies, for this is holy ground, and here is the gate of Heaven.

Like a great flame in their hearts, the song's words burn away indifference and estrangement, and let them feel that they were really always there, in the embrace of true, pure faith. They sing the song again and again, wishing for this moment never to end.

The tears turn to real weeping that envelops us all, weeping that no one can hide, or hide from. Weeping that floods the heart and opens a channel to such a high place in the soul that each girl meets her own *neshamah* and knows it is real. And then she can start weeping all over again.

The train stops. It lets us out, red-eyed and blinking, into the fresh breeze. And it feels totally incongruous to come out of that unearthly experience and land on a comfortably padded bus seat with an air-conditioner vent overhead.

"Wait!" says Tanya. "Your mother was in Lodz! Wasn't she put on a train like that? Did she tell you about it?"

Still trembling inside from that intense encounter with the past, with the melody of faith and heroism, I take a couple of deep breaths before answering. Yes, my mother was put on a train like that, and on many other trains. Again and again, the doors were slammed shut and locked behind her. From Pabianitz to Lodz, from Lodz to Auschwitz, from Auschwitz to Hamburg, from Hamburg to Bergen-Belsen. All the years of her adolescence were filled with rides on trains like those, crushed in with hundreds of others, wondering "Where now?" Trying to breathe and wondering if these were her last breaths.

My father, too, was on trains like those. On a train like that he stood, covered with snow, and relinquished his soul into G-d's hands, singing *Nishmas Kol Chai*. Yes, my father was very familiar with trains; he saw them arriving in Auschwitz every day. He heard their earsplitting horns blowing and the cries of the people being roughly pulled and pushed into line. And he knew the meaning of every train that came to the selection ramp: Last stop. No return tickets honored. Welcome to the World of Truth.

The click-clack of train wheels was seared into my mother and father's memories. It was a reminder of the parents who'd been torn from them, of the childhood friends they'd lost, of the harsh shouts of the Germans and their collaborators.

I've heard stories of survivors who went on to build new lives in places where they wouldn't hear a train's whistle blowing, where they wouldn't see railroad tracks, and if they had to travel somewhere they would go by car. And if they didn't have to travel, they'd stay right where they were. But they would never board another train. They'd had more than enough of trains.

But Mama and Papa traveled with us by train at our happiest times. They packed nice bags for us and dressed us in freshly ironed clothes, with warm woolen hats in winter and sandals in summer. They prepared sandwiches wrapped in brown paper, and thick glass bottles of water, and they came with us to the train station. They would buy us something at one of the station shops and make us feel that nothing was more exciting than waiting for a train.

And traveling by train was pure delight! Mama and Papa sat with us, all smiles, relaxed and enjoying our excitement, watching us press our little noses against the window, looking for ducks as we passed the little villages of the countryside.

"But how?" Efrat suddenly asks, and something in her voice says she wants the answer urgently, almost desperately. "What gave them the strength to get on with their lives, to be happy, to laugh and see the good in life, even though life had been so cruel to them?"

I think for a moment. Who would have thought that gentle Efrat had such a fierce thirst. She says, "But how?" and what I hear is, "Give me some of that water that gave life to your parents!"

I try to explain. "You see, the song you were singing before in the train… that was the song of their lives. Even though he tarries, I will wait every day for him to come. The faith you felt when you sang that song was always there for them, even when everything else was gone. It held them in its embrace, it shielded them, it was the answer to all questions, and it gave them all the strength they needed.

"It was the soundtrack of their lives. They chose to sing it and not to cry, to live and not to die. Again and again, they chose faith, and it gave them endless strength."

CHAPTER 51

The Camp Hymn

Summer Camp, Luxembourg, 1970

We've been laughing all day.

We sit on the wide, comfortable beds in the chateau in Luxembourg where we're having Agudah summer camp this year. My Papa was among those who reestablished Agudath Israel in Europe after the war and initiated the summer camp.

Rikki, Sarah, and I should have gone to sleep an hour ago, at "lights out" time, but we just can't; we're too full of laughter. Every time we think of what happened today, we start laughing all over again.

Rikki is wiping away tears of laughter, and Sarah says, "Stop, enough already, I'm getting a stomachache from laughing." Only Jeannette is missing, and boy, did she miss something today. When we think of Jeannette, our convulsions of laughter die down, and we get a little more serious.

"Poor Jeannette," says Sarah, stretching out against her pillow and kicking off her slippers, letting them land where they will. "How can she stand it, missing everything all the time?"

Jeannette is an only child, and her parents guard her so closely, she might as well be a rare blue diamond in the National Museum. They're with her every day when she comes to school, walking her all the way to the classroom like a bodyguard. And we all know that if that's the way they feel about letting her out of their sight, there's no way they'll allow her to go away to camp for a few days of fun and adventure. And indeed they don't. No camp, no sports, no bicycle.

But today, she really missed something. It all started yesterday evening, with an announcement from the camp director that Baron Maurice de Skirais of Luxembourg would be paying a visit today. Since the chateau we were using was built on his ancestral lands, the Baron was interested to see how the Agudath Israel summer camp was run and what standards were being maintained.

The announcement threw us into a panic. The Baron was coming? Here? To this mess? To these littered hallways, to this dining hall with the torn corners of old posters still stuck on the walls? And what about the auditorium, where we'd left the chairs scattered around haphazardly?

We went to bed anxious and worried, and in the morning we got up extra early and scrubbed down the whole chateau. Nobody had to push us; we felt like the servants in a medieval castle, preparing for a grand ball, and trembling before the wrath of our noble master.

The lawns outside were sparkling clean, the chairs were lined up with military precision, all the disorder in the dining room was put away somewhere (banished to the dungeon, maybe?), and the rooms all looked like respectable living quarters again, instead of the wreckage of Noah's Ark on Mount Ararat.

We worked frantically all day, desperate to have everything looking proper before the Baron arrived. By mid-afternoon we were breathless with anticipation. The director announced that his lordship should be here any moment….

We stood waiting for the nobleman to make his grand entrance. Would he come in a horse-drawn carriage or a limousine? Were we supposed to curtsey? Were we dressed nicely enough?

It was too late to worry now. Suddenly, the baron swept in. What a weird surprise… he was wearing an outfit that looked like a costume from a school play: kitschy-looking trousers, a bow tie, long hair and a little goatee. We'd never imagined that a member of Luxembourg's nobility would have such bad taste, but we minded our manners and didn't laugh, because after all, he was the baron, and we were camping on his land....

And then he began to speak in French... and oy vey, what French! Where on earth had he gone to school — in Poland? Where did he get an accent like that? He sounded like our parents! His speech was even weirder than his clothes, and now we really had to bite our lips to keep from laughing. And what was he saying now? Baron Maurice de Something was saying a dvar Torah? Or was this all a dream?

In the middle of his speech, the baron suddenly broke down and started shaking with laughter. The comedy was over. He wasn't a baron, he wasn't a lordship, and he wasn't Maurice de Skirais. He was just the secretary of Agudath Israel, Antwerp, and he and the director had cooked up this whole ingenious plan to get us to tidy the place up properly, once and for all.

The joke was on us, but it was great fun. And now, an hour after "lights out," we're still laughing about it and can't seem to wind down.

"Tomorrow there's a kumzitz," Rikki wails. "I won't be able to stay awake, I'll fall into the campfire, dead asleep! So come on, be quiet already!"

"You be quiet," we tell her, and then we all start laughing again because of the way Sarah and I said the same words in unison.

Finally, we fall asleep, and I dream of kumzitzes and campfires, songs and melodies that somehow all come together into one song in the end, Papa's song: "Ani ma'amin b'emunah sheleimah b'vias haMashiach." Papa sings it with us so often, and it energizes the whole camp. It's the unofficial camp hymn, because it's Papa's anthem, and this is his camp... and I hear it even in my dreams.

CHAPTER 52

Shabbos in Krakow

I PLAN TO TELL THE end of the story on *motzaei Shabbos*, in the lobby of our hotel in Krakow, with its old sofas, upholstered in wine-red, and its Victorian-style rug. The girls sit crowded on the sofas or sprawl on the rug, leaning their heads on each other's shoulders. The atmosphere of Shabbos still lingers in the air and hangs like a curtain around us.

Our Shabbos was inconsistent with everything going on around us. Out on the street and here in the hotel, the secular clock kept on ticking, and it was business as usual. But at our tables in the dining room, it was Shabbos, like being inside a shining bubble.

We lit Shabbos candles on a side table. When I finished praying in their glow, I turned to the girls with a bright smile. "*Shabbat shalom*!" I said. They returned the greeting and wanted to know what I was murmuring there over the Shabbos candles for such a long time. "I was praying for my children and grandchildren," I answered simply, and went to sit in one of the easy chairs. "I prayed for each son and his wife, for each daughter and her husband, and for all their children. I mention each one by name, and any special request I want to make for each one — for the baby who's not feeling well, and the girl who started school this year, that sort of thing. And remember, I have eight families to pray for," I added with a smile.

"And you remember all that by heart?!" They were incredulous. I laughed and started reciting all the names: "My son Yisrael and his wife Michal, and their children..." I rattled off the names in order, adding a particular request with some of the names, and when I was finished, they all seemed to take a deep breath together, as if they'd exhaled all that was old and were taking in something fresh and new. Amazing, the strength of a woman who can stand in front of the Shabbat candles and pray for every single one of her children and grandchildren....

The tables were spread with white cloths, attractive place settings, and challahs, and it stirred my heart to see a reminder of the past that once thrived in this city and was now gone.

Afterward, there was Kiddush and a traditional Shabbos meal with *zemiros* and *divrei Torah*. And after reciting *Birkas ha-Mazon*, we all sat down over Israeli *pitzuchim* — roasted seeds and nuts — for an *oneg Shabbos* conversation.

This Shabbos was a gift to the group, with no strings attached. It was majestic and serene, and everyone was free to choose how far she was willing to step in, and how much of it to take into her life. Some wanted to run with it, and they were asking for guidance every minute: Can I make a cup of coffee in the morning? Is it really all right to open the magnetic door? Others looked on as observers, curious, yet hesitant and fearful that someone would try to rush them into it before they were ready.

After the daytime meal we went out to tour the streets of the old Jewish quarter on foot. That was something special, to walk in the same places where so many Jews once walked and imagine them all walking home from shul at this very hour with their children at their sides.

The weather was cold and gray, but Shabbos painted the scene a bit brighter and gave a sense of the vitality that was once here. It was a different experience, moving about without the bus and the wheels and the stops at gas stations, and instead, breathing a little deeper and just being there, in the Krakow that used to be... before the inferno.

We feel closer now. It's as if Shabbos was a place that we went through together, and the memory of the shared experience connects us.

We've had a Melave Malka and a few more songs, and now the girls are lounging in the Victorian lobby, waiting to see the video clips from a family wedding that I promised to show them after Shabbos. First I show them the group dance performed by the granddaughters. In matching gowns and elegant hairdos, they move to the rhythm of the music, doing the steps they've rehearsed together with so much love. To these graduate students, it looks too surreal to be true. The weddings they're familiar with are so different. To see a group of girls, royally dressed, surrounded by a circle of women only, dancing to Jewish music, is like watching a scene from another planet.

Then I show them the *mitzvah tantz,* the Chassidic custom that Papa would never do without. At the end of the wedding, after most of the guests have left, Papa dances before the bride, while everyone stands in a wide circle around them, moved to tears. They know that for him, this is more than a traditional part of every Chassidic wedding. For Papa, this is a victory dance. He has lived to see one more grandchild marry. A new Jewish family has just been started, another twig on the great tree of our people.

And although I've seen this video countless times, it touches my heart every time to see Papa celebrating his victory.

CHAPTER 53

Liberation

TOMORROW NIGHT WE'RE RETURNING home, and the girls have informed me that I can't leave any stories unfinished. So I try to formulate a closing chapter that will bring all the loose ends together:

As the Allies moved in on German-occupied Poland, the Nazis forced their prisoners to march into Germany, exposed to the freezing cold, and without food or drink. These were the famous death marches. My mother and Rutka barely made it alive to Bergen-Belsen. Many of their companions fell on the way, too weak and exhausted to stand on their feet for one more second, letting the snow take their expiring bodies before their souls ascended to the Heavenly heights.

But Mama was with Rutka, and Rutka was with Mama, and each of them gave to the other what she didn't have for herself.

All conditions were ripe for death in Bergen-Belsen. Many mustered up the last of their strength to survive the marches, only to find their demise in this huge, terrible camp. The days Mama and Rutka spent there were the worst of all. There were no gas chambers in Bergen-Belsen, and no shootings, for the simple reason that there was no need for them. Fifteen thousand women were crowded into barracks that were built to house no more than one-tenth that number. But every day, their numbers dwindled as the dead were carried out, felled by dehydration, disease, and starvation. A few dirty puddles were their only source of water, bringing on even more disease. So there was no need for the Nazis to resort to violence.

There was no forced labor. There was nothing to do but die. All around, women were lying on the ground, finally depleted, waiting for death to redeem them from their suffering. Mama had no way of knowing that her future husband was also here, dragging dead bodies that were tied with ropes to his feet, to a mass grave, feeling that he, too, was living his last moments. He was so weak by then that he easily might have fallen into the pit and joined them. But Mama didn't know about Papa, and he didn't know about Mama.

But G-d in Heaven knew. Their redemption was already in the making.

On the fifteenth of April, 1945, at their lowest point of despair, they were suddenly liberated. They were too weak to rejoice, too captive to feel free, and too dead to live. Like the others, Papa was lying on the ground, ill and close to death. Through a fog, he heard voices speaking English. But that wasn't reason enough to crawl out of the barracks and see what was happening. He felt that he was the last Jew in the world left alive, a lone Chassid, a relic of a lost world. Why stir himself to go out there?

In his mind, he went through the list of all his brothers and sisters. He knew the tragic end of each of them, except his sister Rivka. She was the last one to be taken for forced labor, and he'd heard nothing of her since. Maybe she was still alive.... Hope awakened in him, and like a spark falling on dry straw, it ignited a fire within him.

He dragged himself to his feet, all skin and bones, and began inquiring. Had anyone heard anything about the girls from Krakow?

That group of Beis Yaakov girls?

Yes, yes!

You could try asking in the kitchen.

Papa went to the kitchen of Bergen-Belsen, his heart pounding, holding on tightly to that slim hope that his sister might still be alive. "Is there anyone here from Krakow?" he asked.

"Yes, we're from Krakow!" said a few young women. "Who are you looking for?"

"Rivka Horowitz."

"Rivka Horowitz?!"

One of the girls came toward him. "I'm Rivka Horowitz.... *Gott!* Shulem Duvid!!"

That meeting of brother and sister contained deep wells of sorrow along with incredible heights of happiness. All the rest of their family had been wiped out... but here they were, the two of them reunited. They still had family... they still had something to live for.

The British and Canadian soldiers who came to liberate the camp were shocked and overwhelmed by the sights that met their eyes. They didn't know what to do about the piles of dead and half-dead bodies. In their well-intentioned attempts to feed the starved inmates, they sometimes gave them too much food, or foods that were too rich for their weakened systems to handle. Over the next few weeks, twenty-eight thousand more Jews died, either of illness or of overeating. The inmates were moved to the Bergen-Belsen Displaced Persons Camp, which was set up nearby, and the liberators set fire to the concentration camp. Bergen-Belsen was the biggest of the DP camps, and soon survivors began to arrive from other areas.

"And that," I say, "was when the Holocaust began for Mama."

Before that, there was no room for thoughts and feelings. Mama had spent all her time struggling to survive, to stay alive for the next thirty minutes... but when it was all over, the reality of what had happened hit her.

She found herself standing by the big bulletin board, where the lists of survivors' names were posted, to notify a world in ruins of their existence. Alongside each name was the name of the survivor's home city or *shtetl*. Every day, Mama stood there, intensely scrutinizing the latest notices, hoping to see a line with the words "Horowitz" and "Pabianitz" — even just one! A brother, a sister, maybe one of her parents. Every day, her hope was rekindled, and every night it was painfully extinguished. Eleven siblings and their parents — where were they all? Was there really none left alive besides herself and Rutka? No aunt, uncle, or cousin? Would she really never see her parents again?

She wouldn't give up. Again and again, her finger moved down the columns. Maybe some new names had been added today... maybe she had missed an entry.

But no. Their names weren't there to be found. Mama began to grasp what had happened, the enormity and depth of her loss. And that was when the Holocaust began for her. Now, there was time to grieve. And her grief was immeasurable.

One day, she and Rutka were told that someone wanted to see them. Who? A relative. He was waiting in the main office. They ran there with hearts almost bursting. A young man stood up, bowed slightly in greeting, and said with genuine feeling that he had come there from England. He was Mama's first cousin. He had gotten information that Mama and Rutka were still alive, and he had come to take them back to England with him. He wanted to help them to reestablish their lives. He would provide them with everything they needed; he had a house, a family, and good living conditions.

The two girls looked at him. They sensed that he was sincere and were touched by his offer. It was no small thing to discover a cousin they hadn't known about. But this man was bareheaded. What would their parents have said?

The girls said they were grateful to him for coming all the way here to look for them, and they appreciated his kindness and generosity. But no, they couldn't come to England. He urged them to reconsider. But they stood firm. They were truly grateful and would certainly keep in touch. But they could not go with him.

Mama and Rutka were young, and like all other young survivors, they desperately wanted a means of climbing out of the ruins and starting life anew. Yet, alongside that great desire was something even greater. Was it their upbringing? Was it the pure *neshamah* within them that can always choose what's right? They chose to say no to their cousin from England, and once again they were alone in Bergen-Belsen, alone in the world.

And then they heard that some Beis Yaakov girls in the camp were organizing a study group. The young lady in charge was Rivka Horowitz. Mama and Rutka went to join them. She was six years late, but at last, Mama was a Beis Yaakov student.

Little did she know how much blessing was about to pour into her life.

CHAPTER 54

The Edelweiss of Belgium

Antwerp, 1962

Today I went over to Tante Rivka. I had no homework, and Mama allowed me to go. All she asked was that I should behave nicely and come home in time for supper. I ran to get my coat. It's great to have a real aunt and uncle; hardly any of my friends here in Antwerp have anything but parents, and maybe a couple of brothers and sisters. And there's only one grandmother, the Finkelsteins' Bomama, and we all share her.

I ran all the way to Tante Rivka's house, so as soon as I came through the front door I took in a deep breath. The air was scented with the green, earthy smell of her houseplants, combined with the aroma of her delicious butter cake. Tante Rivka could read my mind, and she knew I could smell the cake. She served me a nice, big slice of it on her pretty milchig china with the blue flowers, and I remembered what Mama said about minding my manners and ate it slowly, savoring every dainty little bite. Meanwhile I watched Tante Rivka watering her plants. We have a few houseplants, too, and some flowers in window boxes, but they never grow as lushly as hers. I felt like a spy who just found out a big secret without even trying. And here's the secret: Tante Rivka's plants are her friends. She goes from flowerpot to flowerpot, talking to each one. "Good afternoon!" she says to the rubber plant. "How are you today? Are you thirsty? Here's some nice water for you." And then she moves on to a pot of violets on the windowsill. "Well, you're looking fresh and pretty today! And I see you have two new flowers. Mazel tov!"

It's funny, because Tante Rivka isn't the flowery, mushy type at all. She organizes lots of things in the Antwerp Jewish community, like the annual fundraising drive of Keren HaYishuv for Eretz Yisrael, and all the ladies think of her as their leader.

She had made a costume for me to wear at the kehillah's big Purim show; I was dressed up like a pushke with "Keren HaYishuv" written on it in big letters, and I had to walk in and say, "Hello, this is the Keren HaYishuv fund." I felt very bashful and silly, but you don't say no to an aunt, and certainly not to Tante Rivka.

I finished up the last bits of cake and got up to put my plate and fork in the sink and to say thank you nicely.

"I'm going to have lots of flowers, too," I promised, after Tante Rivka handed me the watering can and let me take over watering the plants. "And I'll talk to them, just like you, Tante. Isn't that your secret?"

"Of course. You must talk to your plants — who wants to grow if nobody talks to them? Do you talk to the edelweiss I gave you?"

"I don't," I confessed. "I guess that's why it hasn't been growing."

Tante Rivka laughed. Two weeks ago she'd given me a keychain with a little white enamel flower dangling from it — the edelweiss, the national flower of both Switzerland and Austria. The whole family knows that she is madly in love with this flower, and wherever she goes, she picks up little edelweiss souvenirs and hands them out to all of us.

"Why don't you have any edelweiss in your window boxes?" I wondered aloud.

Tante Rivka put away the watering can and began setting the table for supper. She took a folded tablecloth out of a lower cupboard, and as she spread it on the kitchen table, she explained, "The edelweiss only grows high up in the mountains, at heights of two thousand meters or more. It's so small, and its stem is so thin, that to look at it, you'd never think it could survive up there, where it's so cold and windy and there's snow all year. Yet somehow it manages to push its way up through the snow and to bloom. And after a storm, when the wind has blown everything else away, the edelweiss is still there. No storm can destroy it. It will always be there, small and delicate, yet stronger than all the rest."

*While explaining all this to me, Tante Rivka has taken a loaf out of the breadbox and sliced it with a long knife. She's put out the butter dish and the jam, and I wonder, is she really talking with so much passion about a little flower in the Alps? Maybe the edelweiss is a symbol for her, a symbol of someone she knows, someone small and delicate who stood up against storms and survived... but who?**

---

*Tante Rivka herself was certainly an edelweiss. A whole book could be written about her, and indeed, much is written about her in Pearl Benisch's *To Vanquish the Dragon* (Jerusalem, Feldheim Publishers). Mrs. Benisch's book recounts her experiences as part of a group of Bais Yaakov graduates who went through the Holocaust together, and her good friend Rivka Horowitz-Pinkusevitz was one of the leaders of that group.

When I knew Tante Rivka, there were no longer any barbed-wire fences in the background, but she was still an edelweiss, a heroic leader who prevailed where others would submit. Much as she loved flowers, her determination to do the right thing conquered love. In our community in Belgium, when a girl got engaged, she would be swamped with flowers. All of her friends and relatives, and everyone on her fiancé's side, too, would send flower arrangements, bouquets, and flowering potted plants until the bride's home looked like a greenhouse, crowded with flowers covering every surface. The total cost amounted to a small fortune, and of course most of it was wilted a week later. Tante Rivka designed a pretty greeting card with a picture of flowers on it, and in the card she would write, "Mazel tov! In honor of the bride, instead of sending flowers, we donated their cost to a fund that assists poor brides in Eretz Yisrael. And may your living room be filled with cards like this one." That was almost a crazy thing to do in our wealthy, aristocratic community, where an opulent floral arrangement was a status symbol. But gradually, others began to adopt Tante Rivka's practice. Like an edelweiss, she prevailed.

CHAPTER 55

A Shidduch in Bergen-Belsen

IN BEIS YAAKOV OF Bergen-Belsen, no bell summoned the girls to class. They came on their own, grateful to be alive and glad to be together. Like Noah and his family on the mountaintop after the flood, they looked out at the world and saw it in ruins. There was no going back to what was.

Throughout the last few years of endless roll calls, starvation, forced labor, humiliation and abuse, or cowering in stifling bunkers, there was always a sense that when this nightmare was over, someone would be waiting to embrace them with comforting arms. If they were chosen to survive, then one day they would resume their lives as before. But there was no one to embrace them, and no life to resume.

It was all gone. The entire setting in which they'd lived — the streets of the Jewish neighborhoods, the little brothers in their peaked caps and little sisters in their muslin collars, the shuls and yeshivas, the Chassidic courts, the summer camps in the mountains, the trips by train to visit Bubbe and Zeide — had disappeared like a mirage in the desert sand. There was nothing and nobody to return to.

They had survived the Flood and they emerged from the Ark, blinking in the sunlight and wondering, "What now?" Not even a chair to sit on remained from their childhood homes. They were alone in the world, with no possessions but the striped prisoners' dresses on their backs, and no one understood.

Outside the camp, Europe was scrambling to its feet. People were trying to compensate themselves for the deprivations of wartime, and the shop windows were full of fresh, tempting foods — cakes and pastries, candies, fruits, and cheeses, all displayed paradoxically alongside burnt-out ruins of buildings hit by shells.

The girls went out, trying to find their lives. The American occupiers were turning a blind eye and giving their tacit approval to a genteel form of looting called "organizing." The local Germans opened their shops and their homes and stood by fearfully while the Jewish survivors, who'd been robbed of everything, took what they needed. Not that these items could ever compensate them for the losses they'd suffered, but at least they would help them get organized for the challenge of putting their broken lives back together....

The Jews would come in and help themselves to shoes, clothing, some needles and thread, a loaf of bread or an umbrella. They didn't empty out the premises, although no one would have stopped them even if they'd tried to carry a piano away. The tables had been turned, and the Germans knew they were lucky to be let off so easily. They stood by and wondered why the Jews were taking so little. What, only a coat, a hat, and a pair of boots? Now that the Jews had the upper hand, why weren't they slaughtering the Germans wholesale?

The Jews didn't slaughter anyone. They themselves were in shock, walking around as if in a dream. They were shadows of themselves, trying to piece together the fragments of their identity, to navigate an uncharted path to the future.

Once they'd "organized" some decent clothing and basic equipment for themselves, the girls started having their pictures taken. Well dressed and smiling, with their hair styled, they would go to the photographer for a kind of documentation of their existence. They had big collections of pictures from that post-liberation period, confirmation that yes, they were alive.

In all the pictures of Mama, she's wearing a pair of new boots, a gift she had gratefully accepted from her English cousin. She would style her hair, put on a new outfit, and go with Rutka to get her picture taken. Here we are, the pictures said, two smiling young girls, wearing nice clothes and new boots, you see? The accursed war is over.

When she first came to live in Belgium, Mama had to remind herself that the rules were different here. "Nadja, you mustn't take what you can't afford. Everything here has a price tag, and here, you have to pay! We've finished getting organized, and now we're back to normal life." But as long as she was still in Bergen-Belsen, life had an unreal and bizarre quality.

The study group was, in part, a way for the girls to force themselves to return to a normal way of living. No one was giving them report cards or asking for their educational credentials, but they wanted to be there, in their improvised classroom, learning a bit of Chumash and Navi, Jewish thought, and Hebrew. A faint reflection of the seminary in Krakow that was no longer there…

Rivka Horowitz, the leader of that small group, had been a young teacher before the war in the big Beis Yaakov in Krakow where Rabbi Orlean's voice was heard echoing between the rooms. (The best students were encouraged to start teaching while still in their teens.) She'd been a student there when Sarah Schenirer herself had taught the girls.

Mama, on the other hand, had never had a chance to go to Beis Yaakov. Aside from the meetings in the Lodz ghetto, to which she had run so eagerly, clutching one handful of flour and another of sugar, this was her first experience as part of a group such as this. But her charm and excellent traits of character soon earned her a respected place among the seasoned Beis Yaakov girls.

Rivka Horowitz had a brother, right there in Bergen-Belsen, who belonged to the tiny group that was adamant about upholding religious life in the camp. It was they who made sure there would be a kosher kitchen and minyanim for prayer. Shulem Duvid was Rivka's only surviving sibling, and on the day the camp was liberated, the hope of finding her still alive had brought him back from the brink of death.

And now, Rivka had a *shidduch* for her brother: her new student, Nadja. When they met, he knew right away that this was a girl he could have hoped for even in better times. They were the first couple to get engaged in Bergen-Belsen.

The spirits of their parents and siblings hovered around them, to be there at that special moment, to gather up the tears that couldn't be shed, and to wish them *mazel tov.*

Mama and Papa went around in a cloud of happiness. Their *shidduch* was a miracle, and they knew it very well. Everything they'd suffered was now officially over, wrapped up and tied tightly with string, and a window to the future had opened up for them.

And then, one night in Bergen-Belsen, Mama had a vivid and very disturbing dream. Her father was there. How long had it been since she'd last seen him? Was it five years? She'd been separated from him in the ghetto of Pabianitz when she was barely more than a child, but she'd never forgotten him. His image was still strong within her, and it had guided her through the worst times in the Lodz ghetto, in the Hamburg labor camp, in Auschwitz, and here in Bergen-Belsen.

The father she remembered from Pabianitz, the father who had slapped her and kissed her the day they arrived in the ghetto, when she sneaked out at night to bring him his Gemara, was vividly present in her dream. She wanted to reach out and touch him. But he was gazing at her without pleasure. He didn't say a word… or perhaps she forgot what he said. He looked at her with an expression of silent rebuke, the gaze of a parent who is disappointed in his child and expects better.

All she could remember when she woke up was his tangible presence… and that penetrating look. She was distressed. What had she done wrong? Surely her father wasn't displeased with the young man she had chosen. Shulem Duvid was everything her father himself would have wanted for her; she was sure of that.

But she knew if he had come to her in a dream from his blissful place in Gan Eden, there was a reason for it. There was something he wanted from her…. What was it?

As she went about her day, the answer came to her. Yes, it was perfectly clear now. She knew what was disturbing her father's rest.

CHAPTER 56

What Mama's Father Was Trying to Say

THIS IS THE PART that isn't talked about much. The survivors' stories usually end on a somewhat festive note: the fifth of May, the liberation, the celebrations, the transition to a new life. But although people don't like to spoil the story, the truth is that there was an unsavory aspect to life in the DP camps.

The young men and women who survived the years of slaughter found themselves in a surprising new world. Suddenly, everything was permissible. They could walk into shops and take what they fancied. They no longer had to go hungry; the camp kitchen served generous portions of food. They were alive, and they wondered what to do now, in this huge camp where no one made them line up for roll call or forced them to work.

In a normal life, the teenage years are spent preparing for adulthood. These young people had spent their adolescence struggling to survive. Now, all at once, the struggle was over, and there was nobody there to tell them how, in fact, they were supposed to conduct their lives. There were no parents and no teachers, no family structure, no rules of behavior. There was only a desperate need to compensate themselves for those years of misery and terror — to have fun and enjoy life in every possible way.

They wanted only to forget the past, and they couldn't visualize a future. They had the raw drive to live, but their lives had been drained of meaning. There was only the present moment, and they wanted to squeeze it for every ounce of enjoyment it could hold. And so, licentiousness took over.

Mama's parents had instilled strong values in her. But from his abode in Gan Eden, her father saw the environment she was in, and he didn't like it. She and her *chosson* were so young, so thrilled to have found each other, and there they were, both living in the camp, with all that revelry going on around them. Her father didn't want to see his precious surviving daughter spending her engagement in such an atmosphere.

She explained all this to her fiancé. He, too, had values he wouldn't compromise, and he agreed with her. They must find a healthier place to put down roots and start their new life together.

Buses and entry permits were being organized to take some of the survivors to Belgium. The country was almost unknown to them, but people said there was a Jewish community there, trying to reestablish itself, and there wasn't much anti-Semitism. Belgium wasn't Poland or Germany. You could make a life for yourself there, at least for a time, until you could get a certificate from the British authorities to go to Eretz Yisrael. So Papa and Mama signed up for the caravan leaving Bergen-Belsen.

At the last minute, a young lady approached Mama and asked her to give up her place on the bus. She, too, was engaged to be married, and she very much wanted to leave with her fiancé. Although Mama was in the same position as this girl, she kindly agreed to let her take the seat. She could go out with the next group, after all, and meanwhile her *chosson* could try to find a place where they could acclimate.

But the next group didn't go out. Suddenly, the borders were closed, and the refugees found themselves caught on Germany's accursed soil. Staying there permanently was unthinkable, yet they couldn't get out. Eretz Yisrael was still governed by the regime that sank ships carrying illegal immigrants and took the survivors to detention camps in Cyprus. And America was out of the question for Mama and Papa. Rutka had already sailed there with an organized group, and now Mama was alone in Bergen-Belsen, knowing that somewhere in Belgium, a young man with a pure gaze was waiting for her. She was his whole world, and he was hers. But for now, she could only count the long days that turned to weeks and months, and still dragged on and on. She couldn't even get in touch with him; there were no phones, or even an address to write to. She just had to have faith that her *chosson* was waiting for her, just as she was waiting for him. And she found the strength to endure that unbearable limbo only by holding on to that faith.

One day, one of the young men, a friend of Papa's, traveled to Belgium; he had managed to get a visa somehow. Mama gave him a picture of her to bring to Papa, one of the pictures that was taken after the liberation. The friend quickly wrote on the back of it, "A memento from the one most precious to you, who is waiting for you."

That picture eventually found its way into one of Mama and Papa's albums, and those scrawled lines encapsulate all those long months of waiting. Mama waited a year and a month in Bergen-Belsen, engaged to a wonderful young man and unable to reach him.

Finally, after thirteen lonely months, she was able to obtain a visa, and she arrived in Antwerp to be married and come to the room her husband had prepared for her.* He, too, had been waiting and missing her all those months, not knowing when she would find her way there.

Her father had come in a dream with a message to impart,

*Papa had no money to rent an apartment, so he rented a room in the home of the Rebbe of Sert-Vizhnitz, the Makor Baruch *zt"l*. They began married life without a penny to spare. Papa began to learn diamond polishing, and Mama earned some wages sewing shirts.

and she, his little girl, had taken the message to heart. She'd fulfilled his request and protected the sanctity of her engagement, although she'd paid for it with more than a year of heartbreaking uncertainty and worry. Now he could rejoice. It was a small wedding, with just a minyan of guests, and the bride wore a simple gown. But crowded under the *chuppah,* beneath the starry sky, were many unseen guests. Her father and mother were there, and with them were all the bride's siblings, and their spouses and children. The grandparents and great-grandparents joined them. The whole Horowitz clan was there, an illustrious family with roots going back to Rav Yehonasan Eybeschutz. They all wanted to rejoice with the last living shoot on the family tree and pray that from her, a glorious new tree would sprout.

Papa's family was there, too: his parents and grandparents, his brother who was son-in-law to the Rav of Pabianitz. The sisters he had lost during the war and the brother who had called out from the truck, "See you in the *Oilem HaEmes*!" Now, from their places in Gan Eden, they all came to *shep nachas* from the wedding of their surviving son.

Yes, there were many happy and prayerful guests at that little wedding. Many ancestors whose hope for their family's future was all placed in that young couple. Yet, miraculously, a few bits of herring and little cups of schnapps were enough to feed all the guests...*

---

*When my parents' fiftieth anniversary was coming up, we were looking for something special to present at the celebration. We called Tante Rachel in Petach Tikvah, the aunt who had made *aliyah* before the war. She said, "Yes, I have the perfect thing!" It was a letter Papa had written to her right after his wedding to share the experience. He wrote, "It was a bittersweet wedding. I looked to the right for my father, who was no longer in this world, and for my mother, who wasn't there to meet my bride. I looked to the left, and I didn't find my wife's parents there, either. But I know they are happy and content as they look down from Heaven. I found the bride that they would have wanted for me.... and she even covers her hair...."

CHAPTER 57

Meeting Bubbe and Zeide

HALF OF OUR LAST day in Poland is to be spent visiting the Poznanski Palace, built in the nineteenth century by the fabulously wealthy textile magnate and philanthropist Poznanski, at the height of Jewish prosperity in Lodz — the climax of the days in exile when Jews still thought they could build palaces and live like kings.

Our trip leader looks at the day's schedule. "What's today's plan? Palaces!" he says. "We have half a day left in this country. Let's do something worthwhile. If any of you want to see palaces, you can take a pleasure trip to Versailles."

We're all with him. At the moment, palaces interest us about as much as last year's Polish snow. So what shall we do instead?

There's a short consultation among the senior ranks, and the rabbi suggests Chelmno. It's not far from Lodz, and it suits the purpose of our trip.

Chelmno?!

I feel like I've just been hit in the stomach, and I'm crumpling from the pain. Chelmno, of all places? How did they know that something was waiting for me in Chelmno?

After I'd found out what was lurking behind the tightly-closed curtain in my childhood home, I knew I had to do some research. I went to Yad Vashem in Jerusalem to submit some Pages of Testimony for my parents' family members. Seated in front of a computer, I began with basic details: name, age, occupation, and prewar address. I found my grandfather, Yitzchak Aryeh Horowitz, may his blood be avenged, in the database, and I started filling in whatever details I could.

Suddenly I was stuck. "Sent to where?" the computer was asking. When my mother and her younger brother were separated from their parents and the rest of the family, where had all those others been taken? I had no idea. All I knew was that trucks had rumbled into the ghetto of Pabianitz. My mother, a fourteen-year-old girl at the time, had watched as her family had been made to board those trucks. The trucks had rumbled away, and she'd never seen or heard from them again.

A Yad Vashem employee came over to assist me. "What year was it when they were taken from the ghetto?"

"1942."

"Which way were the trucks headed? Toward Auschwitz?"

I really had no idea. I left the forms incomplete, and the question continued to gnaw at me. Most of the ghetto residents had been taken to the same place. There must be someone who knew where they'd all been taken.

In my parents' house there was a "Yizkor Book," a thick, gloomy volume commemorating the Jewish community of Pabianitz. All the Holocaust survivors had books like that, each for his own family's town, sacred to the memory of those who perished. For the most part, the books were left on the shelf, untouched, but now, I was the detective, on the hunt for clues. I asked my mother for permission, and I began leafing through the book. All in Yiddish, it was a chilling memorial to the lives and deaths of the Jews of Pabianitz. I found my grandfather's name: "The pious rabbi who gave a daily *shiur* on Daf Yomi." I don't think even my mother knew that detail about him. I browsed further in the book. "May, 1942. A selection took place. The young people were taken to the Lodz ghetto, and all the rest were taken to Chelmno."

I turned pale.

I knew the terrible story of Chelmno. The victims of Chelmno were murdered in a grisly precursor to the gas chambers. After being told by white-coated personnel that they must undergo a medical examination prior to being taken to Germany to join work crews, they gave up their clothing and possessions in exchange for "receipts." Then they walked down a ramp into the back of a truck, which was closed and sealed when filled to capacity. The truck's motor was started, and the exhaust fumes were diverted via a hose into the sealed van, killing the victims by asphyxiation.

So that had been the fate of my grandparents. That had been the end of my uncles and aunts and cousins. They had all been murdered in one week, perhaps all on the same day in May of 1942.

I had no reason to be surprised, yet the sudden revelation came as a shock. After my heartbeat was back to normal, I asked Mama if her family had been killed in Chelmno.

"Chelmno?" The name meant nothing to her. "Why? What's there in Chelmno?" I told her there's nothing there now. Maybe a mass grave… perhaps not even that.

Before my trip, Mama asked me, "What about that place, Chelmno?" I said it wasn't on our itinerary.

And now, suddenly the Poznanski Palace has morphed into Chelmno, and I can barely breathe.

I tell my little story to the students and the staff, and that strengthens the rabbi's determination to take us all to Chelmno.

The bus makes a careful U-turn, and we're on the road to Chelmno. I feel my blood rushing wildly, pumping me with fear. I'm not ready to face this. The bus stops. I step down, feeling as if my knees are about to buckle under me.

What am I about to see?

The sight that meets my eyes is depressing. Sheets of plastic are stretched over the ground, covering human remains. Foundations of bombed buildings. Gaping pits. That is what's left of this great killing ground. I stand on this desolate spot and say *Tehillim*. A heavy silence hovers.... The rabbi begins to speak.... The violinist plays.... The group starts singing something.... They cry.... what a sad end to our trip. They head back toward the bus. I turn to follow them, feeling as though I weigh a ton and I haven't found a place to lay down the burden I'm carrying inside me.

We're only a few meters from the bus when Shaked turns to me. "Chana," she says, "what did you say that little town was called, where your mother came from?"

"Pabianitz," I say.

"Pabianitz?" A spark of excitement ignites her eyes. "Come here," she says. "I've got to show you something." She leads me to a big wall and beckons to me as she disappears behind it. I follow her. A large metal plaque stands there amid the wreckage, engraved in Hebrew and Polish.

I can't believe it. I start to cry. The sign says:

In memory of the Jews of Pabianitz
who were murdered here
and whose remains lie buried here in a mass grave.
Honor to their memory!
Jewish ex-residents of Pabianitz
May 1942

The rest of the girls come to see what the drama is about. They stand in stunned silence, amazed at the discovery and the Heavenly Hand that led us here.

"You found them," they murmur.

After a few moments I recover my wits and take out my camera. "For you, Mama," I think to myself. "Here is the gift I promised you. G-d sent it straight to my hands."*

---

*When I went to see my mother in Bnei Brak after the trip, I had a print of the picture in hand. "Mama," I said, "do you remember when I mentioned

Chelmno, and I said it wasn't included in our itinerary? Well, there was a last-minute change of plans, and we ended up going there." She stared at me in suspense. "What did you see there?" she asked. I handed her the picture. She gazed at it, trembling, and then burst into tears. For so many years, she hadn't known where — or if — her parents were buried. Now she had a focal point for her tears. And then she said three words: "Take me there."

I promised I would.

Less than a year later, a granddaughter of our very good friends in Antwerp, the Finkelsteins, got engaged, and Mama was making plans to fly out for the wedding. This was my opportunity. I called Nefesh Yehudi and found out how to get in touch with the Polish guide who had taken us to Chelmno. I called him and asked if he would be able to take my mother and me from Warsaw to Chelmno. No problem, he said. Just give me a date and time. I arranged for him to pick us up at the airport in Warsaw, shortly after our landing. Next, I had to get Mama's agreement to make the trip one day earlier, with a stopover in Poland, instead of flying directly to Antwerp. She was puzzled. Why should we do that? "It's a surprise, Mama!" I said, and right away I realized I'd probably given away the secret. We flew out one day in June, straight from the broiling heat of Israel to the dreary rain of Poland. We put on the silly plastic raincoats we bought from the Polish peddlers, found our driver, and arrived in Chelmno with the rain washing away our tears. Mama was shaking, and the drenching rain only made the scene more dismal.

We were the only visitors to that abandoned killing ground. No one else was with us to cushion the impact. And no one was there to guide me to the memorial plaque. We trudged this way and that way in the rain, but I couldn't seem to find it.

"Where could it be?" I wondered in frustration. "Surely it couldn't have disappeared...." If I hadn't photographed it, I would have started thinking I'd dreamed it. I took another look at the picture and discerned the stone base the plaque rested on. I looked for some stone like that, and suddenly I found it, somewhere way back behind everything else at the site.

Mama stood facing the memorial, silent and still. She had never known with certainty what became of her parents. Now, for the first time, she was at their burial place. We lit candles, recited *Tehillim,* and finally returned to the car, wet with rain and saturated with emotion.

Our one-day detour through Poland was well worthwhile, and Mama was very grateful. "Every time I say Krias Shema," she told me one day, "I feel that this is my parents' Kaddish, and then I picture that plaque in my mind's eye, and I can almost see them."

CHAPTER 58

Aliyah

TODAY WE'RE FLYING HOME. The girls pack their bags and form little groups, smiling for the souvenir pictures.

Shaked is going home to her dog, and Yael to her big house in Rechovot. Ilanit will go back to the memory of her Holocaust-survivor grandmother, and Shir will go back to mothering her children.

Each one will resume her life at the point where she left it. The train will pick her up at the same station where she got off… but she will be different.

They all look the same externally, with their jeans, their colorful scarves, their smiles and their long hair. But on the inside, each one of them has traveled to a new depth, and life can never be quite the same again.

All around me are duffel bags of all sizes, hugs and laughter, and the feeling of final moments together. Graduate students from all over Israel have bonded into one group of friends, snapping pictures and promising to stay in touch.

Something new was born here, in the cold air of Poland. New thoughts were born, and old thoughts died. Hearts have been cleansed and pump fresh blood to cells that never knew how thirsty they were.

Tanya comes over to me, a huge suitcase in one hand and a

small backpack in the other. She sets them down on the pavement next to the bus and says, "So how does it feel, going back like this?"

"Like what?" I ask.

"Like this," she says. Her gray-blue eyes sparkle more than ever. "After everything we've all been through together, everything we've said and felt and thought, all the tears, the friends we've made, to just get up now and say goodbye? I don't know how anyone can do it."

I don't think anyone here knows. We all seem a bit stunned by the realization that it's time to return to everything we left behind in another world. The group leader promised us a Shabbat reunion in a few weeks' time, and that's a very slight balm for the heartbreak we're feeling right now.

Last night, we gathered for a final symposium. Everyone had a chance to share her reflections on the trip, and there were plenty of tears and emotion. Tanya asked to speak first.

"You may not believe me, but this week I finally made *aliyah* to Eretz Yisrael," she said. "I first came to Israel when I was twelve years old. My parents had decided it wasn't good to be Jewish in Moldova, and Eretz Yisrael was waiting for them... so they packed up and took me along, too, as if I were just another suitcase. And there I was in that annoying country where I couldn't understand a word they were saying, and the kids were raised without manners, and the teachers couldn't keep a class under control, and I had a cramped little bedroom that couldn't even try to compete with the beautiful room I used to have.

"I hated everything. Why did they have to bring me here? What was wrong with Moldova, where I had my best friend Katya and all the kids in my tennis club? I was a good student back at home, and popular, too. Every year I was reelected as a class representative, and we were a consolidated group; we had a party for everybody's birthday, and all that sort of thing. And now I was a newcomer in a foreign country. I spoke Hebrew with a heavy accent and lots of mistakes, school was very hard for me, and I didn't know how to adapt to the new social circle. Why did my parents do this to me? What did I care about this Eretz Yisrael and all the Jews who lived here? What was Jewish about me? Was it my fault that that they suddenly remembered something Jewish in their DNA? I wasn't interested, and nobody ever asked for my opinion. They just put me on a plane and said welcome to Israel!

"Physically, I was in Israel, but my heart and soul were still in Moldova. I hadn't made *aliyah*. Not yet.

"But now, I've made *aliyah*!"

Tanya blushed, which made her even cuter.

"After spending a week here and hearing all the stories from the rabbis, from the *madrichot*, and from Chana, I realize who my people really are, what I'm really connected to, and what a responsibility I carry on my back as a member of this elite group.

"Suddenly, I feel that this is where I belong. Here with this persecuted nation that all the other nations want to destroy, because they can't bear to see its power and strength. A people that can stay strong even when others try every way of breaking it. A people that fasts on Yom Kippur even when it's dying of hunger and puts on tefillin even when it sees the smoke rising from the crematoria. This is the people I belong to. Its mission in the world amazes me. The challenge of being a Jew is something new to me, and I want to be a part of all this.

"Now, I'm ready to make *aliyah*. Now I'm ready to be a Jewish woman."

A hearty round of applause. Several girls got up to hug her. Tanya shed a few tears, and all of us were with her.

Other girls stood up to speak. Rotem spoke about her sudden desire to keep kosher.

"My parents are non-religious, but my grandmother used to light candles for Shabbat. They came from Iraq after it was modernized, and they weren't observing much of Judaism anymore or placing any importance on it. They kept minimally kosher, but I gave it all up. To me it seemed archaic and pointless, and I felt that my parents just didn't have enough courage to give it up, despite their higher education and modern outlook. But on this trip, something shifted inside me. I just couldn't bring myself to touch non-kosher food — especially here, where my people suffered so much for their Jewish faith. Chana's uncle was just a young boy, and he wouldn't touch the non-kosher meat they handed out in the Lodz ghetto even when he was wasting away with hunger. Can I — almost twenty-five, healthy, well fed, and in comfortable circumstances — can I desecrate his memory, and the memory of all those heroes, so casually? Can I betray the covenant between the Jewish people and G-d? I can't, and I hope I'll be able to keep up my resolve.... Please pray for me...."

More tears and hugs.

Yael also spoke, about the anger she felt when she first saw me. "I wanted a real Holocaust survivor, someone old and wrinkled with a number on his arm, someone who would point and say, 'I was here!' And instead, this lovely, well-dressed lady with a million-dollar smile comes along and says she's a second generation survivor and she's got so-o-o many amazing stories to tell...

"I didn't want amazing stories. I wanted to be plunged into a black depression, I wanted to cry like I could never stop, and experience the kind the pain and anguish that cuts into your heart. And that's what I ended up feeling. Chana's amazing, inspiring stories gave me the deep emotional experience I was looking for."

For hours, the girls shared their reflections, their feelings, their tears. Doors that nobody knew about were opened; words that nobody knew about were said. Stories suddenly had different endings, and a new light shone on all of us.

With weary heads and full hearts, we said good night at last. But who could sleep?

CHAPTER 59

Cherry Pits

WE'RE IN WARSAW AGAIN, on our way to the airport, that great city that likes to play dumb.

The roads are new and smooth, and the streets are beautiful and oh, so clean. People walk by serenely, trams come and go, shop windows sparkle. Once again, I feel angry about the terrible serenity that covers over so much suffering and weeping, so much fire and smoke. It's as if nothing ever happened... because the Jews are gone, and the Poles can go on smiling.

"Warsaw is beautiful," says Yael, sitting beside me.

"I wouldn't get carried away," says Tanya. "It may be modern, but beauty isn't its strong point."

"Nobody can say it's not clean," says Shaked.

"To us Israelis, that's very striking," laughs Efrat.

"I'd rather be Israeli and live in Tel Aviv with popsicle wrappers on the sidewalks, drivers leaning on their horns, and peddlers' stalls on the streets, than be Polish with a fake smile and a frozen heart," says Yael.

A memory suddenly comes back to me, like a little window opening. Where was it? In Warsaw? Or was it Krakow? I can't remember, but I feel what Yael is saying.

The cleanliness vexes me, somehow. It's as if all the blood

has been washed away, and now we can all put on innocent faces and pretend that nothing happened here.

I was in Poland once before, with my parents. My two sisters and I stood in front of a great mound of cherries. A Polish woman was selling them in brown paper bags for a few zlotys. The cherries shone as if they'd been lacquered.

Papa's eyes sparkled like they always did when something reminded him of the happy times before the war. "Come, let's buy some cherries," he said. "They're just like the ones we used to eat when I was a boy... cherries with cream." You could see on his face that he was transported back to his childhood, with his mother pouring cream from a glass pitcher over a bowl of cherries when he came home from *cheder*.

He bought bags of cherries for everyone, and they really were delicious. Suddenly Tzili pulled me aside, taking advantage of a moment when Mama and Papa were talking with some woman in Polish. "Yuck," she whispered. "I can't stand these Polish people and their hypocrisy, them and their clean sidewalks, and all the anti-Semitism that's still here."

Suddenly, she had an idea. "Let's not leave their sidewalk clean," she said to me and Esty, dropping her cherry pits on the ground. I dropped mine on the sidewalk, too, after making sure Mama and Papa weren't looking. And somehow, with that childish gesture, those little cherry pits seemed to say something. It wasn't revenge or punishment. They simply made a statement about something we couldn't tolerate.

I tell this little anecdote to the girls. "If you see any cherry pits on the sidewalk somewhere, they're ours!" I say.

"So why didn't you tell us?" Yael demands, fixing her black eyes on me.

"Why didn't I tell you what? Stories about littering the street with cherry pits?!"

"No," she laughs. "But why didn't you tell us you'd been to Poland before?"

"True, I didn't tell you."

"We got the impression that this was your first time in Poland."

"That's right. This was my first time, even though I'd been here before."

"All right, then," says the twenty-seven-year-old little girl, settling back in her chair. "So now tell us the whole thing from the beginning. How do you go to Poland without being there? We're all ears!" She takes the remaining earphone out of her other ear and looks at me with big, expectant eyes.

CHAPTER 60

In Poland, but Not There

PAPA AND MAMA DIDN'T leave cherry pits on the sidewalk in Poland.

Papa's way was to take well-calculated leaps over the dark chasms in the landscape of his life, going straight to the nice parts — the cherries and cream, the big, accomplished family in Krakow, the friends who would come to learn Torah with him and stay until late in the evening. Mama didn't remember much from before the war. She'd been so young, and the upheaval had been so traumatic, that sometimes she wondered if she'd ever really had a family, with parents, siblings, a house, and all those things that people take for granted. Was there really a time in her life when there was warm milk for breakfast, a mother waiting in the kitchen when she came home from school, and candied apples in the cupboard, ready to be handed out on Shabbos? She knew there had been such a time, but the memory was so faded and blurry that the question would burst out painfully every once in a while.

One day, after I'd seen what lay behind the curtain that was drawn across my childhood and knew what my parents had hidden from us for our own protection, I decided it was time for a trip to Poland.

Papa and Mama shook their heads doubtfully. Did they have the strength to go back there and face the past? Could they look at the barracks where they'd slept, at the barbed-wire enclosures where they'd stood for roll call, at the homes they'd been torn away from?

I went ahead and consulted the family calendars, wondering if there was any window of time when no one was getting married, no one was due to give birth or had anything else tying them down, and lo and behold, I found a suitable week for the trip.

And so, one foggy summer day, we found ourselves rolling our suitcases along on Polish territory, as quietly as we could, as if afraid of breaking a fragile silence in the atmosphere. My parents were there, along with my husband and me, my son Nechemiah and his wife Chaya, who'd come from Vienna to join us, my sister Tzili and her son, my sister Esty, and two of our Pinkusewitz cousins from Antwerp, Avraham Mordechai* and his sister Bluma.

Papa and Mama were back in the country of their childhood. The rest of us felt a bit removed from the whole experience, cautiously accompanying them on a journey into a part of their past that was foreign to us. Suddenly, we were aware of the gap between our world and theirs. They were speaking to people in Polish, and we were like little children, constantly asking, "Papa, what did he say?"

Actually, when we were children we rarely had to ask that

---

*Avraham Mordechai had learned that he had siblings he had never known: his father's three children from his previous marriage, who perished in Majdanek. It was Avraham Mordechai who summoned up the nerve to ask Papa, "Oncle Shulem, what was the worst part of all?"

We all cringed a bit, afraid of how Papa might react. But he answered with calm assurance, "Bergen-Belsen was the worst. It was Gehinnom within Gehinnom; only the *Satan* could have invented such a place."

question. More often it was Mama or Papa who asked us to explain in Yiddish what someone had just said in French, with that slight embarrassment of parents whose children are ahead of them in some area.

We were in Jordanow, a resort town in the Carpathian Mountains of southern Poland. Papa had been there for summer camp as a boy with his *cheder* group, just a few months before the German invasion had put an abrupt end to their tranquil existence. But then, none of them knew of the horrors closing in on them. They were young teenagers, delighting in the cool mountain air, and they thought their happiness would last forever....

It was hard to locate the houses Papa remembered. Poland was moving ahead rapidly, and the wooden houses of former days were being replaced by beautiful new ones made of stone. In some cases the wooden houses were kept for backyard storage. But Papa was on the scent of a mystery, and he wasn't about to give up easily. He spoke with anyone who would listen to him, asking them in Polish if they could tell him where Jaczek's or Stashek's house used to be, and what had happened to the Polish lady who kept the cow that they would come and milk for *cholov Yisroel*.

Papa had met this lady twenty years earlier on a trip to Poland for Agudath Israel. He had introduced himself and chatted about old times, and he even remembered the cow's name — Krasula.

The old woman was stunned. Seized with excitement, she'd disappeared into the house to look for something she could give to the young boy — now a mature man — who still remembered her and her cow. She came back, apologizing and carrying a few eggs, quite a princely gift in those days of Communism.

But the Communist regime was gone now, and modern Poland was erasing the vestiges of those old days. After many inquiries, Papa found the house. The elderly lady was no longer living, but her children remembered Papa from his last visit.

"Oh, yes — she gave you some eggs, didn't she? She was so excited to see you..."

In Krakow, Papa hired a tourist carriage for a few zlotys, but when the tour guide on board started showing us the sights and describing them in English, Papa requested to take over that role. He dismissed the guide and began telling us in warm Yiddish about his hometown, his family, his friends, and the shul. He knew every corner of the city and every house. Here is where we used to buy milk, and that's where we would go sledding in the winter, this is where our neighbor's store was, and over there is the street where we would walk home late in the evening, after hours of learning Torah.

After that, we went to our hotel, a perfectly ordinary building with a standard lobby and reception desk. But Papa was very agitated. He kept going in and out, looking closely at the entrance and scrutinizing the sidewalk. "What's the matter, Papa?" we asked him worriedly.

Papa could hardly speak. "Right here was our fruit store," he blurted out. "Right where you're standing, my parents used to sell fancy and exotic fruits... this hotel was built over our shop..."

We went to the reception clerk and asked her if she knew anything about the history of the hotel. When was it built, and what was here before? Because his parents' shop used to be here...

The young Polish clerk gave a frightened reply: "Oh, no, I never did anything..."

The next day, we went to see Papa's house. It was still standing, just as it had been when he was a boy and would jump down the front steps two at a time. We climbed those steps and looked at the mailbox. Even the handsome front door was still the same. But we never got past the door. The Polish man who opened it looked fearful.

"We'd just like to see the house, if you don't mind. Our family used to live here."

The man turned a bit threatening. "No," he said sharply. "You can't come in."

There was nothing we could do but turn around and leave. And now, we, too, felt the pain of knowing that Papa had been robbed of everything, and we'd even been denied a chance to see his childhood home.

Papa also took us to Ger, Góra Kalwaria in Polish, the original seat of Gerrer Chassidus where his young soul had been ignited with a flame that was never extinguished, even in frigid Auschwitz. Ger, which had given him the strength to remain a *chossid* in spite of every attempt to destroy him. "Here," he said, pointing to a desolate street in the sleepy town, "the whole street used to be one great mass of black, it was so full of Chassidim. And the road under their feet seemed to move on its own. The train bringing them here was so full, you couldn't even see it, because people were hanging on to the doors and windows from the outside, traveling through the air on wings of love for their Rebbe. The police would throw their hands up in despair. What could they do with all those Jews when they were traveling to the 'Rabbin'?"

We went to the big *beis midrash*, too, which now stood silent, like all the sleeping buildings in the area. "Here," said Papa, laying a hand on a window frame, "we used to climb onto each other's shoulders to get a glimpse of the Rebbe's face, even if only for a moment. We'd tie ourselves to the window bars with our *gartlech* to keep from falling."

Papa was carried back to those days of flaming fervor and youthful passion. He pointed to the spot where he would stand outside, listening as the Rebbe led the prayers, his voice blending with the booming responses of the huge congregation. "This is where the Rebbe sat. He would come in from that door, and this is where he davened." Papa showed us the exact place on the floor. Once again, he was a prewar Gerrer *chossid*.

In Tarnow, we saw Papa's various hiding places: the factory

where he had darted in and concealed himself to escape an *aktion*, while a Judenrat policeman unknowingly stood guard at the entrance; the paint shop where he and others had hidden for the duration of Rosh Hashanah. He shook with emotion as he pointed to the places where the hand of G-d had saved him against all odds.

"You can make a *brachah* here!" my husband reminded him. And with an overflowing heart, Papa recited the blessing for this rare occasion: "Blessed are You, Hashem, our G-d, King of the Universe, Who performed a miracle for me in this place."

We went to the Forest of the Children on the exact date of the *aktion*, the assumed yahrzeit day of Papa's parents. He sought to recite Kaddish there, but we didn't have a minyan. The sounds of that terrible day in 1942 seemed to hover and whirl around in the clearing between the silent trees — the barks of the Nazi commander, the screams of terror, the cries of *Shema Yisrael*, the machine guns spitting bullets. We said *Tehillim* and shed tears, and when we turned to go, that part of us remained behind.

In Majdanek, all the reminiscing stopped. Silence fell, and we walked on tiptoe, afraid to make any comment, almost afraid to breathe. In places like this, the memories seemed so tangible that we could feel them in the air around us. We were anxious about Mama and Papa, unable to fathom their feelings, afraid of overstepping boundaries, saying the wrong thing and causing them pain. Words were out of place, so we kept silent, choking back our responses — no exclamations, no crying, and no questions. Mama went inside for a moment and came right back out, saying it was too much for her. Papa stayed outside.

They didn't go to Auschwitz; that was beyond their endurance. So Majdanek remained in first place as the best place to keep silent.

And then I was home again, unpacking, handing out presents, and knowing that I was still holding so much inside. All the tears I hadn't shed seemed to fill me from top to bottom, down to the depths of my soul, pressing against the walls of my heart, hurting me. All the tears for what I'd seen quite well, for what I'd only glimpsed, and for what I hadn't allowed myself to see. Tears for all those moments when I'd turned my head too quickly, lying to myself that there was nothing to see here. For everything that had tried to come forward and touch me, to connect with me, but instead I'd said to myself a thousand times a minute, "Be careful, Chana! Don't do anything foolish! No crying! Mama and Papa are here, and you have to protect them." So I kept quiet, pasted on a smile as if we were merely visiting the British Museum, and kept moving. But the tears were all dammed up inside, and I knew that one day they would have to come out.

I needed to reach a sense of closure. Despite all my avoidance, a tangled mass of information had burst into my consciousness with my parents' revelations in those flickering videotapes from Beit HaTefutzot. And after that, I'd begun digging for more information, desperate for answers to all the little mysteries that had slithered past me throughout my childhood. Yet I was playing a double game: wanting to know, but refusing to process the knowledge. I was shielding myself, afraid of breaking the fragile glass that encased my childish perception of Mama and Papa, afraid of hearing the crash and being cut by the splinters. I was afraid of my own private holocaust, afraid of being robbed retroactively of my own happy childhood.

I had traveled to Poland, but I hadn't really been there. I would have to go back again when the right time came along. And when that time came, I would have to confront Poland head-on, feel the truth deep within me, and integrate it. Only then could I hope for real peace of mind.

Yes, I explain to the girls, I've traveled to Poland once before, but I wasn't really here. Now, I've really been here.

The bus lets us off at the airport. A slushy mix of rain and snow is falling. We load our baggage onto the conveyor belt and wait in line for the security check. We walk toward the gates. Announcements come over the loudspeakers in Polish and English, summoning passengers to board their planes. Our flight is ready to depart in half an hour. We're on our way home.

CHAPTER 61

Shabbos Reunion in the Old City

IT'S BEEN JUST TWO months since our trip, and we're about to get together again for a Shabbos in the Jewish Quarter, within the walls of Jerusalem's Old City.

It's late Friday afternoon, and I've brought a whole family group with me: My parents, my husband, my youngest son Aharon, my son Motti, my daughter-in-law Ruti, and my little grandson Yossi.

The narrow streets of the Jewish Quarter whisper two-thousand-year-old secrets to us, and the pleasant breeze of early summer carries a sense of yearning straight to the heart. Papa and Mama are thrilled; they see this special Shabbos as a very great privilege.

We leave our bags and things in our lodgings, and then we walk together to the rebuilt Churva Synagogue. We've heard that it's an incredible experience to be there when everyone recites *Shir HaShirim* together at Kabbalas Shabbos. The circular veranda surrounding the towering dome of the shul is full of little children who came to greet the Sabbath Queen.

Yossi, looking dapper in his freshly ironed Shabbos clothes, clings tightly to his great-grandfather's hand. I walk with Mama and Ruti at my sides. Suddenly I see a smiling woman coming toward me... but somehow it seems impossible. It couldn't be Miri!

But it is. She comes up to me and gives me a hug that leaves no more room for doubt.

Still, I'm surprised. Miri is wearing an elegant blue dress — with a matching long-sleeved shell of the type that's sold only in shops that cater to religious women.

Who would have thought Miri would show up dressed with such modesty and grace? She still has her long blond hair and the green eyes that laugh with optimism. Only her dress does not match her previous self.

On our trip to Poland, her outfits were always at the height of secular fashion. She stood so tall and exuded such confidence that one would think she was the last person who'd be moved to make any changes in her secular life. But here she was, dressed like a seminary girl. How had she come all that way? There was no time to talk about it, though. I invited her to talk after candlelighting, and hurried to shul.

The davening was wonderful. In that imposing synagogue, new, yet with so much history behind it. With the children's angelic singing in my ears and Mama and Ruti beside me, I felt as though I were wrapped in the shining robes of the Shabbos Bride.

After davening, we all sat down in the Simcha Hall adjoining Aish HaTorah, directly overlooking the Western Wall. Papa couldn't stop exclaiming about what a *zechus* it was to be eating a Shabbos meal there, with the Kosel right before our eyes. What a *zechus*, to be here with three generations of his offspring! Who would have believed he would ever see such a day?

When we'd finished our family meal, we went to an *oneg Shabbos* program that was being given for a group of male students who had also been on a Nefesh Yehudi trip to Poland and had eaten in a separate hall. Rabbi Mordechai Neugroschel was in the middle of speaking when we walked in. Fearful of causing an interruption, we stood at the back, as unobtrusively as possible.

Rabbi Neugroschel looked at Papa and said, "What am I

talking for? Here is someone who was there! You can ask him!"

The students took the rabbi's suggestion seriously, and after his talk, they approached Papa and Mama, almost wanting to touch them, these real, live people who were "there" for six whole years of their impressionable youth, and still had genuine smiles in their eyes.

They wanted to hear how Papa had managed to put on tefillin and hear the shofar in Auschwitz. They wanted to know how he could even think of *mishloach manos* in Bergen-Belsen, with dead bodies piled up all around him. How could he retain his faith under those conditions?

Papa wasn't fluent in modern Hebrew, and the young men talked a mile a minute, but he understood them. They understood what he said, too, because they weren't communicating in Hebrew, they were speaking the language of the heart.

We sat there as if in a dream from another world — Papa in his shiny silk *kapote* and tall *spodik*, with his Belgian-Yiddish accent, Mama with her warm smile, sitting straight and well-dressed, answering their questions with me acting as interpreter. And all those boys refusing to leave, wanting to stay a little longer to bask in Papa and Mama's glow and to hear more and more about what it means to be raised with true Jewish faith, true Jewish strength.

Late that night, I sat on a low stone wall with Miri, listening closely as she explained how she came to the point of putting on a modest Shabbos dress.

"I've been through a lot in my life," she said softly.

"Yes, I know... at least part of it," I answered. Miri and I had talked a few times when we sat together on the bus in Poland. Her story was tragic. Her parents had died suddenly, one after the other, leaving her, still very young, to raise two little siblings in the middle of that void.

"I managed to keep it all together seamlessly," Miri said. "I always was the strong, optimistic type... I was born that way. It was a gift from Heaven, the sort of gift that only later do you realize why it was given to you. I didn't break down. Far from it — I felt I was coping very well, and I patted myself on the back for it.

"Then I started going to Nefesh Yehudi programs on campus. I was already working toward my master's degree in educational counseling, and I didn't mind hearing what they had to say about Torah and Judaism. In fact, I enjoyed the lectures very much. They didn't make me feel pressured, they just sort of skimmed the surface in a gentle, soothing way, like a holistic massage. Nobody was trying to take over my mind; they were just offering a taste, a chance to get acquainted with Judaism.

"I went to Poland as part of the program. It was my first time; when my high school had their trip, I didn't go. I felt it wasn't serious enough... mostly horsing around and shopping, interrupted by visits to Holocaust sites. Nefesh Yehudi was offering something different, and I was glad to join them. If I'd known where it would end up leading me" — a smile lit up her green eyes, and she blushed slightly — "maybe I would have thought twice.

"I knew there would be rabbis who would speak from an Orthodox standpoint, and I knew you, an avowed *dossit,* would be there to tell your parents' story. 'That's okay,' I said to myself. 'It will be interesting to hear things from their point of view.' But I found myself on a different road from what I expected. I was on the fast highway, and I couldn't stop in the middle.

"I came to Poland with a good friend, expecting to find some quiet time for self-discovery, but we were speeding ahead, way beyond that. First of all, we were all women. I was used to being in mixed company all the time, which meant hiding behind makeup and saying all the right things even if they weren't true, always trying to make a good impression... and that can get a girl all mixed up about who she really is. And suddenly, there I was, in an all-girl environment, and all that stress was lifted. You wouldn't understand... I mean, you must be used to it," she said, gently poking fun at me, "but it was like suddenly having so much space.

"And then there was the rabbi, and the *madrichot,* and you, of course, and you all told stories about Jewish heroism that I never could have dreamed of. I started to understand what faith really is, how incredibly empowering it is, how people could hold on to it, and it could get them through anything. Their whole world could collapse and turn into a horror movie... but they hung on with their fingernails... screaming, crying, bleeding, but not letting go. It just amazed me.

"All around me, everything was crying out, 'Torah! Life! Meaning!' I wasn't seeing random suffering that just happens. There was always a great hand there, a Divine hand to hold you up and say, 'I'm here, my child. It hurts, but I am here.'

"In Majdanek, we stood by the big stone plaque and sang *Eishet Chayil.* It was quiet, the music played softly, we lit memorial candles, we sang and cried, and cried and sang. It was something we were trying to say to all the women who were murdered there: 'No, it's not like what everybody thinks. They killed your body here, but your *neshamah,* your soul, was above all that. The *neshamah* is greater than that; nobody can take the *neshamah* away. It was in G-d's hands the whole time, always pure.

"At that moment, I felt that I myself was an *eishet chayil* and they were singing the song to me, promising me that my *neshamah* was greater than anything here on this earth.

"And that's how the whole trip was. It was as if we were really meeting the people in the stories, as if we could look them in the eyes and dive into them. They were really present for us. And then there was the music that kept you present and wouldn't let you escape. And the words... I must have heard them somewhere before... everything — the stories and the songs — it all gave me such a strong feeling of déjà vu. I felt as if I already knew it all and was only now remembering it…

"What was it? What was that something that was always there inside me and always knew all these things? What was waking up in me all of a sudden? It was as if someone had been sitting there quietly in the dark for twenty-seven years, and in one week, I suddenly started noticing her. I acknowledged her existence, shone a spotlight on her, brought her something to eat and drink. She was my *neshamah,* and she'd stood up and started making noise, saying, 'Hello, Miri, here I am! I'm the one who's making you feel like crying all the time without knowing why. I'm the reason all those songs sound familiar! I've always known them! You wonder why you were so moved by your first experience of Shabbat? It was because of me, because you opened the door and shone some light on me. You wonder how you could sing songs you'd never heard before? It was I who was singing them, my dear. It was I, your *neshamah.*

"When I returned home from that trip, I couldn't be the same as I was before. Now I was Miri with her *neshamah* set free. A *neshamah* greater than anything on this earth."

CHAPTER 62

A Man with a Number

Darkness envelops us. It's late, and only a few lone figures pass by now and then. Miri's eyes are full of tears, and so are mine. An antique-style street lamp sprinkles a bit of light on us, and the winding alleyways are silent.

"You see, I always thought my own story took up all the space in the world," Miri said. "My losses, my grief, my courage to overcome, my successes, and everything I've become since then. And suddenly I realized that my personal story doesn't matter that much. It's not central — it's just part of one very big journey of the Jewish People. I'm part of a nation that has continuity from the beginning of history until today, and we all have roles to play, destinies to fulfill, and stations along the way.

"And where am I in the script? Did I get any lines? Suddenly I realized how small I was, and how arrogant I was being. Who was I to try to take center stage and take my own direction in this great march of the Jewish People towards its shared destiny? And how could I kick aside everything that I am? Yes, whether I like it or not, it's me, I'm a part of it, and it's my destiny, too.

"This has taken a lot of work, Chana. I'm almost thirty, and I'm about to get my master's degree. I work, I'm successful and popular, and I'm pretty satisfied with myself. It's not easy to put all that aside and say, 'Miri, there's Someone bigger than you charting your path. Listen — you're a Jewish woman, and you have to fulfill your destiny. This is your real story, and if you don't fulfill it, then it won't be fulfilled.

"At the airport terminal, I said to G-d, 'Creator of the Universe, I know You're calling to me. I hear it loud and clear, I feel it in my whole body, and I want to answer it. I won't disappear back into the underground burrow I was living in before, without light or air — and I even used to think that was the whole world.

"'I want to answer You,' I said. 'But how?' I wanted a strong answer that wouldn't allow me to sidestep it, something that would require a commitment.

"I had to jump in somewhere, so I decided to start with the clothes. The last time I wore jeans was on the trip home. Since then, I've only worn dresses. Two weeks later, I signed up at a Midrasha, Netiv Bina, here in Jerusalem. That was what I needed — they just keep dropping the bombshells on you, without giving you a chance to breathe. I've been there for about six weeks, and my *neshamah* hasn't stopped dancing."

We sat there quietly a few minutes longer, immersed in everything Miri had said, just feeling each other's presence. Then I gave her a kiss and wished her good night and *Shabbat shalom*. Something in my face must have made her laugh, and she said, "Hey, Chana, let's not get too heavy here. Under all my long skirts, I'm still not exactly a Bais Yaakov girl! I have a long way to go, but I've taken a new direction, and I have a feeling I may go far."

"Good night, sweetheart. *Shabbat shalom*!"

In the morning, all the girls were waiting to see us. They'd arrived Friday afternoon, but I hadn't seen any of them except for Miri. After prayers at the Western Wall, a family Shabbos meal, and hearing little Yossi's take on the weekly Torah portion, we went to spend some time with them.

When we entered the room, all the girls gazed at Mama and

Papa as if they would swallow them up with their eyes. I could almost read their thoughts: So these are the people Chana told all those stories about... wow.

The rabbi who led the tour in Poland went up to the front to speak. Meanwhile, I looked around at the girls. I saw that Yael's husband was with her. (Really? She'd managed to drag him here? Or had he just come along to keep a watchful eye on her?)* Miri was there, in the dress she'd worn last night, and there was Rotem, winking at me, and Tanya next to her, very serious and attentive. Almost all fifty girls were there, every one of them wonderful.

The rabbi went on to talk about people who survived the Holocaust with their faith intact, and their special closeness to G-d. His voice rose with passion as he related a story about the Satmar Rebbe, Rav Yoelish. When the Rebbe decided to leave

---

*Yael's husband came with her to the Shabbaton and watched their three children while she participated in the group sessions. Whenever he could, he came in to listen to the lectures, all huddled up and silent as a mummy. On *motzaei Shabbos* (Saturday night, after Shabbos ends) he spoke up for the first time. "I came here to see how you brainwash people and practice religious coercion on them. But as the hours went by, I felt myself melting. You took away my ammunition.

The following Tuesday, he called Rabbi Rosen. "I think of myself as a pretty special guy," he said. "I have a university degree, I belonged to the *Shayetet* [an elite unit in the navy, comparable to the US Navy Seals], and now I work at Rafael Advanced Defense Systems. But something happened to me during that Shabbat. Ever since then, my mind has refused to settle down. I was wondering, maybe you know of a *shiur* in my area that would be suitable for me?"

It turned out that Rabbi Rosen was scheduled to give a lecture in their area that same week, so they met again, and after the talk, Yael's husband asked him if he could get someone to come and kasher their kitchen, and if he would find a kollel student to study Torah with him. "I thought I knew everything," he said. "And then I found myself holding a prayer book and not knowing where to begin or what to do, and I realized how ignorant I am. It's terrible! I need to fix this right away!"

Jerusalem for America, his Chassidim besieged him, begging him not to go. "Will the Rebbe leave us here alone? Who will give us *brachos*?" they asked. The Rebbe looked at them and said, "*Brachos*? You want *brachos*? Look for someone who puts on tefillin with a number on his arm, and ask him for *brachos*. His *brachos* will be fulfilled!"

Suddenly, an electric current passed through the room. The rabbi glanced at Papa and said, "We have someone like that right here. This is the opportunity of a lifetime. Come on, everyone, ask him for a *brachah*!"

There was a moment of hesitant silence. These girls take their choices seriously, and I wondered what was coming next. But then, a few girls got up and approached Papa. So what if they were college-educated intellectuals? The rabbi said this was a rare opportunity to be blessed by a holy man with a number on his arm. Didn't they have a *neshamah*, too?

A few seconds later, a long line was forming, each girl in turn shyly or boldly requesting a *brachah*. Papa, the epitome of kindness and humility, didn't know where all this was coming from, but he was more than willing to give whatever he could. He blessed each girl unhurriedly, allowing the words to flow from his heart and soul, with a radiant smile, as if he were blessing his own daughters.

I retreated to the side, not wanting to intrude on this sublime moment. A spark seemed to jump out of one heart and ignite the heart of another. Perhaps that is one way of defining a *brachah*?

Papa didn't repeat formulaic blessings; he blessed each girl individually with a specific, detailed *brachah* that flowed from the inspiration of the moment. The girls sensed the holiness of that moment, and they answered "*Amen*" with lowered eyes.

CHAPTER 63

Papa Vanquishes the Fireworks

AFTER THE *BRACHOS* CAME more questions. With the typical directness of Sabras, the girls pick the hardest questions, and their aim is straight. My daughter-in-law, sitting next to me, cringes a bit, but Papa and Mama are relaxed, explaining everything, finding no question too hard. Papa is asked about Chassidus: did being a *chossid* help him to cope with all the suffering?

Papa retells the story of the saccharine tablet he found on Purim and gave to his friend as *mishloach manos*. They were two young Jews on a death march to Bergen-Belsen after six years of torture and starvation with no end in sight, and the *mishloach manos* was less than minimal. But after sadly wishing each other a happy Purim, they added, "And next year, may we celebrate with the Rebbe."

They had nothing to give but a little tablet of saccharine that couldn't even save them from starvation, but they still had a reason to keep going, to hold onto the thin thread of life. They could still hope to see the Rebbe again one day.

The girls ask about the Chassidic leaders who were rescued through special efforts. How did the ordinary Chassidim feel, knowing that their Rebbe had escaped to safety while they were suffering horribly in the camps?

"It was our hope," Papa replied, with the perspicacity of an elderly Jew who has seen a thing or two in his life. "The Rebbes had to flee. In any case they couldn't continue leading their communities. They were at the top of the Nazis' most-wanted list. Pictures of the Gerrer Rebbe were circulated among every branch of the German police and armed forces, even before they started the deportations. The idea was to take the leaders first, to break the people's spirit and make them lose hope.

"The Rebbes weren't abandoning a sinking ship. They were preparing a lifeboat for those who managed to reach free waters. To a *chossid,* knowing that his Rebbe was alive was a great source of strength. It gave him something to look forward to, a prospect of life after the flood, that vision of eventually rejoining his beloved Rebbe and his community, somewhere on the globe."

They asked him if he'd ever questioned his faith. In the midst of all that horror, hadn't he ever asked, where is G-d? He told them about the day he realized he was on the way to Auschwitz, the perfect peace that enveloped him as he handed over his soul to his Creator, and his anticipation of meeting Him. "I didn't have questions; I had answers. I didn't ask where was G-d; I saw Him, right next to me all the time. I felt His presence protecting me. As the *tzaddik,* the holy Rebbe Aharon of Belze said, every Jew who survived the Holocaust had two angels beside him the whole time."

I looked at my father and was filled with pride and love. Once again I felt like a little girl who believed he was all-powerful. In his arms I would always be safe. He could vanquish all the scary fireworks in the sky. He was no longer the clean-shaven businessman who worked all day in the Diamond Bourse. Now he was an elderly *chossid* whose children were all married, felt there was no reason left to remain in Belgium, and came to live in Eretz Yisrael. Although he was acclimated to life in Belgium, he had never struck roots there; he'd always thought of it as temporary, warranted by circumstances. He bought apartments for all of us in Eretz Yisrael, but he lived in a rented property. He would buy himself a real place to live only in Eretz Yisrael. To him, only Eretz Yisrael was home.

And just when he reached the age at which most people feel settled down, too accustomed to their neighborhood to start over again, Papa bought an apartment in Bnei Brak and began really living.

"I have a ticket to Gan Eden," he would often say. "A VIP ticket. I can't lose it — it's tattooed here on my arm. But what will I do when I get there? All the *tzaddikim* there will be learning Torah, and how will I feel? What kind of Gan Eden is it if you arrive there knowing nothing?* As soon as he retired to Bnei Brak, Papa started learning full time. He wasn't satisfied with going at the leisurely pace typical for his age. No, Papa was one of the lions! It was as if now, at last, he was a young *yeshiva bochur* in Chachmei Lublin, and he was simply continuing where he'd left off before the war.

He got up every morning to learn and went to sleep at night in order to get up and learn. He breathed in order to learn, and visited with his grandchildren and great-grandchildren in order to learn.

---

*Papa knew quite a lot, actually. Long before he retired from the Bourse, he set business aside for weeks at a time to take part in the Ponevezh Yeshiva's Yarchei Kallah intensive Torah study retreats in England and Switzerland. He would review in depth all the pages of Gemara he'd learned as a youth for the entry exam at Yeshivas Chachmei Lublin. He had a great intellectual rapport with Rabbi Berel Povarsky, the Ponevezh Rosh Yeshiva, who gave him *geshmak* (delight) in his learning. He never missed the Yarchei Kallah; they gave him strength for the whole year. One time, my husband and I asked him to be *sandek* for our little son's *bris*. He and Mama flew in specially, but then the *bris* was delayed due to newborn jaundice. "Chana," he said to me, "you know what a *zechus* it is for me to be *sandek* at a grandson's *bris*. But the Yarchei Kallah starts in England on Sunday. If we can't make the *bris* by then, I'll have to go. I may miss the *bris* and lose the privilege of being *sandek*, but I can't give up those days of learning Torah."

Around lunchtime, he would phone my husband to share the ideas that had come to him during the morning's learning session. "What do you think of my *teirutz*?" he would ask... "Rabbi Akiva Eiger says the same as you, but the *Ketzos* says like me." My husband would answer him, and Papa would refute his answer, raise a question about it, or express his delight at the perfect solution. It wasn't just a courtesy call to a son-in-law, and it wasn't just an exchange of knowledge. It was more than an intellectual discussion. The Torah was his lifeline!

If my husband didn't answer the phone, Papa couldn't rest that afternoon — not because he wasn't tired, but because he just couldn't. His mind was engaged in the Torah, and he couldn't rest until he'd settled his thoughts.

One time, my parents had booked a vacation at the Dead Sea. It was one of Papa's favorite places, and to go there with Mama... that was the icing on the cake. But a few days beforehand, he asked her if she'd like to go with a friend or one of us daughters instead. He'd love to go, and it was the perfect vacation spot for him, but how could he miss so many days of learning in the kollel? When would he ever make them up? He wasn't getting younger, and every day that passed was gone forever. So would Mama mind very much...? Was it all right with her if he stayed in Bnei Brak? Mama agreed. Many waters cannot quench love, and Papa loved the Torah more than all the waters of the Dead Sea.

When Papa left Belgium, he left a good reputation as an honest, reliable diamond trader. He also left all his public service activities as Antwerp's local chairman of Agudath Israel and a member of the Agudath Israel World Organization, to which he'd dedicated himself unstintingly for decades. When the Agudah representatives in Israel heard that he was coming on *aliyah*, they asked him to join them in their work on behalf of the public. But Papa just smiled and quietly declined. "I came here to learn," he said. "There are plenty of people who can serve in Agudah instead of me, but no one can learn Torah instead of me."

The girls aren't aware of all this. To them, he's a kindly grandfather who speaks a halting Hebrew, listens to them patiently, and translates the words in his head before he replies. He's the very image of humility and simplicity, and to look at him, no one would ever dream of the strength in him, the strength it took to put on tefillin in Auschwitz, the strength it took to leave all the comforts of Belgium for a little side street in Bnei Brak, a shul where he didn't know anyone, and the anonymity of a retiree who came to learn.

But they can sense that strength, and they rely on it, just as I always did. My father could always vanquish the fireworks. They could fill the sky with their noise and their flames, and it never bothered him. He always looked past them, at the Heavens themselves.

CHAPTER 64

Yes, Mama Can

MAMA KNOWS EVEN LESS Hebrew than Papa, but her presence speaks all languages. She has all the gentleness of a Bubbe from the shtetl, with a touch of the Queen of England. She smiles at all the girls who crowd around her, and it's love at first sight.

They're looking for a powerful takeaway from this meeting. "Mrs. Horowitz," Efrat gushes, "are you real?"

I translate, and Mama smiles.

"How could you stand all that hunger and loneliness?" they ask. "Left alone, without your family, when you were still so young… for all those years, with no end in sight…. Where did you get the strength?"

Mama answers in Yiddish:

"Nisht du 'ich ken nisht,' es iz nor du 'ich vill nisht.'

In der Riboino shel Oilem zol ins nisht oispriven vus a mench ken…"

It loses its charm in translation, but I do my best to tell the girls what Mama just said: "Don't say 'I can't' when you really mean 'I don't want to.' And may G-d never test you to your limits."

A person has tremendous ability; it reaches to the skies, if he only has the will. Difficulties can bring a person to places in himself that he never knew were there, but it's not wise to put yourself to the test if you don't have to.

I'm reminded of the dentist we went to in Holland. Mama needed some very complex dental work, and she sat in that chair for seven hours straight without moving or saying a word. It was grueling and painful, and the dentist was astounded. "Madame Horowitz," he said, "it's all right to groan once in a while."

"Oh, that was nothing," she said to him afterwards. "It didn't hurt." She knew what real pain was.

I don't want to think about it, but I can't help it. Hashem tested her to her limits, and she showed how much *"a mench ken."*

Mama was always a woman who "could." Even when our circumstances became more comfortable and she was able to dress well, hire help, take us on vacation at the seaside, and furnish the house nicely, she didn't sit back and relax. She always demanded more of herself.

I remember accompanying Mama, somewhat against my will, on her visits to the Jewish old-age home in Antwerp. She would adopt a lonely old woman and treat her like a mother, bringing her cakes and freshly-squeezed juice, chatting with her and leaving a nice picture of the "grandchildren" on the bureau. We played along with the whole charade. We would come around to bring her something or just to say hello, until the lady passed on to a better world, and then Mama would adopt someone new.

After I moved to Eretz Yisrael, she learned that many *talmidei chachomim* here have large families and little income. Some have difficulty making ends meet. Mama began to collect children's clothing from her friends in Belgium, everything from coats to pajamas, even shoes and tights. It was all from the best French brands, the iconic Petit Bateau for example, and Mama would fold every item neatly and lovingly, so as to present it in a respectable manner that would make the recipients feel good. Then she would pack it all into big boxes and mail them to me. The clerk at my local post office soon learned to recognize these parcels, and whenever they arrived he would phone me and say, "Mrs. Rotenberg, some more parcels just came in from your mother. Please come and pick them up quickly — they're blocking the passageway here!"*

I would sort the clothing by size, wrap it up, and give it to the families. The recipients would tell me, "These clothes bring sunshine into our lives."

Belgium was never a world leader in the field of medicine, but in recent years it has become a hub for all sorts of transplants, and as a result people began coming from Israel to the Antwerp Medical Center. Mama would go and visit those patients and the family members who accompanied them. She didn't speak their language, and she never was very talkative anyway, but she knew how to be supportive without words. I asked her once how she passed the time with these people and she said. "I listen to them. People need someone to listen to them..."

---

*There's another story behind this whole project of Mama's. It was quite costly to send these big parcels abroad, and Mama began to realize she needed a special budget for the purpose. Then she thought of Papa's *grammen* (amusing and touching rhymes chanted at weddings and other celebrations, specially composed for and about the central figures in the celebration). Papa dedicated his talent for writing *grammen* to the mitzvah of *simchas chosson v'kallah* (going all-out to create a joyful atmosphere at a wedding celebration). Many people wanted to pay him for his *grammen*, which were a major feature of every wedding in Antwerp. But Papa preferred to give his services free of charge, purely for the sake of the mitzvah. One day, however, Mama asked him to consider taking payment for his *grammen*, in order to finance the shipping of her clothing parcels to poor families in Eretz Yisrael. For that mitzvah, Papa was happy to take payment from the prosperous families of Antwerp. From then on, he charged a fair price for his *grammen* and put the money in Mama's parcel fund. Problem solved. And in my parents' shared merit, another little girl received a fashionable dress for the holidays, and another little boy proudly went to shul in his European-made suit.

Sometimes travelers from Israel came alone on various types of business, and sometimes young families would come to try their luck in the land of chocolate. Mama helped them all in every way she could. One time she heard about a recently arrived family in need of furniture. Someone told her that a neighbor was about to replace his living-room furniture and had some pieces to give away. Without missing a beat, Mama climbed the stairs to the neighbor's apartment, glanced at the little coffee table, thought it looked about right, and picked it up in her two hands, shocking the owner, a proper Belgian in a necktie. "Mrs. Horowitz," he said, "surely you don't mean to carry that yourself!"

"Of course not," she said soothingly. "There's a driver outside..." The family in need lived down the street, and Mama schlepped the table to their door. "Mrs. Horowitz!" they gasped. "You didn't carry this here yourself, did you?"

"Of course not," she chuckled. "The driver carried it." Relieved, the family thanked her profusely.

After my brother Mottel passed away in Eretz Yisrael, and we got up from sitting shivah, Mama wiped away her tears, put on a nice outfit, and went to the hospital with a tray of filled chocolates and little gifts, all beautifully arranged. The medical staff was stunned to see her there, bringing them gifts, just seven days after losing her only son, and they didn't know what to say to her. But she spoke to them: she'd just come to express her gratitude to the wonderful doctors and nurses who had taken care of her son so devotedly until the end.

I still go to Bnei Brak now and then on *erev Shabbos* and drop in on my mother. She isn't a young woman, and she has to watch her sugar consumption, but every Friday, her kitchen counters are covered with long logs of chocolate babka. An hour after they're baked and cooled, there's barely a slice left. She hands it all out to whoever needs it. Half a loaf, for example, went to the shoemaker who worked in a little booth at the end of the street. Once, Mama had him sew an outer pocket onto her leather bag for her mobile phone. She paid him, and added half a loaf of babka as a tip. He thanked her, and she was touched to see he had tears in his eyes. From then on, she's brought him half a loaf every Friday, and that's his Shabbos cake. There are widows, elderly and young, who Mama visits once a week, and women with new babies who she checks on, to see how things are going. She attends three different Torah *shiurim* regularly, in Yiddish and in French, and there are phone calls that must be made. The ladies look forward to those weekly calls from the only person who shows an interest in them. If she flies to Belgium once in a while, she leaves me a list as long as the exile, detailing all the people I must call on her behalf and why, how the cake is to be distributed, who is to received the meat patties she left in the freezer, and which elderly lady absolutely must be visited. At her advanced age, my mother manages to do much more than most people can handle.

"I was small and frail as a little girl," Mama tells the students, and I translate. "I was short, and my older siblings thought of me as a baby. In a family of eleven children, nine of them older than I, I almost felt redundant. But apparently I was capable of more — out of all of us, I was the only one who survived. Never say you can't; when Hashem is with you, you can..."

Once again, there isn't a dry eye in the room, and the man who came to sing for us wants to dedicate a song to Mama — the classic Yiddish song *Oyfn Pripetchik* about the little shtetl children learning *alef-beis.* Then he sings *A Yiddishe Mamme,* and everyone feels that she certainly deserves the tribute — she, and all the other women who "can."

One Last Story, but Not the End

by Miriam Aflalo

I NEVER KNEW THERE WERE streets like this in Jerusalem.

It looks like someone cut-and-pasted a charming Italian village and put it right here in Ramot Beit, two streets above the main road I've traveled on a thousand times, never knowing this was here...

Beautiful stone pavement, arched trellises of greenery over painted wrought-iron gates, pretty name plates on front doors flanked by gaily colored flowers in pots, perfect quiet, the distant bark of a dog, and more quiet, a fresh morning wind...

I had thought I'd meet with Miri in a café somewhere, or in an office at the school where I teach, but when I called, she said she had a six-week-old baby and wasn't able to get out very much. "But you're more than welcome to come and visit," she added.

"Oh, mazal tov!" I said. So Miri was a married woman now, and with a baby, too. Not the restless, searching student I'd imagined. But after all, it *had* been six years since her trip to Poland. "So where do you live, and when would be a good time?" I asked.

"Just a moment," she said. I could hear children's voices chirping in the background. "I'm picking up my bigger ones from preschool. Can we talk later?"

We spoke on the phone again afterwards, and I learned that Miri lived in Ramot Beit, had three children, worked as an educational counselor for charedi youth, and was currently on maternity leave. The trip to Poland six years ago had been the big turning point in her life....

Now, two weeks after Miri invited me, I was finally here, on the lovely, narrow street where she lives, looking for the house number she gave me and thinking that even the name of the street — She'ar Yashuv — was apropos.

I knocked at the metal gate, and Miri came out, shoeless, to answer. Green eyes in the face of a young girl, her head wrapped in a scarf... she looked like one of my friends from seminary. She must have read my thoughts, because she smiled and said, "Six years ago, if someone had shown me a picture of how I would look today, I would have run the other way."

We laughed. She led me inside. I expected to see toys scattered all over the living room and the remains of breakfast cereal in the kitchen, but everything was clean and neat to perfection, and furnished in the vintage style I love.

From the big picture window I could see all the way to Giv'at Shaul and the graceful lines of the Chords Bridge at the entrance of Yerushalayim, and in an infant seat on the rug lay a perfect little baby, as cute as his mother and as pure as only G-d can make. I liked everything I saw: the house, Miri, and everything that was in her eyes. Just the right happy ending for Chana's story.

Miri told me how the trip to Poland had affected her, about the *brachah* Chana's father had given her, and the amazing way it had all come true... how she'd met her husband, an Israeli who'd grown up in Singapore, of all places, where his family had relocated because of his father's job. In some population registry somewhere, he was on record as being a Jew, and that was all he knew about the subject.* She told me how a group of women

---

*He flew to America, where he was enrolled in a university, and one time he was asked to be part of a minyan. "A minyan? What's that?" he asked. The men

who'd been on the trip had formed their own community. Many of them had started keeping Shabbos, and they would host each other. Family friendships had formed, and when they got together they would talk about their children and many other topics. It was also a chance to vent about the harder aspects of their new lives.

"It's not easy," she said, "to take a whole new direction in life when you're almost thirty, and you're so proud of everything you've achieved up until then. On your former path, you got lots of recognition, and now you're just a raw beginner, and on top of that you have new obstacles that you have to remove or get past."

She told me how she'd begun as a confident graduate student, attending lectures on Jewish identity on the side, just to get a taste, but then, after the trip, finding herself in up to the neck. Once she started studying at the Midrasha, it was a whole new world, learning things that pertained directly to her as a Jewish woman: a new, value-based style of dressing… the Torah allows you to prepare food this way on Shabbos, but not that way… *d'Oraisa* and *d'Rabbanan*… and the thrill of finding new meaning in life, which kept coming in high-frequency waves.

Miri spoke in strong, elevated terms, yet without preaching or

---

asked him again if he was Jewish, and he said yes, that he knew for sure. But he'd never heard of a minyan before. They explained that it was a group of men who get together for Jewish prayer. They needed a tenth man. Would he mind helping them out? He said, "Sorry, I don't know how." "That's okay," they said. "It's enough if you just want to be part of the group. It'll take about ten minutes." Well, he was a kindhearted type and willing to help out so they could pray. They went inside and began. The *chazzan* said something, and all the other men responded. But then, there was total silence. Everyone was standing still and not saying a word. The long silence made him nervous. What was going on? Did they want him to leave? Was he allowed to ask someone how long they were going to stand silently like that? It seemed to go on forever… but at last it was over. By the time they finished praying, he realized one thing: he needed to know more. Soon he knew much more, and the rest is family history.

hitting anyone over the head with her words. And even though her early encounters with Judaism — and especially with her Jewish self — had been so dazzling, the educational counselor in her knew how to moderate the experience.

"And all this resulted from a ten-day trip?" I asked, feeling a bit skeptical.

"No," she said. "It's not the trip, or even the stories you hear during the trip. It's the truth that's there inside you, that's brought out by the trip and the stories, so strongly that you can't escape it, and all you want to do is fulfill it!"

By the time I get up to say goodbye, the baby has fallen asleep in his mother's arms, so I tell her in a whisper how impressed I am. I look at that little one who's lived only two months in this world, and I realize he has no idea how much he owes his existence to other people he's never met, and to things they experienced long ago.

I go out, and once again I'm surrounded by arched, blooming trellises, creamy-white Jerusalem stone, and the bright, midday sun.

Some stories never end; they just pass, like a torch, from one person to another, and the fire keeps burning perpetually....

Epilogue

Cheshvan, 5772

Several months after the Shabbos reunion, I went with my seminary students on a school trip to the Negev. It was interrupted by a phone call from my sister Esty. "Papa isn't feeling well," she said. "He's in the hospital."

A bit later, Tzili called. "Chana," she said, "I know you're on a *tiyul,* but I have to tell you that Papa had a mild stroke."

I was worried, but life had taught me that Papa was strong. He would overcome this, too.

We were at the Dead Sea when my husband called and said, "Take a taxi and come to Tel HaShomer."

I arrived at the hospital and found Mama sitting there with her *Tehillim,* without a trace of hysteria in her manner. She was happy to see me.

Tzili said, "Come and see him." I recoiled at that idea, knowing that he was unconscious. "What for?" I said, but Tzili took me by the arm and brought me in. She drew back the curtain, and there he was, a picture of tranquility, his features smooth and relaxed. It was mind-boggling.

A nurse stopped us in the corridor. "That's your father?" she asked.

We said yes, and with awe in her voice, she said, "I saw the number… he has a number on his arm…."

On Friday, we were in Bnei Brak, and two hours before Shabbos we received the news: Papa had gone to the Heavenly heights, his soul taken painlessly by a "Divine kiss," just as he would have chosen and just as he deserved.

We knew that in the upper realms, his whole departed family was now greeting him, and thousands upon thousands of angels created from all the mitzvos he'd done, all the Torah he'd learned, and all the suffering he'd borne with firm faith. But we were left alone, bereft of his strong, illuminating presence. During the shivah, the house was crowded with pained visitors who came to offer consolation.

And then, a lady brought us three folded pages. It was an article she'd written for Aish HaTorah's Hebrew website, about an elderly Jew from Bnei Brak who enthralled everyone in the *shtiebel* with his dancing on Simchas Torah. It was to be his last dance in a world where he never stopped dancing. She hadn't known who he was at the time, and we hadn't known about the dance. It was the most beautiful final chapter that Papa himself could have written about his life.

> Simchas Torah in our shul is a real celebration, and I've written about it before. A diverse and fascinating group of worshippers makes up our congregation....
>
> One of the relative newcomers is an elderly Jew who came on *aliyah* from Belgium not long ago, bought an apartment near the shul, and began coming regularly. Established members of the shul say he was born in Poland, experienced the terrors of World War II, and eventually ended up in Belgium where he married, raised a family, and built a life. After all his children married and settled in Israel, he decided there was no longer anything to keep him on foreign soil. His wife, who came from a background much like his own and also survived the Shoah, agreed with him wholeheartedly, and they relocated to our city, Bnei Brak. I meet her now and then in the neighborhood grocery or at the vegetable store. She speaks mainly a juicy Yiddish and understands Hebrew, and I'm just the reverse: Hebrew is my native tongue, and I understand Yiddish because my grandmother speaks it in almost the exact same accent, as they both came originally from Poland.
>
> We exchange a few polite words, asking how's the family

and such, sending regards to the few acquaintances we have in common, and saying goodbye, with a friendly handshake, see you again soon....

When I came to shul this Yom Kippur for Kol Nidrei, I found I was sharing a bench with this same elderly lady. She greeted me warmly and then opened her *machzor*. An old, musty smell wafted from it. It was quite large, and different from any other edition I'd ever seen. The prayers in Hebrew were printed on one side, and on the facing page was a Yiddish translation. She alternated between the two languages, davening some parts from the Hebrew side, and then switching to the Yiddish.

Once in a while she lost her place and turned to me for help, pointing apologetically to the small hearing aid in her ear and explaining, "You see, *maidele,* I don't know the davening that well; I never went to high school or seminary. There was a war going on. And my hearing isn't that good these days, either..."

By the end of Yom Kippur we were close friends. From then on, her smile when we met at the grocer's was broader, and we parted with a hug.

The holy day had passed, and the busy days of preparation for Succos were over, too. *Lulavim, esroigim...* and even the *aravos* were already beaten on the floor. Simchas Torah was waiting in the wings.

In our shul, everything is organized ahead of time for Simchas Torah so the congregants can spend most of the day in shul. For the festive midday meal, everyone is assigned a different dish to bring, and after all the davening, dancing, and *aliyos* for one and all, the tables are set, Kiddush is made, and a royal feast is served to the whole congregation.

In the evening after Havdalah, the hustle and bustle begins right away as the men set up for *Hakafos Shniyos*. Benches and tables are pushed aside, musical instruments are brought in, and the sound system is plugged in.

A musical arranger who davens at our shul leads the band, a few young men with nice voices serve as the singers, and everyone else is in charge of the dancing. All the men hold hands and dance the night away as if they hadn't just spent the last twenty-four hours dancing.

Their fatigue is forgotten, and once again they rejoice in the *simchah* of Torah, unwilling to let go of the unique celebration that was self-prescribed by the Jewish people.

During the dancing this year, a small circle of three men began to dance in the middle of the main circle: the Rav of the shul, a highly regarded *maggid shiur*, and the Jew from Belgium who had recently joined us.

The keyboard player was outdoing himself, and the crowd was lustily singing *"Ki oirech yomim u'shenois chaim..."* The elderly Jew shut his eyes tightly and almost seemed to rise up from the floor as he danced. His face was flushed and then pale, flushed and then pale, and the people around him noticed it and began to worry that he might be unwell.

While they were still wondering whether they should stop everything and call for medical aid, he pushed up his sleeve and raised his left arm high in air, so that everyone could see the number tattooed there — and he danced.

Instead of singing the verse along with the crowd, he started singing, *"Hundert ein un zechtzig, tzvei hundert draisig! Eins! Zeks! Eins! Tzvei! Drei! Nul!* (One hundred sixty-one, two hundred thirty! One! Six! One! Two! Three! Zero!)" Again and again, with all his might, he sang out the numbers etched into his flesh, his constant companions since those terrible days.

The congregation stopped their singing and stood stockstill. Only he and the Rav, who was the first baby born after that dreadful destruction, continued dancing, holding on to each other with tears streaming as they sang out the numbers.

One of the men came out of his momentary shock, handed him the microphone, and asked him to say a few words to the young congregants who looked on, wiping away tears and knowing mainly that they were witnessing something great. They should hear it and remember it:

"I thank the *Ribboino shel Oilam*... I thank Him for the good He has repaid me... *Ashrai!* How fortunate I am to have merited this! How fortunate I am to have reached this day... G-d, I have won! *Yodu la'Shem Chassdoi!"*

Simchas Torah ended like Purim, with tears, with dancing, with one circle united and unique, and all voices in unison singing the words that marked the end of the festival: "Wipe out the memory of Amalek from under the heavens — do not forget!"

APPENDICES

Mexico

FOR YEARS WE STAYED peacefully in our little corner of Jerusalem. At the beginning, I went out to work part time, teaching English, and later on I started organizing sales from home now and then, but my main occupation was raising the eight wonderful treasures the Creator had given me.

My husband, Rabbi Yeshayahu Rotenberg *shlita*, taught in Kol Yaakov, the well-known yeshiva headed by Rav Yehuda Ades *shlita*; he was the Rosh Kollel of the yeshiva alumni. During that period, many students from Latin American countries came to the yeshiva. After they married, many of them stayed and banded together into a fine little community of their own, and they developed a warm relationship with my husband, who was much more than a Rosh Kollel to them. Those who returned to Latin America would often relay warm invitations to him to visit their countries and give a series of *shiurim* in their communities, to reawaken in their souls the joyful days they'd spent learning Torah in Eretz Yisrael.

My husband consulted with Rav Ades *shlita*, and after much deliberation, they decided on a plan. He would go to Mexico, visiting every Jewish community there and giving a series of *shiurim* — a total of seventy-two *shiurim* in a week and a half. He was to run a one-man marathon on a trail paved with love of Torah by the Jews of Mexico.

For my part, I packed a suitcase for my husband, tucking in a few homemade treats, and waited for the week and a half to go by.... But before the time was up, a call came in from Mexico. One of the community representatives was on the line. "Chana," he said, "the thirst for Torah here is tremendous. It can't be quenched in just a week and a half. I feel that your husband ought to come here for a longer time, to establish more Torah learning and strengthen the people spiritually. It's a duty that can't be shirked. The people here are asking him to come for at least three months."

He handed the phone to my husband.

"For three months you'll be in Mexico on your own?" I said, gripping the receiver tightly.

"Of course not," he said. "We'll all come. We'll bring the children here for three months — Sivan, Tammuz, and Av. They'll be on summer vacation for a lot of that time, and they won't miss much school. We'll look at it as a long vacation. Maybe we'll visit your parents in Belgium on the way…." That was a nice bit of bait, and it was tempting…. "Let me think it over a little," I said.

Three months, I said to myself, and I went to look for Mexico in the atlas. Where was it, exactly?

We ended up going, of course. We boarded a plane to Belgium (yes, I'd taken the bait), and a taxi took us to Mama and Papa. They were stunned by our plans to travel on to Mexico.

What on earth were we looking for in Mexico? Wasn't it some kind of Third World country with Indians, and a new ruler taking over by military coup every two weeks?

How would we manage? We didn't speak Spanish, and where would we get kosher food? As always, they only wanted what was best for us, and Mexico didn't seem to fit the bill….

We explained that many Jews lived in Mexico, and we were going there to fulfill a sacred duty, to teach Torah to our people and fill their souls with Yiddishkeit.

Ah, that was different! To sacrifice for ideals was something they had no difficulty understanding. We left for Mexico City with their blessing.

The Jewish community there greeted us with open arms. They were warm, wonderful people, and they took good care of us, going all out to help us get settled and adjusted. A wealthy community and proud to be Jewish, they gave everything they could for the honor of Torah.

It turned out that we stayed longer than three months — a year and a half, in fact! We flew home for a break once in a while, but we couldn't leave the Mexican community. My husband was their Rav, and without meaning to, I became their Rebbetzin. I organized *shiurim* on *shemiras halashon* and on raising children, and I started advising the wonderful women who came knocking on my door about matters of *shalom bayis.*

We got to know the Saba family, one of the most influential families in Mexico. Their wealth had not blinded them, and they remained generous, warm, and firmly attached to their roots.

We invited my parents to visit, and they happily accepted. No longer was Mexico some far-flung Spanish colony on the other side of the world, but a fine place where their son-in-law taught Torah and brought the Jewish people closer to their Father in Heaven. When they arrived, they were treated like royalty. "The Rav's father-in-law," they whispered excitedly, and they placed him at the head of the table.

We were sitting with the Saba family in Cuernavaca, a beautiful vacation spot south of Mexico City. Papa was full of *nachas* from everything he'd seen, and everyone was happy. The weather was hot, and Papa rolled up his sleeves. Moshe Saba, the head of the family, blinked, and leaning toward my husband, he asked quietly, "*HaRav,* was your father-in-law in the camps? He has a number on his arm..."

My husband nodded. Mr. Saba was electrified. To the Sephardic Jews of Mexico, the Holocaust was something distant. They knew about it, like everyone, but they'd never met any survivors and didn't live among them. "Maybe your father-in-law could tell us something about it?" he asked, eager for the opportunity to learn firsthand.

And Papa agreed. He told his best stories, about the tefillin and the shofar in Auschwitz, and a few other things, and

I translated. Moshe Saba was astounded; he just couldn't calm down. He kept on repeating, "How can someone live through all that? How? And to come out of it with his faith still perfect? Incredible!"

Years later, Mr. Saba was flying in his private helicopter, accompanied by his wife, his older son, and his son's wife. In a sudden, tragic accident, the helicopter burst into flames, killing everyone on board.

The news was a terrible shock to us. We'd had a close relationship with them, and they'd helped us in so many ways. I was haunted by the thought that almost that entire beautiful family had been killed in one moment. I can still picture Mr. Saba's incredulous face and hear him murmuring, "How can someone live through all that? How?"

After a year and a half in Mexico, we returned home. Our children really needed to get back to their own schools and their native peer group. Only the Spanish we'd learned to speak remained with us as a souvenir.

A few years ago, we received a call from Argentina. They wanted my husband to come and start a yeshiva on the outskirts of Buenos Aires, near the city of Mercedes. By that time we were at another stage of life. Most of the children were married, and there was no one we had to take with us. My husband would go there for two weeks at a time, and then come home for two weeks, and sometimes I would join him for a short time. Alone at home, I found myself with long, empty evenings to fill. It was during this time that the curtain of my childhood was pulled back, and I found myself floundering in a sea of new information. Those quiet evenings were devoted to Holocaust research, reading, listening to various *shiurim*, and also giving lectures myself. I would come home to my empty house exhausted in body and mind, feeling as if I'd just swum across the sea.

My husband commuted between Jerusalem and Argentina for two years, and at the end of that time, this book began.

A Thank-You Letter following My First Nefesh Yehudi Trip to Poland

2 March, 2008
25 Adar I 5768

Dear Chana,

In the eight days we spent together in Poland, which really felt as if they couldn't be quantified, you showed greatness. You mustered all your powers and succeeded in touching the inquiring heart, the wondering soul, and the uncomprehending mind of each one of us.

It was a journey into the past and into the hidden recesses of the soul. Each of us felt that lives that were snuffed out more than sixty years ago breathed once again in our own bodies because of the stories you told about your family: your parents, your aunts and uncles, your grandparents, and other family members who were picked up along the way.

Through those sacred stories, you blew life into those cold, desolate places where our people's blood cries out from the earth. You showed us living examples of true Jewish heroism and taught us that it can come to the fore even at the lowest points in our history and in the worst situations a person can be thrown into.

For all this, you deserve great appreciation, and one expression encompasses it all — thank you.

Thank you for allowing us to peek into your life and your family history, through your stories, through all the relaxed conversations we had with you on the bus, at meals, and in the hotels. Whenever our glances met yours, we knew there was a genuine meeting of hearts there.

Thank you for your honesty, your sharing, your openness, and your candor.

Thank you for the song you sang to us at Auschwitz, which blew life into the bitter memories of that place.

Thank you for enabling us, through your tears, to reach real Jews who lived through all those things that we could only try, helplessly, to understand.

Thank you for not sparing yourself, or us, and bringing out into the open all the events that our suffering people have tried to forget.

Thank you for exposing us to the spiritual side of being Jewish, and for helping us to strike roots that connect to our distant past and our Jewish identity.

Thanks to you, we learned that the spirit really can vanquish the dragon.

We can't help but be amazed at the skiing moves you demonstrated and the lessons you gave us, which saved many legs that surely would have been doomed to destruction, had you not stepped in to give us a basic education in the art of skiing.

Tzvi Yannai wisely said, "There are no eternal loves, and no immortal ideas. Everything is in transition and in a process of change. Great flames eventually become torches alongside the tracks on which the train moves." Yes, those great flames turned to torches, but they turned back into great flames again when you carried out your mission with us in Poland, born of your admirable sense of moral obligation toward your family and your people.

With great appreciation and esteem for your endless sensitivity and giving,

The Students of the
Nefesh Yehudi Trip to Poland

A Letter of Appreciation to My Parents after the Shabbos Reunion

February 2008

To our honored friends,
Rabbi and Mrs. Shalom Horowitz *shlita*

We hope this letter finds you well and enjoying every blessing.

We would like to express our heartfelt appreciation and gratitude for your participation in the Nefesh Yehudi students' gathering in the Jewish Quarter on the Shabbos of *Parashas Beha'alosecha*.

Your words, which emanated from warm and caring Jewish hearts, penetrated deeply into the hearts of the students. Through the trip organized for them by Nefesh Yehudi, the students saw remnants of the past and were able to find commonality with the Jewish communities that once thrived in Europe. But seeing the remnants of the past cannot compare with meeting people like you, who link the past to the present. Their understanding was immeasurably deepened by hearing first-person accounts and conversing with people who were there, and are here with us, whole in spirit, in Torah, and in faith.

Your sincere and straightforward words, with their message of real Jewish faith, connected them to the Jew and the Judaism of today. Their encounter with you showed them that Judaism is full of vitality, present, and enduring. It survives all attempts at physical and spiritual eradication, rising from the ashes every time, to bring forth new generations of believing Jews who continue on a path that began millennia ago, through Torah study, faith, and keeping the mitzvos with pride and heroism.

It was a great privilege to have you as our guests, to hear your words, and to see and feel the fulfillment of the Divine promise that the Jewish People is eternal and the Torah "will not be forgotten from the mouth of his progeny."

May Hashem grant you many more good years of robust health and strength, and may you merit bringing more soldiers to Torah and faith and shedding your light on the Jewish People.

With appreciation and gratitude,
Eliyahu Ilani
Nefesh Yehudi

A Letter Handed to Me by a Student during a Trip to Poland, a Few Moments before Candlelighting

4-5 Adar II 5774
6-7 March 2014

Dear Chana,

I'm not really sure how to begin, and the reason I'm writing instead of saying this to you is that I think I might make you feel uncomfortable.

I'd like to tell you a few things, first of all. Every time you tell us about your family's experiences, I'm sure it is very hard for you, and the mask that you always say you wear really does its job, because you look so strong and brave (and I'm sure you really are like that under the mask, too).

The Holocaust isn't part of my family background, but it was still very important to me to come on this trip, to understand better, to be with my brethren, my people. And thanks to you, this trip is especially amazing (I know the word sounds ironic, but I'm not sure how to describe it)!! Your strength and the stories you tell open my eyes more — for better or worse — to the fear and the joy and happiness of moments I will never really know, and I pray that no one will ever know them again.

I'm writing a journal this week, trying to describe what I'm seeing and hearing so that I won't forget it, and it will be on record for the distant years that will come, and I was just writing about you. The stories you tell about your father touch me. The more you tell about him, the sorrier I am that I never had a chance to meet him. And I went on to write about the feelings of envy I have toward him.

Sometimes I feel a sort of emptiness inside, a lack of connection to certain things, most of them having to do with my religion. I grew up in a traditional home, went to religious schools through twelfth grade, and I was even in Bnei Akiva. But in recent years I stopped feeling connected. The holidays no longer felt meaningful to me, even though I love and enjoy them, and when you tell about your father, who never for a moment stopped believing in Hashem and in His will, that everything is under His direction, and His path is the path of truth, it makes me envious. I believe that a person needs to be "larger than life," and that some people have the merit and the gift of feeling that way. I wish that I could learn more from your father and the rest of your family, and manage, like him, not to give in and to know there is always a guiding hand, and at every moment, be it hard or easy, Hashem's hand is leading us in the right direction.

I'm writing this to you on Thursday evening, and if you look at the date above, you'll see that I added tomorrow's date, too. The reason for this is that on Friday afternoon, before Shabbat, I wanted to add a few words of encouragement, support, and thanks to you, most of all for the words you say to me and to all of us, and for having the courage to come again and again to a place that's not easy to be in, and still remain strong in your belief.

I'm not sure that these words really express what I feel, but I hope I've succeeded in saying at least part of it.

I'd like to wish you and your family only joy and happiness, and that you should all know how to continue on the path of your father, who sounds like someone who's head-and-shoulders above the crowd, simply amazing! May you continue to be courageous and strong, and an amazing woman in your own right! It's a privilege for me to be here with you, and you make such a difference!

May you have a *Shabbat shalom*, and always remember that even in the most terrible place on earth, there is always a ray of light, and at the most difficult moments there is always something beyond that situation — but then again, you're the one who taught me that…

Have an amazing Shabbat!

Mor Eliyahu
(Be'er Sheva)
The Journey to….

Tears of Bliss

Dovid Zaritzky

Originally published in the monthly journal Bais Yaakov,
Cheshvan 5728 (November 1967)

WHY DOES THE IMAGE of that Jew who danced with tears on his face last Chol Hamoed, keep reappearing in my mind?

I said to myself, here is a Jew crying for joy, and he didn't know about these tears when he was in the Diaspora, in the death camps. When did he attain them, when did he see himself dancing together with those tears in a huge circle by the Western Wall?

Perhaps he didn't notice the tear rolling out and falling on his blissful face; perhaps he was so happy, he didn't recognize his happiness, like a rich man who has so much money, he doesn't know the sum. I saw this Jew in that great circle, and he was dancing as his forefathers danced when they went out to be burned at the stake.

I saw that Jew dancing, and he didn't know a thing. He didn't even see his own tears, and I said to myself, perhaps that Jew doesn't recognize his own happiness, and it's up to me to point it out to him.

I joined the circle of dancers. I looked at his feet, and they were singing *Omdos hayu ragleinu b'shearayich Yerushalayim*. I looked at his hands, and they were enfolded in the hands of other Jews, and I could hear them singing *Yad Hashem asah zos, hi niflas b'eineinu*. I took hold of his *kapote* and tucked my hands into his wide sash, and I could hear the garments singing *Ki hilbishani bigdei yesha*. I said to myself, surely I know this Jew, who is dancing for the first time beside the Kosel, and now he is bringing his first *korban,* a thanksgiving offering for having been burned in Auschwitz, and having gathered up the ashes, and having come here to dance by the Wall.

I went and stood near him, and I peered into his face — of course I knew him, this was my friend Reb Shulem Duvid, from Antwerp. Why, I wondered, did I suddenly spot his face among the thousands of faces here that were moving, crying, dancing with joy on that night of Chol Hamoed by the Wall? It must be because he was so calm, with no sign of crying on his face or in his eyes.

I stopped him and said, my dear Reb Shulem, from where are these beautiful tears that I see in your eyes, and that run down your blissful face and fall from there to the ground of the Kosel that was just cleared after two thousand years? In *chutz la'aretz,* even in Antwerp where there is a flawless Jewish community, no one sees such tears as these, that have no trace of complaint in them and contain not the smallest drop of water, but derive purely from the tears of Adam HaRishon as he stood at the threshold of Gan Eden.

Reb Shulem from Antwerp stood and gazed at me and said in great surprise, am I crying? And why would I cry, after I've come to such happiness as this? And I saw his tears increasing, wetting his whole face, and he didn't even try to dry them, for he wasn't aware of them, because those tears did not flow from the same source as all other tears. He, Reb Shulem Horowitz, had reached the peak of bliss that was waiting for him. Tears did not find him in the furnaces of Treblinka, and not when he walked barefoot on snow-covered roads, starved to death and expecting every moment to be his last. Being orphaned and bereaved did not draw these tears from him, from the marrow of his bones.

But those moments at the Kosel, as one of thousands dancing that night of Chol Hamoed, they drew forth these tears.

He continued to move among the dancers, and the tears

continued to flow, very slowly, with great concentration, from his eyes. The gentle breeze, which had also been sanctified before coming to the Kosel by immersion, licked them away one by one. He was not singing; it seemed there was no room left for anything but the tears of bliss that filled his whole being, that covered him as water covers the seabed. He did not sing, he did not look at anything. His eyes poured out tears, and from time to time they were fixed on the great stones of the Kosel, and then his lips moved. Was he entreating, praying, saying something he had been saving all his life for this great moment? Was he praising, or thanking, or just tossing out some words, intelligible only to his innermost soul and all the torment he had suffered?

And when the dancing ended, my friend Reb Shulem stood with his hands stretched out as if holding other hands, his feet not moving, but I saw that he was still dancing, just as his eyes did not weep, but the tears kept on flowing.

Threads of Light in Jordanow

Yehudit Golan

Originally published in Mishpacha magazine (Hebrew edition), Pesach supplement, 5765 (2005)

Poland, 5697 (1937)

The forest loved the voices of the children that brought cheer to its dark corners. It waited patiently all winter, as quiet as the black tree trunks awaiting the order to bring forth their buds, and when spring arrived, it got all dressed up to receive them, overjoyed to see them like an old man whose grandchildren come to visit.

Matisyahu (Mattis) Gelman loved the forest of Jordanow. The trees, so firmly planted in the ground, gave him a feeling of rootedness, compensating for the well-rooted genealogical tree that he lacked.

Shulem Duvid Horowitz loved this forest, too. In Krakow, it was the object of dreams that were almost tangible. The yearly vacation in the shade of those whispering trees painted his summer in exuberant colors. Even after seven decades, the sweet taste of those days in Jordanow has not faded.

"There's Mattis," said Avrum Leib, Shulem Duvid's older brother, when they arrived with their bundles at the *dacha* in the forest. The two words were uttered in an awed undertone, but Mattis was wrapped up in his own meditations. His ardent striving and seeking, his stormy fight to reach the peak of ultimate truth, and his exhausting struggle with his parents — all these found an outlet here among the trees. Here, almost palpably, he felt G-d's presence all around him, wrapping him in endless swaths of compassion.

His father was so far from here!

This was the father who'd held him close to his heart in the family pictures, who'd taught him the rules of chess and followed his achievements with pride, the father who had woven dreams of academic advancement for his son and sought out the best gymnasium in Vienna for him.

But his rich, successful father hadn't felt the venom of being called a "dirty Jew" by his classmate Stashek, with the pent-up hatred of two thousand years.

Was it the latest prize he'd received in an official state ceremony that had turned his friend's heart against him, or was it, perhaps, the compliment from their literature teacher on his beautiful German that made his compositions a delight to the ear?

Mattis looked himself over. He wasn't dirty, and he didn't look Jewish, either, yet this was the name his classmate had chosen to call him. He found himself wandering the streets of Vienna, inexplicably attracted to the Jewish enclave to assess its cleanliness. And then came his encounter with Rav Meir Shapiro, the head of Yeshivas Chachmei Lublin.

Now, in the forest, Mattis could almost touch the *hashgachah pratis* that led him to the house where the Rav was staying, and the conversation that had come about so naturally between them, as if a conversation between a Polish *rosh yeshiva* and a Viennese gymnasium student were an everyday occurrence.

The handshake of the man who became his Rav infused him with powers he'd never been aware of, powers that effervesced within him and turned him into a burning torch of *avodas Hashem* with a charisma that drew other youths, with similar aspirations, to him.

Mattis left Vienna and made Krakow his headquarters, heading straight for the heart of Chassidus, and invigorated by the flame that burned in him, he sat hour after hour learning Torah, exuding joy, a strong sense of fellowship, and clear recognition that "there is nothing besides Him."

Reb Leibel Yud, an elder among Gerrer Chassidim, remembers the quick steps of the black-haired, blue-eyed youth. "Every day, he would climb up to the loft, and after a short time, we would hear the muffled sobs of a son throwing himself into his father's embrace, crying over the lost years he'd spent without Torah and Chassidus."

The forest, too, was a good place to cry, to bathe one's soul in forty *se'ah* of purifying tears, cleanse it of stubborn rust that still clung to it here and there. The trees didn't sympathize, they didn't listen or comfort, they were simply there, his partners, bathing in the tears of their own dew.

Mattis wrote...

My dear father,

Forgive me for not writing sooner. The z'man has started already, and I am very much occupied. We study with great diligence here, and in these few weeks, I have really come alive spiritually. As I saw in your letter, you are not at all pleased about my studying in a yeshiva, and you want me to come home. Why should you get upset and suffer needlessly? I left home and family out of complete devotion, without considering myself or others. I sneaked across two borders, only for the sake of attaining my desired goal of learning Torah. And now I should go back? And anyway, isn't it better to study under the Rav, a world-renowned genius, among young men who know hundreds and thousands of pages of Gemara by heart — and some of them have written seforim — than under that hypocritical teacher Leinsdorf?

I am so far from that now that I don't understand why I didn't get up in the middle of a lesson, throw it all away, and run away already then... I ask you once again not to distress yourself and Mother for nothing, but to understand my situation and not cause me anguish.

Wishing you well and sending you a kiss,
The son you don't understand,
Matti

Herr Gelman's hands trembled with rage when he read this letter and saw the dream of "his son, the lawyer" vanishing behind the Polish border.

Doggedly, he fought a one-man culture war. His campaign brought him all the way to the Gerrer Rebbe himself, who answered him calmly, "Your son says his soul yearns for the Torah, and how can his argument be refuted?"

Shulem Duvid went to unpack and arrange his things, anticipating two weeks of delightful tranquility in the forest of Jordanow.

His devoted sister Rivka had made sure he brought warm blankets. "Sometimes it gets very cold there at night," she'd said knowingly. And indeed she knew the capriciousness of the mountain air, from the wonderful weeks she'd spent with Frau Sarah Schenirer. The Carpathians made a lovely setting for seminars, summer camps, and early morning hikes — but the nights were cold.

The cabin smelled sweetly of unfinished wood. Three of them were to share it: Avrum Leib, Shulem Duvid, and... Mattis.

Avrum Leib was already bonded to Gur with every fiber of his being. Mattis was an uncompromising *kommandant* (leader of a group in Gerrer Chassidus), but the *bochurim* weren't deterred by the lofty standards he set. Shulem Duvid, the younger brother, wasn't yet officially a Gerrer *chossid,* but he learned in a Chassidic yeshiva.

The forest looked at the youths who had come seeking its shelter, and it smiled as if hiding a secret. Between its pathways, ancient roots formed bumps on the ground and sent their shoots relentlessly into the fertile earth, listening eagerly for the quick footsteps that would drum on their back. Overhead, the green canopy smiled to itself, waiting to see what would happen.

The perfumed late-afternoon brought the chirps of all sorts of songbirds preparing to settle down for the night in the treetops, weary leaves seeking respite from their day's work, and small animals scurrying to their burrows.

Suddenly, Mattis turned to Shulem Duvid and said, "Would you like to go out, and talk a bit?"

The evening wind sent a slight chill down the young boy's back, but Mattis put an arm around his shoulders. The sky had not yet darkened when the moon came up, large and bright. And suddenly it was above the trees, sending beams that drew fine lines in the dimness of the forest, so that it now looked like a magical maze.

The trees didn't eavesdrop. Still standing tall, they slept, immersed in their dreams. Shulem Duvid and Mattis walked beside them, conversing in measured words surrounded by long silences. Under the graying trees came the echoes of Kotzk and Gur, Krakow and Lodz, and as if they were fresh leaves, Mattis would spread them out little by little, beautifully arranged for the young lad who walked at his side, gazing up at him thirstily.

The truth of Gur screamed in the growing quiet of the forest, sending echo after echo through the woody silence, and each echo penetrated deeper, reaching tiny points that Shulem Duvid had never known were there....

Mattis was painfully genuine. He didn't wrap himself in optimistic complacency, he didn't look at the crowd wallowing in noisy vanity, and he didn't pat himself on the back. No! Mattis kept his soul on the move, showed it heights to aspire to, opened windows to breathtaking views, sketched out paths, built agendas, and the boy with him looked on, astonished.

Gates of wisdom, of a world he'd never known before, opened before him as the forest fell into its slumber.

At darkness descended, they returned to the cabin, the flame of Gur blazing in their souls. But the fire did not stay in the forests of Jordanow.

One cold morning in Krakow, as Shulem Duvid was preparing to go out early to the *beis midrash,* someone came knocking briskly at the door.

"It's six in the morning, who could it be?" he wondered. He went quickly to open the door, and standing there was one of the Mattisovitches. "Mattis says please come right away to the *shtiebel*!"

Surprised, Shulem Duvid followed the youth. At this hour, there were few people in the streets, but the *shtiebel* was already full of young men who were always at the *beis midrash* at five-thirty, like soldiers at their posts, bent over their Gemaras.

"Come, let's learn," Mattis said to him simply, and on the thread that had been formed in the forest of Jordanow, he now began to string more pearls.

The page of Gemara that Mattis explained so well that day became Shulem Duvid's prized possession, and he never lost it, not in the ghetto, nor in the camps, nor on the death march, and he still has it with him today, sixty years after.

"What is this world, anyway, that we should give any importance to it?" Mattis said to the young men of his *chavurah*. "It is nothing! Less than a bagatelle! We must choose one or the other: Either to be crushed under it, or to rise above it!

"Man is dust and ashes; today he says one thing, tomorrow, another. And if you seek to satisfy him, you'll never fulfill the mission. There is only one obligation, and that is toward Heaven! To seek, without respite, to know what G-d wants, and to do it without fear!

"The main thing is not to be disturbed by any man... examine yourselves to see whether you have made this principle your own."

The dark waters of the Vistula River looked quietly at the group of young men walking across the Podgórski Bridge, softly singing a Chassidic melody as they returned from their Purim night gathering.

Mattis, dressed in a long kaftan and a *spodik* and holding a pipe in his mouth, walked among them, exuding majesty like a Rebbe. Suddenly he stopped next to the Krakow Gasworks and gave the command, "Maariv!"

In a moment, as if they were in the *shtiebel* and not on a street in the heart of a Polish city, the *chavurah* was standing in prayer, elevated above everything and everyone around them, fixing their hearts on Hashem alone.

"Not everyone agreed with him," Reb Shulem Duvid says, "but the real test came later. Then everyone knew that these boys' intentions were pure. Their heroism of spirit in those dark times was awe-inspiring. They occupied themselves with Torah learning, paying no attention to the world around them, unafraid to die as martyrs. And they refused to give up one iota of their *tzelem Elokim*. That was their real test, and every one of them withstood it, without exception.

When the Jews of Krakow were driven into the ghetto, Matisyahu Gelman's *chavurah* was among them. As much as possible, they continued their lives just as they had before, devoting all their time to Torah study. They didn't sign up for work, and they kept their beards and *peyos*. Since they had no food vouchers, they subsisted on a bare minimum.

"I went into the building where the Talmud Torah had been," Reb Shulem Duvid relates, "and I was stunned to come upon a group of *Chassidishe bochurim* sitting there learning, bent over their Gemaras, immersed in the world of Abbaye and Rava, as if Hitler *yimach shemo* didn't exist and everything was normal... I could see, though, that they knew quite well what that murderous regime was like. One of the married men had half of his beard torn out and shorn off, others among the *bochurim* had only one *peah;* some Nazi thug must have chopped off the other one.... But they were sitting there learning diligently as if everything going on outside had nothing to do with them at all. I stood there astonished, and I envied them, because I'd had to go to work some time ago, along with my sister, to support our family. Those *bochurim* and *avreichim* were like something from a higher realm. It was no wonder that when the Rebbes of Gur and Belz met in Eretz Yisrael a few years later, the Belzer Rebbe said to the Gerrer Rebbe, "Your *bochurim* were *mekadesh Shem Shamayim*!"

At first, the Mattisovitches were sharply criticized for their conduct. "It's irresponsible!" many argued. "You can't be confrontational with conquerors, you have to play along with them."

There were those who mocked the young men who would sometimes walk around openly in their Chassidic garb, which made them stand out as Jews even from a distance. But gradually, their attitude changed to admiration. People began to help the *bochurim*, to bring them food that was cooked especially for them, and to respect them more and more for the way they clung to their customs and the mutual aid that characterized the group. When the group was broken up and spread out among different camps, there, too, they became role models.

Mattis was often joined by his Chassidim in his forays between the ghettos, when they would take up a collection in one town for the benefit of *bochurim* in another town who were in dire straits, or even *bochurim* who had been caught and put to forced labor. They came to Tarnow, too, to collect money for their friends in trouble, and there they met their younger friend,

Shulem Duvid, who was residing temporarily in the ghetto there with his family.

"Does anybody donate money in times like these?" Shulem Duvid asked them incredulously. "People don't have money even for their own necessities..."

"You'd be surprised," they told him, "but Jews, *rachmanim b'nei rachmanim*, are asked, and they give — sometimes their last pennies!"

"But you're endangering your lives," Shulem Duvid argued.

"True, but this is an instance of real *pikuach nefesh*. Several of our friends in the Lodz ghetto need this help! And what's all the fuss? When so many Jews are endangering their lives in order to get their livelihood, all the more so we ought to do anything to save people who are starving to death."

Their words were sincere and straight from the heart, and Shulem Duvid made the rounds with them among his acquaintances, helping them to collect whatever they could. And then they vanished from Tarnow, just as mysteriously as they'd arrived.

In the years that followed, no youthful laughter was heard in the forests of Jordanow. The *dacha* was desolate, bereft of its cheerful visitors, and the green leaves that had waited impatiently packed up their colors when fall arrived and landed on the hard ground with wrinkled, disappointed faces.

No one came. Not in 1940, and not in 1941.

Not in 1942, or 1943, or 1944.

Mattis moved from ghetto to ghetto.

In the town of Radom, according to a member of his *chavurah* who survived the inferno, he was caught when the Nazis burst into an apartment in search of a prominent personality who was residing there. Mattis, who was also staying there, was taken away and never seen again.

May Hashem avenge his blood.

In Memory of Reb Shulem Duvid HaLevi Horowitz *z"l*

Moshe Yaakov Kanner

Originally published in Hamodia, Cheshvan 5773

ON *SHABBOS KODESH PARASHAS TOLDOS*, 5772, around midday, I was sitting at a family *simchah* with a good friend from Montreal, Reb Yaakov Abramchik. During the meal, Reb Yaakov mentioned something he'd recently heard about some heroic Jews who had fashioned a shofar for themselves at Auschwitz and blown the *teki'os* on Rosh Hashanah, risking their lives for the mitzvah. "Reb Yaakov," I said to him, "you're a close friend of Reb Shulem Duvid Horowitz, aren't you? Just this past *erev Rosh Hashanah* he was telling me that he had three *zechuyos* to take with him before the Heavenly Tribunal, and one of them was that he heard the shofar in Auschwitz, on that very occasion you just mentioned."

That *motzaei Shabbos*, a friend called me from Europe. "Have you heard? A few hours ago the *levayah* of Reb Shulem Duvid Horowitz took place in Eretz Yisrael. What an irreplaceable loss!"

Reb Shulem Duvid was gone? I was stunned. How could it be? A man so full of vitality, so accomplished, healthy in body, mind, and soul, so full of joy, was no longer with us? A living limb had been torn from the Gerrer community and from Agudath Israel. Another extraordinary figure from the old generation had left us. An amiable and elevated man who saw only good in every situation he was in, and never ceased thanking G-d for all His kindness.

What a terrible loss, especially for us, the protégés he had nurtured in our youth in Antwerp. He had played such a big role in our spiritual life. And to think that my friend and I had just been talking about him on Shabbos! The heart of a friend senses things, even from afar… in our time zone [in North America], it was still the middle of Shabbos while the funeral was taking place in Eretz Yisrael. At the very moment when we were talking about his *zechuyos*, his many relatives, friends, and admirers were parting from him in Israel. We'd been inspired from Above to mention his merits at that moment of his departure from the world — and amid joyful feelings, for Reb Shulem Duvid had been a joyful man all his life…

Once again I recalled the conversation we'd had a few weeks previously, when we'd wished each other a good year, the last time I ever spoke with him. It was a warm, friendly conversation, and we'd reminisced about old times. And then, for some reason, he'd said, *"Moishele, drei zochen nem ich mit zich oiben* — I'm taking three things Up There with me…" Who ever thought those would be his parting words to me…

The first of those three merits was the fact that he'd taken part in the shofar-blowing in the Auschwitz death camp, with the shofar obtained by Reb Nissan Leizer, today an esteemed member of New York's Bobover community. It wasn't only an act of heroism, it was a statement of complete recognition of G-d's Kingship, even there in that netherworld. The shofar blasts declare that the Creator is our King, and these saintly young men made that declaration under the boot of murder and humiliation — they took out the shofar and blew the blasts of *malchus*, to proclaim their belief in the King of all kings, and that no place is devoid of Him, even there within those barbed-wire fences. Those murderers fancy themselves rulers over us, but the truth is that "You are King over all the earth… for You are the G-d of Truth and Your word endures forever… for You hear the sound of the shofar and listen to the blast, and there is none like You."

The second merit was his loving acceptance of G-d's judgment when he lost his only son, Reb Mordechai Tzvi *z"l*, or Mottel, as everyone affectionately called him… the unforgettable Mottel! A young *avreich* of noble spirit, a *chossid* and a *lamdan* with an inward focus, always in pursuit of the truth, outstanding in *chessed*, good and doing good, performing physical acts of kindness, and generous with his money. We all looked up to him; he walked among us, yet remained focused on his goals, pleasant, yet serious. How hard he toiled over his Gemara and *sifrei Chassidus*. I remember one *seudas Purim* that the *bochurim* made in the *shtiebel*, and he was also there, still a *bochur* learning in Yeshivas Tchebin. The elevated atmosphere at that *seudah* was indescribable. Mottel didn't talk much, but just by being there he lifted us all to the heights. And when Reb Mottel went to his eternal rest at the age of twenty-six, after a protracted illness (he passed away on 25 Iyar 5736, on the day of *hod sheb'yesod* in the Sefirah), our hearts were torn over the loss. He left a family with three little orphans. Extraordinary things were said about his last days, in particular. On the last Purim of his life, he got out of his hospital bed to fulfill the mitzvah of *mishloach manos*, which his father, too, had made superhuman efforts to fulfill on his last Purim in Buchenwald. Neither the father nor the son would pass up this mitzvah of joy and friendship, even at the hardest of times. The words of the Rebbe, the Beis Yisrael *zy"a*, echoed in the void: "*A shud, es iz avek a gute neshomeh, a reiner yungerman* (a pity, he was a good soul, a pure young man)." Our hearts ached especially for his parents, Reb Shulem Duvid and his family, who had lost someone so precious to them. I took part in the *levayah* in Bnei Brak, and a feeling of dark anguish enveloped us all. But Reb Shulem Duvid displayed uncommon strength. He made a great *kiddush Hashem* when he publicly accepted Hashem's decree and thanked Him for the gift he'd been granted for twenty-six years, pointing out the fact that at the time of the *churban* in Europe, he never thought he would live to marry and have a family. And over the years afterward, whenever he mentioned his exceptional son, no sadness showed on his face; he spoke of him in a simple, natural way, feeling with complete *emunah* that his Mottel was alive and well in the upper spheres.

The third merit that Reb Shulem Duvid planned to bring with him before the Heavenly Tribunal on Rosh Hashanah was his regular practice of being *ma'avir al middosav* (letting things go, not demanding one's full due from others). Amazingly, the Shlah Hakadosh, to whom Reb Shulem Duvid was related, mentions this quality in connection with *Parashas Toldos*, which was read on the day of Reb Shulem Duvid's *petirah*. He writes that we learn the principle of being *ma'avir al middosav* from the episode in *Parashas Toldos* between Yitzchak Avinu and the shepherds of Gerar: "And these are the most desirable qualities, that a person should seek peace, *veya'avir al middosav* with a forgiving attitude toward everyone, and show them much love."

Those are the *zechuyos* that Reb Shulem Duvid mentioned to me in our last conversation. He was tested in all of them, and he withstood every test.

And He Spoke Peace to All His Progeny

Reb Shulem Duvid, you said you were bringing three merits before the Heavenly Tribunal. I beg your pardon, beloved one! In your humility, you found only those three. But truth be told, there were a thousand more, whether you knew it or not. Your every bone was saturated with simple, pure *emunah*. You emerged from your terrible suffering in the camps even stronger in your faith, although those troubles overtook you when you were still very young. *"Uvechol zos Shimcha lo shachachnu"* was your motto. You not only heard the shofar there with *mesirus nefesh*, but you fulfilled many mitzvos. And on many occasions you said the merit of being among those who suffered the horrors of the war is something you wouldn't sell for all the money in the world.

In all your ways, your main goal was to please our Father in Heaven. For many years you occupied yourself with Torah at every available moment, and even more in your later years, when you toiled over your learning all day, like a young kollel scholar. How sweet you found it to delve into the depths of Torah! You effaced yourself completely before *tzaddikim*, and every word from their mouths was sacred to you. From something hinted in the words of the Beis Yisrael, you learned that you were left alive after all the atrocities in order to act, to build and restore. And this became your soul's desire and life's ambition. You worked energetically and tirelessly, *l'shem Shamayim* and not for reward or praise, to establish and strengthen Jewish observance. You worked day and night for the *Klal*, and in Antwerp in particular, to rebuild the ruins in the way of our fathers. With all your might, you gave yourself for the sake of Torah institutions in the Holy Land and abroad, and for Agudath Israel, which was your very essence. You built a *bayis ne'eman* with your exemplary wife *tlch"a*, who has so many accomplishments to her credit, a home founded on the principle of acts of kindness for others. You established an exceptional family, generations of *chachamim* and *sofrim*. Every achievement in Torah by your offspring, every *sefer* they authored, filled your heart with great joy. You found bliss in every page of Gemara you learned, in every *chiddush* and every idea. You had an *ayin tovah*, always glad to see others happy and fortunate, for your *ahavas Yisrael* was extended to every individual. You had an open, sympathetic ear to people's troubles. Whenever the opportunity came up, you engaged in the Heavenly task of suggesting *shidduchim*. You were a fountain of joy, always *b'simchah* and bringing *simchah* to others, particularly at weddings, with your charming *grammen*. In the fullest sense of the words, you were *oheiv es habri'os* — you loved people as G-d's creations.

To the young generation, and particularly to the boys of our *shtiebel,* Reb Shulem Duvid gave from his treasure-house of *yir'ah,* memories, and the lessons of his youth, with wonderful warmth and friendliness. Let us add a few words here about the home of Gerrer Chassidus in Antwerp, where Reb Shulem Duvid lived, davened, learned, and achieved. Our *shtiebel* was, and still is, a "precious cornerstone" of Torah and Chassidus. Men of piety, Torah, and extraordinary character, survivors of the flames and the sword, found their place there, and among them was my father and teacher *z"l.* The *shtiebel's* walls were saturated with the voice of Torah and the fragrance of Chassidus. From early morning they were there, learning exuberantly, and at night, too, the singsong of the Gemara did not cease. At every available moment we went there to learn, to sit down together to a meal in *Chossidishe* fellowship, and also to play, talk, and get a bit wild, but all within the walls of the *shtiebel,* which was like a second home to us. And Reb Shulem Duvid stood over us, smiling and sharing in all our experiences.

I'll take this opportunity to thank Hashem and publicly praise Him for saving my life on the night of Rosh Chodesh Kislev, 5734 (1973). I was on my way to the *shtiebel* to hear a *shiur* on *Maseches Ta'anis* when I was hit by a tram. I was struck on the head with a blow that sent me flying through the air, and I landed on the opposite tracks (another miracle, that the tracks were clear the whole time I lay there). With Hashem's help, I managed to get up after a few minutes.

Miraculously, I was fine. I continued straight to the *shtiebel,* where everyone was happy to see me, and of course Reb Shulem Duvid was overjoyed to hear how I was saved… *Hodu laShem ki tov, ki l'olam chasdo!*

For us boys and young men, Reb Shulem Duvid was a *ner tamid* in the *shtiebel.* His radiant face never dimmed. He drew many youths toward the path of Torah and *yir'as Shamayim,* but for us boys in the Antwerp *shtiebel* especially, he was like a beloved uncle. The friendly face he showed to each one of us illuminated the way as we started out on our paths in life. In Antwerp, it rains often and heavily. The gray skies, raging winds, and pouring rain affect people's state of mind, especially for a child who must slog to school and back every day in the gloom. But Reb Shulem Duvid always greeted us with a captivating smile. To him, every day was a beautiful day, and the sky above him was always clear and bright. The sun always shone on him, and he looked positively at every situation. This had a strong influence on us.

Even though Reb Shulem Duvid was well known in his time for his many important achievements in the public sphere, it is befitting to emphasize this point, his *kiruv* of local youth, and even to mention little details that are forever engraved on my heart and that say so much about who he was. Every child and adolescent boy was close to his heart and soul. He would inquire about all the Jewish boys in town to discover whom else he might bring close to Torah and *yir'as Shamayim,* and nurture his talents. I want to emphasize this quality of his, because we really have no idea how important it is to a boy to get attention from an adult, especially a distinguished person, and how much difference a kind, encouraging word can make to him for the rest of his life. That one moment of feeling important can lift a child up, free him from his doubts, and change his direction.

The *gaon* Rav Manoach Hendel, author of *Chochmas Manoach,* expresses this idea in his annotations on *Megillas Esther*. The final verse in the Megillah says that Mordechai "spoke peace to all his progeny." For all his status and importance as leader of the Jews and viceroy to the king, Mordechai would greet every child, inquire after his wellbeing, and draw him close with "words of love and friendship," and he did not feel he was lowering himself. Reb Shulem Duvid filled that role for us all the time; he would talk to us anytime about anything, and especially about the days of his youth in Poland. He vividly described for us the court of the Imrei Emes in Gur, he told us about his older brother Rav Chaim Eliezer (son-in-law of the holy *gaon* Rav Mendele of Pabianitz, may Hashem avenge their blood), about the Mattisovitches — a group of young war heroes led by Reb Mattis Gelman, may his blood be avenged, who sanctified the Name of Heaven in their lives, openly and in hiding, about his hometown of Krakow and its *lamdanim* and Chassidim, worth far beyond their weight in gold.

He did all this with natural humility, with genuine *ahavas Yisrael*. I was just a boy when I wrote a little poem about Avraham Avinu. Reb Shulem Duvid read it with interest and put it in his pocket, as if that childish effort were an important document. "Moishele wrote this," he said with warm affection, and his eyes shone with happiness. Who can say how much that little incident influenced my writing in the future? Many times he implored me to call him by his given name, simply Shulem Duvid and nothing more. I hope he forgave me for not acceding to his wishes on that point. When I was about twelve years old, I received a gift from him, an anthology of writings by the legendary leader Rav Yaakov Rosenheim. On the flyleaf he wrote me a dedication that began with the word *l'yedidi...*"

Dear Reb Shulem Duvid! If you only knew how many times that boy read that dedication, and how many times he drew encouragement and strength from it... Here was an important man, well-known in the city, a pillar of the community and of Agudath Israel, and of course, one of the "faces" of the *shtiebel*, and he, with his own hand, was writing to me, a young boy thirty-five years his junior and addressing me as his friend... and he meant it sincerely. It was inculcated in Gerrer Chassidim that age differences mean nothing, especially in matters of *ruchnius* — *"Zekeinim im n'arim yehallelu es Sheim Hashem..."*

There was another fine boy, a few years younger than I, whom Reb Shulem Duvid befriended and encouraged to come to the *shtiebel*, and over time that boy rose to high levels and became a *gaon* in Torah and a *baal madreigah*. Reb Shulem Duvid had a very great part in planting that mighty tree. Yet he took no credit for himself, and in fact he considered the younger man his rabbi and effaced himself before him. That was always his way, to efface himself before *talmidei chachomim* and to honor them without limit.

A year has passed, Reb Shulem Duvid, and the tears of your friends have not dried. Your image, in all its warmth and splendor, stands living before our eyes. Your years were full of vitality and enveloped in pure, unshakable faith. They were years of Torah, Chassidus, *tzedakah* and *chessed*, and public service for the sake of Heaven. In the eyes of so many Jews you were the symbol of *yedid kol Beis Yisrael*, crowned with the good name of *ahuv laShamayim v'ahuv labri'os*. To our sorrow, our crown has been taken away, but we take comfort in the outstanding offspring you left, who maintain your eternal legacy. May your memory be blessed.

Glossary

The following glossary provides a partial explanation of some of the Hebrew, Yiddish (Y.), Aramaic (A.), German (Ger.), French (Fr.), and Italian (It.) words and phrases used in this book. The spellings and explanations reflect the way the specific word is used herein. Often, there are alternate spellings and meanings for the words.

A CAPELLA (It.): choir.

AKDAMOS (A.): a liturgical poem in Aramaic, said or sung on Shavuos before the Torah Reading.

AKTION (Ger.): literally "action": a violent operation against Jewish civilians (or other perceived enemies of the Reich) by German security forces.

AM YISRAEL, CHAI VEKAYAM!: "The Jewish People, alive and enduring!"

APPELLPLATZ (Ger.): the outdoor area where roll call took place in the concentration camps.

ASHRAI!: How fortunate I am!

BASAR LAVAN: lit., "white meat"; an Israeli euphemism for pork.

BEIS MIDRASH: a room, large or small, where men gather for Torah study.

BEKIUS: study focused on acquiring a broader base of knowledge, but with less depth.

BOCHUR: a young, single man.

BUBBE (Y.): grandmother.

CHEDER (Y.): also called Talmud Torah. A school for young Jewish boys where Torah is the main subject studied.

CHEVRA KADDISHA (A.): burial society.

CHOLOV YISROEL: To ensure that milk comes from a kosher animal and conforms to the strictest level of kashruth, the milking should be done by, or in the presence of, a Torah-observant Jew. Milk produced under this close level of supervision is called cholov Yisroel.

CHOSSON: bridegroom, fiancé.

CHUPPAH: wedding canopy.

DAVENING (Y.): prayer.

DEVEIKUS: closeness (literally, clinging) to G-d.

DIVREI TORAH: lit., "words of Torah"; a discussion of a verse or a concept from the Torah.

DOSSIT: the feminine form of doss, a mildly pejorative Israeli term for a charedi Jew. The term is being used ironically. It is based on a garbled attempt to mimic the Ashkenazi pronunciation of the modern Hebrew word dati, which means "religious."

EMUNAH: faith, belief.

EREV SHABBOS: Friday, the day before Shabbos.

GAN EDEN: Paradise.

GARTLECH (Y.): plural of gartel, the sash worn by Chassidim during prayer.

GERRER CHOSSID: a follower of the dynasty of Rebbes from the Polish city of Góra Kalwaria (Ger in Yiddish), one of the largest Chassidic groups in the world.

GYMNASIUM (Ger.): In Europe, an academy that prepares students for university.

HAKADOSH BARUCH HU: the Holy One, blessed be He.

IYUN: deep, analytical study.

KALLAH: bride.

KASKET (Y.): cap worn by Chassidic Polish boys.

KEZAYIS: a measure of volume, the minimal amount that is considered a meal.

KODESH: sacred matters; religious studies.

KOSEL: (also pronounced Kotel) the Western Wall.

MIDRASHA: an institute of Jewish studies for women.

MISHLOACH MANOS: one of the mitzvos of Purim, to send portions of food to one's friends.

MOTZAEI SHABBOS: Saturday night, after Shabbos.

NISAYON: a test of faith and character.

NISHMAS KOL CHAI: a prayer of thanksgiving said in the morning service on the Sabbath and festival days.

OILEM HAEMES: the World of Truth, the Next World (Hebrew, as pronounced in Yiddish).

ONCLE (Fr.): uncle.

ONEG SHABBOS: the mitzvah of "delighting in the Sabbath"; often refers to a social gathering on Shabbos night after the meal.

PUSHKE (Y.): charity box with a slot for coins.

ROSH CHODESH AV: the first day of the month of Av and the Nine Days of mourning the destruction of the Holy Temple, culminating on Tishah B'Av.

SEGULAH (pl. SEGULOS): a talisman or an act, based on Kabbalistic or Talmudic tradition rather than science, meant to effect a remedy, a particular benefit, or protection from harm.

SHABBOS GOY: a non-Jew whose job is to do certain tasks on the Jewish Sabbath that the Torah forbids Jews to do, but may be done for them by a gentile under certain conditions.

SHABBOS TIMER: a device that is set before the Sabbath to turn lights on and off automatically at predetermined times.

SHADCHAN: matchmaker.

SHALOM BAYIS: maintaining harmony and love in marriage.

SHELO ASANI GOY: "[Blessed are You, G-d, King of the Universe,] Who did not make me a gentile."

SHEMITTAH YEAR: the Sabbatical year, when the Torah commands that the Holy Land be left uncultivated. Produce grown in accordance with halachah could be hard to come by.

SHIDDUCH: match.

SHMIRAS HALASHON: guarding against evil speech.

SHTIEBEL (Y.): a small shul, apart from the main synagogue.

SHVIGGER (Y.): mother-in-law.

SIDDUR: prayer book.

SIYUM: celebration upon completing a section of the Torah.

SPODIK (Y.): a black fur hat, taller than the more common shtreimel, worn by many Chassidim of Poland, especially Gerrer Chassidim, for Shabbos and special occasions.

SUCCAH: A temporary dwelling for the Festival of Succos (Tabernacles). The basic requirements for a succah are specified in the Mishnah.

TALMID CHACHAM: a Torah scholar.

TANTE (Fr.): aunt.

TECHIYAS HAMEISIM: the revival of the dead.

TEHILLIM: Psalms.

TISCH (Y.): lit., table. A gathering of Chassidim around the Rebbe's table to hear him speak words of Torah, to sing uplifting songs together, and to partake of small samples of food and drink handed out by the Rebbe.

TREIF (Y.): not kosher.

TZELEM ELOKIM: the image of G-d in which man was created.

YODU LA'SHEM CHASSDOI!: Let Hashem's pious ones thank Him.

YOM HASHOAH: Holocaust Remembrance Day.

Z'MAN: In the yeshiva world, the year is divided into *z'manim.* "Elul *z'man*" starts on the first day of the Hebrew month of Elul and ends with Yom Kippur; "winter *z'man*" is from the first day of Cheshvan until the end of the month of Adar; and "summer *z'man*" is from the first day of Iyar until Tishah B'Av. The vacations are known as *bein haz'manim* (lit., between sessions).

ZECHUS: privilege or merit.

ZEMIROS: liturgical songs sung at the meals in honor of Shabbos.

ZOGT DI HEILIGE GEMARA (Y.): "The holy Gemara says..."

Before the War

My father's parents, Reb Mordechai Tzvi and Frumet Horowitz *Hy"d*

My mother's mother, Tzirel Faigel Horowitz *Hy"d*

My father as a young boy with his sister Chana *Hy"d*

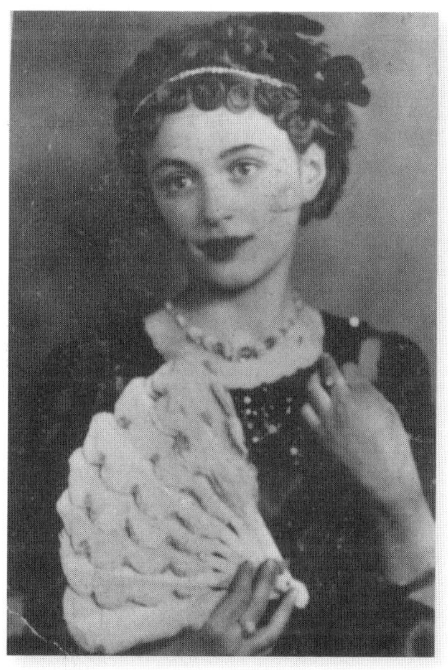

My mother as a little girl, dressed up for Purim

Women of my mother's extended family at a *sheva brachos* celebration for her sister in Alexander, Poland

My father's older brother, HaRav Chaim Eliezer Horowitz *Hy"d*, at his inauguration as Rav of Belchatov

After Liberation

My mother with her niece Rutke, who survived along with her

My mother, after the liberation

Left to right: my Aunt Rivka, my mother, and Pearl Benisch

Beis Yaakov girls in the Bergen-Belsen DP camp.
Sitting, second from left, is my mother.

Activists on the Rescue Committee in the DP camps.
Third from left is my uncle, Leibel Pinkusewitz.

My parents on their wedding day — Antwerp, 1946.

My parents after their engagement in Bergen-Belsen. Sitting between them is the matchmaker, my Aunt Rivka.

At the wedding meal. To the left of the *chosson* is the Vizhnitzer Rebbe, the Imrei Chaim *zt"l*.

My sister Tzili with a doll from America

My parents in Antwerp after their wedding

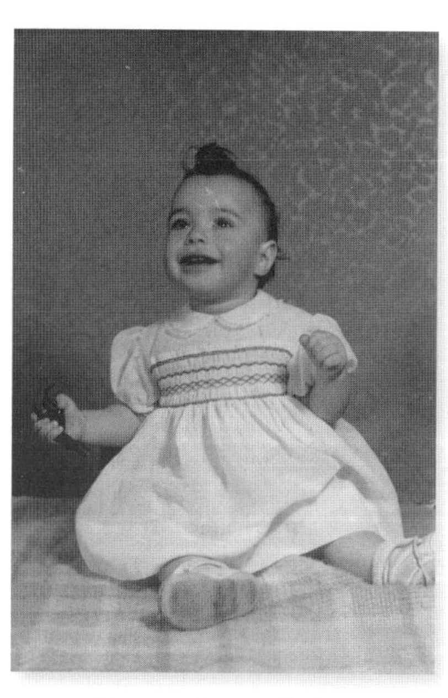

Me — a happy baby

In our living room in Antwerp: From left, my brother Mottel, my sister Esty, my sister Tzili, and myself

My brother Mottel with his violin

At my brother's bar mitzvah. Second from right is my Uncle Leibel.

"The Baron" at the Bnos Agudath Israel camp in Luxembourg

In my *tzedakah* box costume, for Keren HaYishuv

A family picture

My father speaking at an Agudath Israel Conference

My father at a public-service function

With Rabbi Moshe Sherer *z"l*, president of Agudath Israel of America

With the Gerrer Rebbe *shlita*

With the Rebbe of Gur, the Pnei Menachem *zt"l*

Above: My parents on our first trip to Poland in 1984, in front of the Yeshivas Chachmei Lublin building. Second from left is Rabbi Yehuda Meir Abramowitz.

My father in front of the gates of Auschwitz, showing the number on his arm

The new fence around the Jewish cemetery in Lublin

At a *hachnossas Sefer Torah*. Left to right, Rabbi Nissan Leizer from New York, my father, and Moshe Horowitz from Montreal. The three of them were together in Auschwitz.

Aunt Rivka at my bas mitzvah

At a family celebration — from left to right, Aunt Rivka, Dr. Judith Grunfeld of London, and Pearl Benisch

My father with Elie Wiesel, when they met at Davos

My parents celebrating their 50th wedding anniversary, Kislev 5757

A journey back to our roots, summer 2005. In front of the original Gerrer *beis midrash*, right to left, my son Nechemiah, my husband, myself, my parents, my sister Tzili, my daughter-in-law Chaya, my sister Esty, and my cousin Bluma Carmel.

On the ramp in Auschwitz. First from right is my cousin Avraham Mordechai Pinkusewitz.

My father in Jordanow

University students on a Nefesh Yehudi trip to Poland, winter 2008

My mother and I at the site of the mass grave in Chelmno, summer 2010

The memorial plaque dedicated to the Jews of Pabianitz
over their mass grave in Chelmno

At the inauguration of my husband as Rav of the Gr"a shul in Bayit Vegan

My father performing the famous *mitzvah tantz* at one of the grandchildren's weddings

Engrossed in Torah study,
a month before his passing

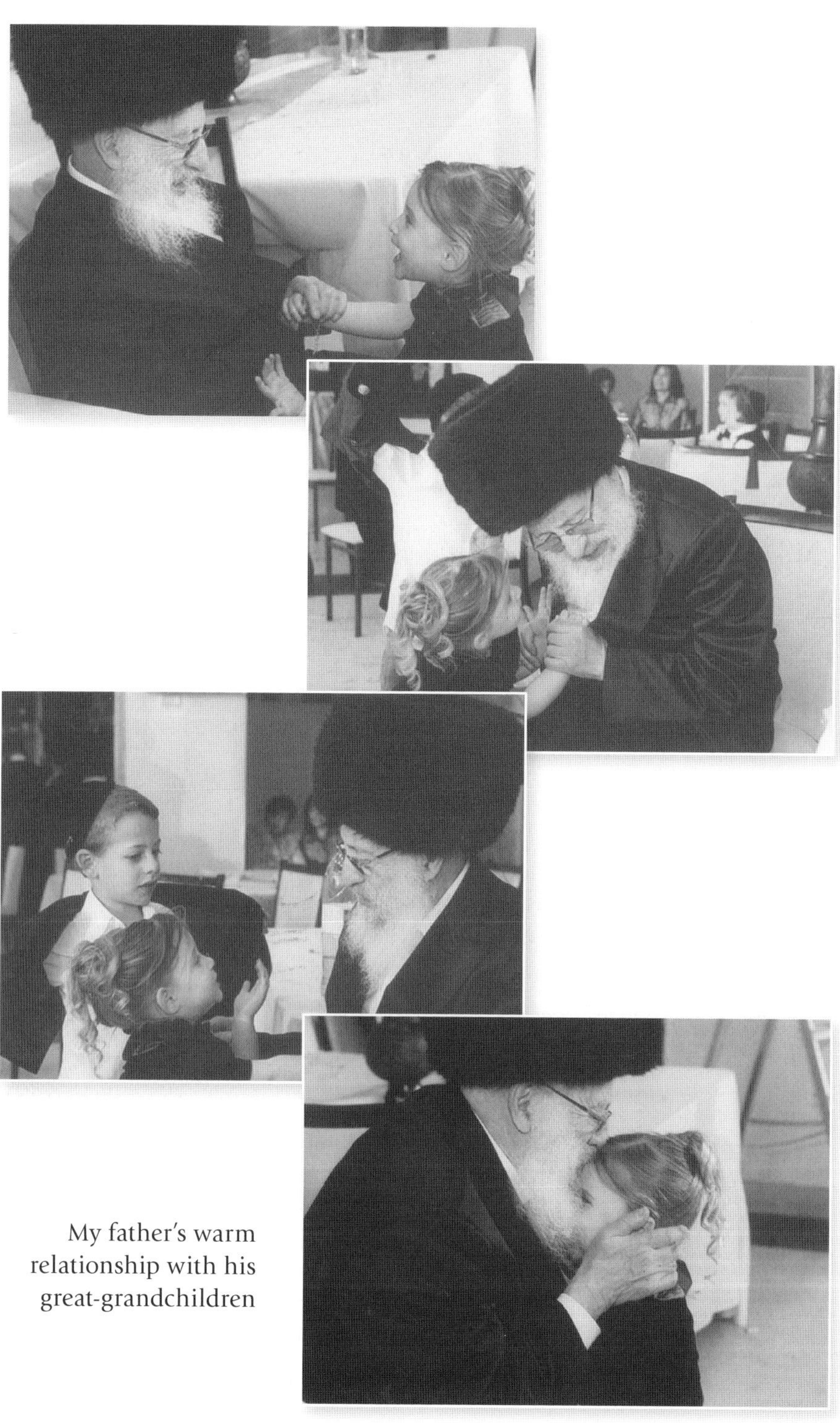

My father's warm relationship with his great-grandchildren

My family at my granddaughter's wedding

My older sister, Tzili Eitan, and her family

My younger sister, Esty Rappaport, and her family

My brother Mottel *z"l*

Mottel's son,
Yehoshua Horowitz

Mottel's son,
Chaim Horowitz

Mottel's son,
Aryeh Horowitz

Family Graves Discovered Only Recently in Poland

The grave of my mother's brother, Meir Horowitz *z"l*, in Pabianitz

The grave of my father's grandmother, Sarah Braun *z"l*, in Tarnow